TOWARD A BETTER WORLD

TOWARD A BETTER WORLD

MIKHAIL S. GORBACHEV

Introduction by
the Rt Hon Denis Healey

Hutchinson
London Melbourne Auckland Johannesburg

This edition first published in Great Britain in 1987 by Hutchinson,
an imprint of Century Hutchinson Ltd, Brrokmount House,
62–65 Chandos Place, London WC2N 4NW

Century Hutchinson Australia Pty Ltd
PO Box 496, 16–22 Church Street, Hawthorn, Victoria 3122,
Australia

Century Hutchinson New Zealand Limited
PO Box 40-086, Glenfield, Auckland 10, New Zealand

Century Hutchinson South Africa (Pty) Ltd
PO Box 337, Bergvlei, 2012 South Africa

British Library Cataloguing in Publication Data

Gorbachev, M.S.
    Toward a better world.
    1. Soviet Union — Politics and government
    — 1953–
    I. Title
    947.085'4'0924   PK290.3.G6

    ISBN 0-09-173601-3

Printed and bound in Great Britain by
Butler & Tanner Ltd, Frome and London

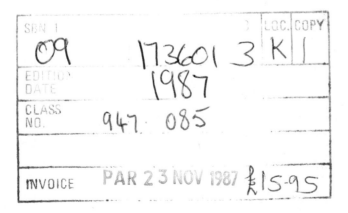

CONTENTS

INTRODUCTION

Six stimulating hours with Mihail Gorbachev during his visit to Britain just before the death of Chernenko left me with a question which later meetings in Moscow have failed to answer. His education, culture and open-mindedness were not uncommon among the young generation of Soviet leaders who were spared the worst traumas left by Stalin and the war; but beyond his exceptional charm and relaxed humanity he seemed also to be genuinely nice. How could such a man hope to become leader of an arthritic and corrupt dictatorship which condemned dissidents to labour camps and psychiatric wards? And if he did succeed, how long could he survive?

In fact fierce battles between progressives and conservatives have been fought inside the crumbling structure of Soviet totalitarianism ever since 1917. After Khrushchev and Kosygin Gorbachev is the third post-war reformist, representing a constituency which resembles theirs. He had powerful sponsors, above all Andropov, who showed the perception to choose Kadar as Hungary's leader after the tragedy of 1956. Perhaps the KGB has played a more constructive role in recent Soviet affairs than Western demonology can admit; after all, it knows the weaknesses of the system better than any other institution, and is the only institution which need not fear the KGB.

When Gromyko proposed Gorbachev's election he is said to have warned: 'He has a nice smile but his teeth are steel.' The steel teeth were soon at work devouring hostile, corrupt or incompetent members of the leadership in both State and Party, in Moscow and outside.

So far as we know, Gorbachev was not involved in foreign policy until he joined the Politburo shortly before becoming leader. But his earlier experience taught him that, although still a military giant, the Soviet Union was fast becoming an economic and political dwarf. From the moment he became General Secretary he recognised that it would be difficult to restructure the economy unless he could reduce the military drain on scarce human and material resources particularly in the new technologies.

He has often stressed that economic priorities must determine Soviet foreign policy, but as Chairman of the Defence Council, with full access to all the facts of modern warfare, he seems like Kennedy and Nixon in the United States to have developed a deep sense of his unique responsibility as one of the two men on earth who could unleash the nuclear holocaust. Chernobyl reinforced this feeling; but he seems to have drawn far wider lessons than that 'a nuclear war cannot be won and must never be fought.' His speeches imply that even conventional war cannot be an instrument of policy between the superpowers.

This in turn has led to a conclusion which supersedes the fundamental principle of Soviet foreign policy since Lenin – the assumption of a struggle to the death between the Two Camps. In his keynote speech to the Party Congress in 1986 he used the jargon of Marxist dialectic to predict a synthesis between the Two Camps: 'This is precisely the way, through the struggle of opposites, through arduous effort, groping in the dark to some extent as it were, that the controversial but *interdependent and in many ways integral* world is taking shape.' Although Malenkov was the first Soviet leader to reject war as the inevitable conclusion to the struggle, no one before Gorbachev dared to suggest that, as cooperation replaced competition between the two Camps, they would come to form a single world society.

The style is as remarkable as the content here. What earlier Soviet leader, indeed how many Western leaders today, would dare to describe themselves as 'groping in the dark' on such an issue? The humility which allows Gorbachev to admit uncertainty, to confess in other speeches that he may well be wrong, stems from the inner self-confidence of an exceptionally stable personality. When I met earlier Soviet leaders in a delegation, they would open by laying down the law in a long speech written by an official. At Gorbachev's meeting with British MPs in 1986 he simply asked us to raise any questions which concerned us, made pencil notes and replied in detail to every point we raised.

He is at his best on informal occasions or when improvising, as in his press conferences at Geneva and Rejkavik. His Report to the Party Congress contains long passages from the Kremlin word-processor which sit uneasily with his personal style. The essential targets of his television speeches are potential critics inside his own country: Soviet leaders have to campaign after they are elected, not before.

To foreign audiences, Gorbachev can speak with the confidence not only that the Soviet Union is now effectively equal with the United States in every dimension of military power but also that in the age of overkill equality may be more than enough. He can offer Mitterand a unilateral cut in those areas of conventional strength where the Red Army is superior. And he can offer to give up over five times more medium-range nuclear warheads than the United States in order to secure the political benefits of a disarmament agreement. For he believes that Soviet security now depends more on politics than on weaponry.

These speeches are the fruit of Gorbachev's second year as leader; he has already carried their message further, notably in his speech to the Moscow Peace Forum in February 1987. His restless experimentation is pushing out the frontiers of Soviet foreign policy in all directions, from the Pacific to Latin America. A sensitive and uninhibited intelligence is constantly modifying traditional doctrines in the light of personal observation and experience. When this century ends he will still be younger than any earlier Soviet leader at the close of his career. His own people will not be the only beneficiaries of his success and his survival.

Denis Healey
1987

I

TO THE AMERICAN READER

Before you, respected reader, is the third collection of my speeches published in the United States. It is a continuation, as it were, of the dialogue begun between us a year ago, a dialogue at the center of which stand the most urgent problems of world politics, namely international security and Soviet-American relations. These are problems shared by both of us. And we should think about them together and agree on how best to solve them to our mutual benefit.

The works included in this collection (covering the period February–December 1986) concern various subjects and fields, from the most specific to the very broad, both domestic and worldwide. And still, it is my firm conviction that they are born of one idea: we can no longer live and think as we have in the past. Attempts to push tomorrow back to yesterday are too dangerous, especially in our day and age, and especially as they concern military affairs, where the price of a single error is irreversible catastrophe.

Each century, while giving birth to new ideas, gains new perceptions. Indeed, each and every one of us looks at the world differently than our fathers, grandfathers, and great-grandfathers did. Likewise, our children, not to mention our grandchildren, won't be able to understand many of today's cares and concerns. Such is the way things are.

The 20th century, however, is unique: it has witnessed the appearance of a range of new factors that compel us to perceive differently the effect that decisions taken by individual governments would have on the future of civilization, the relationship between the extension of our knowledge and the way we use it, and time and space themselves. Power politics that does not go beyond the use of gunpowder is one thing, and power politics based on a potential capable of making the myth about the world's end come true in a matter of minutes is quite another. Or, say, it is one thing when a handful of workshops emit smoke into the air, and quite another when we have overall air pollution threatening the world with an ecological disaster. Life itself demands that each national economy, and the world economy as a whole, be restructured, whether we like it or not.

In short, the time has come to ask ourselves and one another many questions, including unpleasant ones, for not all of them fit in with our customary notions of things that are so readily presented as "axioms" or "age-old truths." But it is quite unnecessary for anyone to abandon his own faith and to adopt one that is alien to him. Let each live by his own convictions and worship his own God. We must calmly sum up the collective experience of humankind, and draw objective conclusions from objective premises.

There is no reason why anyone should assume the role of an omniscient, implacable oracle. There is no state that has nothing to learn from others. We are all teachers and pupils in one way or another. But reality often has a way of becoming distorted in the human consciousness.

Innumerable are the times when domestic crises have given rise to international and even world crises; how often have people vented their anger on others when they are beset by internal difficulties. They have learned to drape even the most blatant, vulgar greediness in national colors, wrap it in high-flown rhetoric. Is it not self-evident that justice, social and ethnic justice in particular, lies at the foundation of democracy in any country. It is the cornerstone of harmonious inter-state relations—not superficial or elitist justice but that which embraces each and every one.

Consider the underlying ideological and moral conception of our 27th Party Congress, and of the new edition of the Party Program adopted at the Congress. In our view the competition between the two systems takes place simultaneously with a growing tendency toward the interdependence of states in the world community; herein lies the dialectics of the development of the modern world. A contradictory, but interdependent and in many ways integral, world is emerging in which the struggle between capitalism and socialism should take the form only of peaceful competition and peaceful rivalry. In this world, the guarantee of security is increasingly becoming a political rather than a military task.

Security, if we speak of the USSR and the U.S.A., can only be mutual, or, if we take international relations as a whole, only universal.

There will always be disputes over the nature of freedom, just as there will always be debates over the question of what is love. Each person, and even more so each generation, has its own standards of measurement and its own perceptions of these and similar matters. They depend on many circumstances, both transient and permanent, on one's temperament and state of health, on whether one is rich or poor. We have an old saying: A sated man does not understand a hungry one. Soviet people find it difficult to accept the idea that one man is destined to be sated, while the lot of another is to live hand-to-mouth. Americans probably have their own parable about the fat man and the thin one, their own disputes denying infallibility.

But one thing is certain: peace and life are inseparably linked. Only in conditions of peace can people take part in heated discussions about rights and freedoms, preferences and biases. Owing to the logic of historical development, a yearning for peace has come to occupy the highest position in the hierarchy of human values and political priorities. For the vast majority of people today, peace has become the criterion for judging what is permissible and what is not, what is lawful and what is not. In a nuclear age one's rights are not determined by what one "wants," since power permits one to "want," but by humanity's obligation to the present and future inhabitants of our planet. All can and must act together following this approach—in my view the only correct, moral, and forward-looking approach—to the problem of war and peace. This means everyone—people of all countries and nationalities, people with different world outlooks and convictions, people of different religious faiths and social status.

The United Nations proclaimed 1986 the Year of Peace. The Soviet Union sincerely supported this decision, supported it in deed and in action. Throughout this year silence has reigned at our nuclear testing sites. And we are not testing strike systems or their components in outer space. The USSR has put forward a whole range of businesslike proposals for bringing about a fundamental improvement in the world situation.

Almost all of our initiatives are outlined in this book. At this point I will mention only the most important among them:

—on January 15, 1986, we put forward a proposal on the step-by-step, strictly controlled elimination of nuclear arms by the year 2000;

—in late February we formulated the basic principles of an all-embracing system of international security that covers the military, political, economic, and humanitarian fields;

—at the Soviet-American negotiations we presented a package of detailed and balanced proposals on nuclear and space weapons;

—jointly with its Warsaw Treaty allies, the USSR has advanced a program to reduce armed forces and conventional armaments in Europe;

—the Soviet Union has outlined a wide-ranging plan before the countries of the Asia-Pacific region aimed at ensuring peace and cooperation in that part of the world;

—throughout the year, the task of ending experimental nuclear explosions under strict international control has not been removed from the agenda. In an effort to solve the problem, the USSR has extended its unilateral moratorium four times.

It's easy to brand our initiatives as "propaganda" without taking the trouble to consider them carefully. It's the easiest thing to do, especially when one doesn't really want to solve the problems. But let us ask ourselves, without prejudice, what it is that we are "propagandizing"?:

An end to nuclear tests. The elimination of nuclear weapons under effective control in any form. The dismantlement of military bases outside a country's national frontiers. The reduction of conventional armaments and, eventually, complete disarmament. A halt to propaganda of hate toward other peoples. The building of good-neighborly relations and cooperation between all countries in the name of life itself.

Is that so bad? Why is it that some prefer to advertise violence and cruelty, idolize weapons, turn diplomacy into an instrument of power politics and interstate relations into confrontation bristling with arms? Some people are trying to prove that military technology is the answer to the eternal question of "to be or not to be." Those who call for the use of force believe that "one nail drives out another." But that is suicidal self-deception. It is an ill-intentioned attempt to clothe vice as virtue so as to *prevent* people from recognizing (instead of helping them to recognize) an elementary truth: if there is to be life, weapons must cease to be.

It is not easy for adults to relearn. That is so. But nothing can be done about it; this is the demand of the times. The no-to-weapons signal will be flashed more and more often before the world's nations and their leaders. And no one should regard this objective necessity as an encroachment on national sovereignty and prestige or national pride, especially when they are intricately connected with force.

Is it right to deride common sense continually, to test people's nerves and keep them in a constant state of fear?

Is it permissible to take the planet's resources without moderation, to pollute its atmosphere and bodies of water, to destroy nature, and to overstrain ecological systems?

Is it a responsible thing to do to put national egoism before everything else, an egoism that knows no restrictions or even self-restrictions, be it under the flag of consumerism or "supreme interests"?

What must be done to make our common home on earth a safe one for all nations, and not just a well-appointed dwelling for one or two of them who happen to be luckier? The Soviet Union thinks that we should answer the challenges of our time together. And "together" does not mean doing things at the expense or to the detriment of one another. It means to try to see, first of all, what unites us and makes each of us part of one whole, not what divides us and puts us at opposite poles.

Who has thought up the stereotype, the idea that the USSR is America's enemy? How long has it been sowing confusion in people's minds? It would be interesting to know. Russia didn't meddle in the American revolution; in fact, it helped it in some way. Russia's "attentive neutrality" was beneficial to the struggle of the North American colonies for their liberation. The United States, as is known, "greeted" our revolution in October 1917 quite differently. When the American interventionists, along with others, had to withdraw from Soviet territory, those who stood at the helm in the United States were deeply offended; so much so that they did not recognize the USSR for sixteen years.

In general, I would like to note the following. Whenever one reads books on American history, one begins to wonder: where has the old, virtuous America gone? Where has the reverse come from—the idea of "not recognizing" another country, of "punishing" it, even with hunger; of deciding arbitrarily what is "good" and what is "bad," and of wishing others ill. It is indeed true that people hate those whom they have wronged.

I'm not trying to reproach anyone. Nothing could be further from my mind. Even in family relations reproaches are harmful, let alone in relations between states. I'm only calling for reflection without prejudice, setting aside timeworn myths and falsehoods.

I'm moved by different considerations. Why, for instance, does the development of Soviet-American relations nearly always lag behind world development? Why are we roused to constructive joint action mainly by terrible and dangerous events and not by normal realistic thinking? Why do peals of thunder prove more convincing than arguments prompted by common sense?

Yes, we have a socialist system, and our people prefer this system to any other—a system they have won through revolution and have defended in wars against interventionist forces and fascists, through the sacrifice of scores of millions of lives. We do not believe that our present system is perfect in every respect and are making a big effort to make our life better, brighter, and richer, both spiritually and materially. All right, we are different. But is this reason for enmity, for trying to impose on others one's own system, one's own way of life, one's own yardstick for measuring freedom? And why such an arrogant claim to being "perfect"? It is a dangerous, very dangerous claim, I would say.

Today we again have a common enemy. This enemy is more terrible than German fascism or Japanese militarism during the Second World War, when our two countries fought side by side. This enemy is nuclear war. In fighting against it the USSR and the U.S.A. must be on the same side, unconditionally. In an alliance formed to combat the threat of nuclear catastrophe, no one should have to sacrifice his cherished ideals, let alone his interests. Nuclear weapons are essentially immoral and inhuman. Their existence can find no justification in any religion or theory or in life itself. What can be proved by nuclear might? Only one thing: that man is foolish and imperfect, that he has deeply ingrained atavistic instincts. However, if the worst should happen, there would be no one left to prove this to. After such a war there will be no preachers or believers; neither rural Russian homes nor New York skyscrapers, neither the Kremlin nor the White House; neither man nor beast will survive. There will be no living thing left!

Soviet society is ready for peaceful competition with the capitalist system. We do not fear such competition. Nothing in our philosophy prevents the conclusion of the most radical agreements on disarmament, including complete demilitarization of the world under international control. Call it historical optimism or anything you like, but the fact remains that in all our creative undertakings peace is our chief ally and helper. I say this loud and clear, without reservations. The arms race, the military confrontation, the muscle-flexing— none of these is our choice, our kind of policy. It may be recalled that right after the revolution we did not even have an army and were not going to set one up. It came into being only when our land had been invaded.

How do we start ridding the earth of the scourge of militarism? It would be most practical, in our view, to begin from the beginning—by ending nuclear tests. After that, military arsenals should be reduced. At the same time, confidence between states should be built up and civilized relations cultivated. All that can be achieved only if we realize that in a nuclear age an essentially new approach to the question of war is needed. Psychologically, the possession of nuclear power gives rise to and sustains the hope of achieving world domination, of making other countries live according to the laws of those who wield a nuclear sword. This is, of course, an illusion, for nuclear war will inevitably destroy the very notion of "domination," together with those aspiring to it. But this is something that still needs to be understood. And policies must be shaped patiently and purposefully in quite a different direction than the one in which they are being formed today.

In order that people should have things under control, the Soviet Union has persistently been urging governments to set a limit to the militarization of science, to curtail work on the development of new military technologies and, as a first step, to stop nuclear testing. In August 1985 the USSR announced a unilateral moratorium on all nuclear explosions. Quiet has reigned at our test sites, although Western powers have continued to explode one charge after another.

In introducing the moratorium we were aware that Washington might start maneuvering, referring to "verification difficulties" and "a lack of confidence," and then, when the propaganda impact of such arguments has been spent, sweep aside all excuses and pretexts and say: "We must do what we must do in the interest of national security, and that's that!" Such a possibility existed from the outset. Still, one liked to think that common sense would prevail. After all, for the moratorium to become bilateral and then universal, no material outlays or special efforts were needed. In fact, nothing was needed except political will and a sense of responsibility for the present state and future of humanity. Between the ending of tests and the drafting of an agreement there was only half a step, for the document would only have formalized the actual state of affairs.

Thus, not only weapons and the latest technological ideas are being tested in Nevada. It is a test primarily of the policies of states, of how serious are their declarations renouncing nuclear war and promising a nuclear-free world, a test of their historical maturity. There is no need to be cunning here—to try to develop *postnuclear* weapons while testing nuclear ones. It is all rather obvious.

In this context it seems pertinent to recall something from the past, both recent and not so recent. How did the present vicious circle of an arms race come about? Over 25 types of the most horrible weapons—nuclear arms and munitions, strategic bombers, atomic submarines, multiple-warhead missiles, the neutron bomb, etc.—have been created since 1945 and introduced into world politics by the United States. The Soviet Union has been forced to catch up with the United States, to bridge gaps, while putting off many of its urgent tasks until later.

But such "militarist success" has cost the United States itself dearly. Economically, according to official statistics, total U.S. military spending in the years 1946–1986 came close to 3,400,000 million dollars. Surely this amount of money could have been spent in ways that would have benefitted the American people. The cost was also high, extremely high, militarily and politically, from the point of view of that country's effective security.

Each new weapon system added to the U.S. arsenal has increased the risk- and fear-factor. As a result the United States has ceased to be invulnerable, and the oceans around it no longer serve as its "guardian angels." To have created such a situation U.S. militarism has inflicted the greatest blow to the interests of the American people as well.

If one doesn't stop, this will go on and on. Action will produce counteraction. Let's say the USSR makes a first move; you will at once try to catch up. If the Americans start a new round of the arms race, we will find an antidote for it. But when will it stop? How long must this tug-of-war go on before common sense takes the upper hand, thus preventing the irreparable from happening? A peculiar feature of the present situation is that the Soviet Union possesses a wide range of responsive measures. Duplication of U.S. achievements—something that suited the United States very well—is now ruled out. This is both better and worse. Better, because it will mean less expenditure for us. Worse, because the technological incompatibility this leads to will further complicate arms control or will even make the problem insoluble from a technical point of view.

And now the main question: what have we got to quarrel over? Why should we be enemies—do we have anything to divide between us? We do not compete on the world market. Our interests do not conflict geographically. There are no Soviet bases close to your borders. We have many ideological and political differences, but they should not be a reason for mutual destruction. Why then seek trouble?

I read American newspapers and magazines regularly and listen to the radio, and so receive a mass of information. And I never cease wondering: why this hostility, this hatred toward us? What is the cause of it, what motives lie behind it? Can it be that jingoism—that refuge of ignorance—has become a mass ideology? For when one talks with Americans (and I have had many such talks) one usually feels nothing of the kind—neither hatred, nor bloodthirsty aggressiveness. One feels a desire for cooperation, peace, and good-neighborliness. So what is happening? Apparently someone wants us to be enemies. But who?

Some people say that the Soviet Union cannot be trusted. If there are people in the United States who really believe that, let's sort things out together. Why cannot the Soviet Union be trusted? What is the basis for such mistrust? Let us calmly, without unnecessary polemics and without giving in to emotions that drown out the voice of reason, recall the history of our countries, the history of our relations, and clear up the perplexities and misunderstandings—since they exist. Let us also find out if a mountain is not really a molehill. And if that is the case (and we believe it is exactly so), who needs this and why? And what can and must be done to stop this unwise practice?

I want to make this quite clear: in the Soviet Union, too, many are troubled by the problem of trust. They say quite frankly that the United States is not to be trusted. And they back up their position by referring to facts. For sixteen years the Soviet Union was not recognized by the United States. It is the Soviet Union, not the United States, that has been encircled with war bases. We were not the first to develop new means of warfare. It was against us that definite dates for a preemptive nuclear attack were set; it was our country that was divided on the map into occupation zones, and even the kind of state system it should have was predetermined. Documents of the National Security Council relating to this subject have been declassified. One can now read them. We were subjected to all sorts of insults, and "punished." It has been suggested that we be relegated to the scrap heap of history. And so on and so forth. I shall not go on with the list of facts that nourish our profound mistrust. But at times I ask myself: how would matters stand if we, and not the United States, were guilty of all the things mentioned and much else? How would you, esteemed Americans, feel about it? What would your reaction be?

The Soviet leadership believes that ruthlessness has no future in foreign policy (although certain U.S. circles have a thirst for it), and that confrontation is of no use economically, ideologically, or militarily. But sometimes a really dead-end situation develops, and one asks oneself: What more can one do when all one hears is the same stereotyped, cheerless "No."

My frankness might be surprising and perplexing. Nothing has apparently happened to warrant such a candid discussion. Perhaps the motive is the obvious disappointment in the course of events since the Geneva summit meeting. Although in words we came closer together after Geneva, the division in actions and in positions has grown wider. Thus far no new agreements have been reached, while there is a rush to bury previous agreements. The U.S.A. has announced plans to abandon the SALT-I Agreement and the SALT-II Treaty. The public is being prepared for a cancellation of the treaty, which has no time limit, on ballistic missile systems (ABM). The Star Wars program is being carried out at an accelerated pace. Work outside the laboratory has begun on the anti-satellite system ASAT. Judging by certain facts, the U.S.A. is testing in Nevada nuclear devices of third generation and fundamentally new strike systems using the energy of nuclear explosions. It follows from several highly authoritative statements that the United States is developing an entire set of technology for an actual, full-scale nuclear war.

Generally speaking, there are sufficient grounds for disappointment. Another matter for thought is the purpose which the American political lexicon serves—is it to express certain ideas or to cover up those ideas? No less disturbing is the unwillingness of Western politicians to look facts in the face, as well as their attempts to draw people's attention away from these facts with various ruses, rhetoric, and demagogy. Peace-loving verbiage doesn't at all inhibit the preaching of force or the singing of praises to nuclear weapons as a basis for a "deterrence strategy." Some people say that all of this is for domestic consumption. I will not make any judgments as to the morality of such an attitude, but it is high time to realize that today the entire world is being drawn into a discussion on life and death, and attitudes differ.

The radiation from an explosion of the smallest charge is more than three times as great as that of the Chernobyl accident. The use of even a small portion of the existing nuclear weapons—and over fifty thousand units of such weapons have been stockpiled to date—will be tantamount to catastrophe. I often recall the cruel saying of the ancients—you can take everything away from a man except death. He who strikes first will destroy himself. He will die even without a retaliatory blow, as a consequence of the explosion of the very warheads which he himself has detonated. I wish to thank the doctors, both American and Soviet, for disclosing that truth, for having calculated, using mathematical models, the outcome of a nuclear war. It was the politicians' turn to say this.

And during my meeting with U.S. President Ronald Reagan in Reykjavik on October 11 and 12, 1986, the Soviet Union stated that truth. But unfortunately, the United States did not share that view, and so we could not work toward a common goal. And it was not our fault. A turning-point in world history did not take place, even though it could have and we were as close to it as we have ever been before. A unique, historical opportunity has perhaps passed us by. Regrettably, there was a definite lack of a new approach on the part of the Americans.

We brought to Reykjavik a whole package of concrete proposals. Acceptance of these proposals could have become a driving force for the establishment of a nuclear-free world. What did the USSR propose to the U.S.A.?

1. To reduce strategic defensive arms by 50 percent on both sides in the coming five years, by the end of 1991. To eliminate the remaining 50 percent during the next five years, by the end of 1996.

2. To eliminate completely Soviet and American medium-range missiles in Europe. Furthermore, in contrast to our previous proposals, we did not insist this time that the powerful nuclear potential of Great Britain and France be included in the general count.

3. To establish three-way control—with national means, international methods and on-site inspection—over the process of eliminating nuclear weapons and over the strict observance by both sides of the agreements reached.

4. We proposed that in the course of the next ten years the USSR and the U.S.A. undertake to refrain from using their right to withdraw from the ABM Treaty, which is of unlimited duration, and to observe strictly all of its provisions; to refrain from testing space elements of antimissile defense systems in outer space, and to keep all testing and research within the boundaries of the laboratory.

5. To begin without delay talks with the aim of completely banning nuclear testing.

We offered the most large-scale compromises which, in the event of their being accepted, would have placed Soviet-American relations on a stable foundation. But these compromises also have their limits. If we disarm on earth, we cannot at the same time arm in outer space.

If SDI, as the American side has declared several times, is to render nuclear weapons useless, the question arises as to what will be rendered useless if, under three-way control, nuclear warheads and carriers are to be destroyed. A convincing answer to this question has not been given. Have the people obsessed with SDI worked out a postulate that domination in outer space implies domination on earth? Whatever the case may be, we naturally could not agree to the ABM Treaty being dropped from the set of disarmament accords. And indeed we had no right to act otherwise: the Soviet people would never agree to this.

And thus SDI—a program for achieving military superiority through militarization of outer space—wrecked actual agreements. We have been convinced again and again that SDI is not a defense system. Rather it is an attempt to replace or to supplement nuclear arms with even more destructive and insidious weapons. It is a new technological wrapping for the same old claims on world leadership and hegemony.

On the advertising boards SDI is depicted as all but an "insurance policy" for the American people. Appropriations for the SDI program are in fact expenditures on the universal funeral of all humanity. It sounds harsh, but truth doesn't always sound pretty.

SDI does not frighten us in military terms. The USSR can develop an anti-SDI program that will not be a duplication of the U.S.A.'s program, and not as expensive. Furthermore we can develop it sooner than the American Star Wars program will be carried out. But we don't want to do this. SDI and anti-SDI will mean an endless arms race that can get out of control.

What is to be done then? The would-be experts on international affairs, primitive enough to examine everything through a prism of anti-Sovietism, are ready to light the fireworks because in Reykjavik we didn't manage to reach an agreement. They cling to the lack of success and talk about Reykjavik as a failure.

I categorically reject this interpretation that turns the facts inside out. Reykjavik was an important and significant event. The meeting was useful in many ways. Ideas were reevaluated. Issues were discussed on a qualitatively new level. It was found that all the material means for building an enduring peace, a peace that is worthy of mankind, are available and that the most dangerous weapon systems can be scrapped.

At the same time, the American Administration's obstinacy shed new light on declarations and statements that the U.S.A. is supposedly no longer striving for superiority, on the worth of its declarations that no one can win a nuclear war, that reasonable compromises should not be rejected out of hand, etc. But, it turned out that the U.S.A. is still dreaming of superiority and cherishing the hope of victory in Star Wars and in a war on earth. And by compromise it has in mind mainly concessions by others. There is an absolute polarity between their words and actions.

The world must definitely change if civilization is to continue to exist. People are tired of words. They want action—constructive action. Action that will take into consideration equally the legitimate interests of each and all. This is the aim of Soviet policy, a policy of peace and disarmament. We stand for the continuation of the Geneva and Reykjavik dialogues—in Washington, Moscow, or any other place in the world.

We have reached a crossroads. For us to go to war—that is out of the question. The USSR and the U.S.A., every government and every nation, remaining as they are, must conduct their affairs in the international arena prudently and properly, and must live in a civilized manner. There is still time to choose the direction we will take. But time is not an inexhaustible resource. It is being depleted constantly. It shrinks before our very eyes. We must not lose this time. Political activity must proceed more quickly in order to reach at last the level scientific thought has attained and to outstrip the technical development of the arms race as much as possible.

We take matches away from children so they won't burn down the house or burn themselves. Today we must take nuclear weapons away from the adults so they won't burn down the universal home—earth—and so that they won't murder mankind.

A most important task is to work out a new mode of political thought and probably a new international law. A new way of thinking must develop that is characterized by respect for people and nations whose social coloring and social beliefs are different from ours. International law must be purged of double standards and categorically condemn aggressive wars and all other forms of international violence. In a future world community that will be different from the one we have today we will have to work together again to find ways of distributing wealth among all the countries of the world.

I have in mind especially the developing countries with a total population of more than two billion. Here we have a whole region of poverty. The national income of the former mother countries is eleven times higher than that of the former colonies. This gap is not narrowing but widening. It is a most acute problem. Its solution calls for constructive and creative cooperation between governments and nations on a world scale.

In the old days corporals warned young recruits that once a year guns fire by themselves. Today, when we rely heavily on computers, generals and politicians assure us that the opposite is true. So are we to wait for an accident to happen? And meanwhile are we to continue to pile up huge mountains of weapons on earth and prepare for their deployment in outer space? And then, if we can manage it, are we to establish military bases on the Moon and force Mars to justify its name as the God of War? In the meantime, the earth will be left to rot. And indeed why should we worry about what happens to the earth if politicians have acknowledged their inability to forestall the worst, thus condemning the planet to extinction?

And can we really continue to live like this?

Today it is not man who is asking nature to show mercy, rather nature is appealing to man to be merciful. Everyone is indebted to nature, you as well as we. But you are the more indebted: producing 53 percent of all goods manufactured in the world, developed capitalism accounts for 63 percent of all ecological refuse.

These figures can only roughly or theoretically be translated into rubles or dollars. For how can we calculate that which is priceless? For example, how can we estimate the price of the death of animals and vegetation? Valuable genetic stock is being depleted, many types of flora and fauna have become extinct, and the delicate balance of nature has been upset.

We may recall the plight of modern agriculture from which a hundred states are suffering. The Sahara, overrunning traditional farming lands, is moving headlong southward. It is possible to stop the spread of deserts, which have already taken over five billion hectares of land—one hectare for every inhabitant of the planet. According to specialists, to do this seventy billion dollars must be spent before the end of the century. In the next 15 years, if nothing changes, 15,000 billion dollars will be spent on the arms race. If military allocations were reduced only by a fraction, it would be possible to attack this threatening malady that is spreading like wildfire.

The world economy annually discharges into the atmosphere 200 million tons of carbon monoxide, more than 50 million tons of different hydrocarbons, 120 million tons of cinder and 150 million tons of sulphur dioxide that turns into "acid rain." Acid rain is quickly turning Europe into a "balding continent." Coniferous trees are dying out from the Mediterranean to the Baltic Sea. We are distressed by this calamity, which has also hit our own northern forest tracts.

The pollution level of the westerly winds in the European part of the USSR is about ten times higher than that of the easterly winds. But we are not condemning anyone. We propose cooperation. And that is why we are saddened when our tragedy—the accident at the Chernobyl nuclear power plant—has brought out in certain people in the West a malicious delight in the misfortune of others, an enthusiasm for everything anti-Soviet and a spate of primitive passions.

Man rose above all other living creatures on earth on the wings of humanism. Today five billion people living on this planet need humanism more than anything else. They need it for establishing good-neighborly relations between individuals and states. The fostering of a new way of thinking is, in my opinion, instrumental in bringing about a radical turn in the life of the world community. Revolutions always begin in the mind. The way to save civilization and life itself does not lie in thinking up new technologies for ever more accurate and lethal weapon systems, but rather in liberating the mind from prejudices—political and social, national and racial—from arrogance, self-conceit and the cult of force and violence.

In conclusion I would like to say that our era is marked by sharp changes. So many events and transformations are taking place within a very short period of time in our country, in your country and in the world as a whole. It is true that "time is money." But above all time is life—in the literal sense, and today in the political sense as well. We must make haste to remove the fears and threats looming over us, our children and our descendants. We in our country are changing and altering our mode of political thought and are adapting to the present realities, the realities of the nuclear age, the space age, and the computer age. We are waiting for this from everyone else; from you, the American people.

Let me say this: we have no evil or secret designs against your country; we are not hostile to the American people. And if anyone asserts otherwise, he is simply acting with bad intentions. We regard the people of the United States with respect.

I would like to use this opportunity to wish each of my readers, his near ones, and the great American people happiness and prosperity.

Mikhail Gorbachev

Mikhail Gorbachev in conversation with Andrei Gromyko. 1986.
Photo Courtesy of the author.

President and Mrs. Mitterrand in Moscow with Mikhail Gorbachev
and Mrs. Gorbachev.

Visiting Mother, Mikhail Gorbachev and Raisa Gorbachev flank Mr. Gorbachev's mother. The others are relatives and friends. 1986. Photo Courtesy of the author.

Mikhail Gorbachev in Vladivostok. 1986.

Mikhail Gorbachev and Anatoli Dobrynin with Armand Hammer (at left) and Dr. Robert Gale (arms folded). Dr. Gale went to the Soviet Union to treat Chernobyl workers exposed to radiation. 1986.

Mikhail Gorbachev and Stewart Richardson, of Richardson & Steirman in Moscow. He is holding a leatherbound copy of *The Coming Century of Peace*. 1986.

Raisa Gorbachev with children. 1986.

A recent portrait of Mikhail Gorbachev. 1986.

II

PRESS CONFERENCE

Reykjavik, Iceland, October 12, 1986

Good evening, ladies and gentlemen, comrades, greetings to you all.

Our meeting with the U.S. President, Mr. Reagan, ended about an hour ago. It had lasted a little longer than we had planned. This was made necessary by business in hand. So I want to make my apologies to you for not being able to come for the press conference at the appointed time.

You already know that the meeting took place on the initiative of the Soviet leadership. But, naturally, there would have been no meeting if Mr. Reagan had not agreed to it. That is why, I would say, it was our joint decision to have that meeting in Reykjavik.

Now it is over. It is sometimes said that when you talk to someone face to face, you can't see his face. I've just emerged from a meeting which, especially in its closing stage, passed in heated debates. And I am still under the impression of those debates. Nevertheless, I will try now not only to share my impressions but also to sort out what took place. Yet it will be the first impressions and evaluations, the first analysis. The meeting as a whole is yet to be evaluated more thoroughly.

It was an important meeting and you yourselves will realize this when I describe its contents, the problems which were the subject of a very broad, very intensive, and very serious discussion.

The atmosphere at the meeting was friendly. We had an opportunity to present our views freely and without restrictions. This enabled us to deepen our understanding concerning many major problems of world politics, bilateral relations, primarily those questions which are in the focus of world attention, problems of war and peace and the ending of the nuclear arms race, in short, the entire complex of questions coming under that subject.

I am a regular reader of the world press and I've seen in the last few days what a broad response the news of the meeting has evoked. A good deal was said in this connection both about the General Secretary of the CPSU Central Committee and about the U.S. President. The question was asked whether they had not been too hasty, whether there was any need for such a meeting, who made concessions to whom, who outplayed whom, and so on. But you know, the reason why we made our proposal to the U.S. President to have a meeting without delay and his decision to respond to our invitation positively were very important.

I would now like to recall Geneva where we met for the first time. That was a major dialogue and now, after quite some time, we continue to regard the Geneva meeting that way.

At that time, if you remember, we recognized the special responsibility of the USSR and the United States of America for safeguarding peace, and declared jointly that nuclear war should never be unleashed and that there could be no winners in it. That was a statement of immense importance. We also declared that neither side would seek military superiority. That was also a very important statement.

Almost a year has passed since Geneva. The Soviet leadership has remained loyal to the commitments it assumed there. Having returned from Geneva, we extended our moratorium: it was to remain in effect till January 1 this year. Silence has reigned at our test sites for 14 months now—is this not evidence of our commitment to the Geneva accords and of our sense of responsibility for the destinies of peace? Those were not easy decisions to make since tests in Nevada continued at that time and are going on now. On January 15 we made a major statement in which a program for the elimination of nuclear weapons by the end of this century was set forth.

Last June the Warsaw Treaty countries put forward a major comprehensive program for large-scale reductions in conventional armaments and armed forces in Europe. That was also a major step in view of the concern voiced by the West Europeans and the United States.

Drawing the lesson of the Chernobyl tragedy, we proposed the convening of an emergency session of the IAEA General Conference in Vienna. It took place and you know about its results—they are very promising. Now we have an international mechanism which makes it possible to resolve many important questions concerning the safety of nuclear power engineering.

In other words, in the period under review—and I don't think I am exaggerating in making such an evaluation of our policy since what I speak of is facts, not mere intentions—we have been doing everything possible to help bring about a new way of thinking in this nuclear age. It gives us pleasure to note that the shoots of this new thinking are sprouting, especially on European soil. This was evidenced, among other things, by the success of the Stockholm meeting.

Now I'll probably conclude the list of the concrete actions that we have taken, guided by the letter and spirit of the Geneva accords with President Reagan. The facts themselves, I think, enable you to form your own judgments as to the seriousness of our attitude to these accords.

Still, why was the Reykjavik meeting necessary, what were the motives for our initiative?

The fact is that the hopes for major changes in the world situation, which we all entertained, began to evaporate shortly after the Geneva meeting, and, in my opinion, not without cause.

Much has been said, perhaps too much, at the Soviet-U.S. talks; between fifty and one hundred variants of proposals have been afloat, as I told the President yesterday. This fact alone raises doubts as to the fruitfulness of the discussions under way there. If there were one or two, even three variants, which would make it possible to narrow somehow the scope of discussions and concentrate the search on some major directions, one could then expect that the search would lead to concrete agreements and proposals to the governments. But nothing of this kind is taking place at Geneva, although the discussion there is concerned with key issues of world politics.

Frankly speaking, these negotiations have recently been marking time, in fact, they are practically deadlocked. The arms race has not been stopped, and it is becoming increasingly clear that developments are approaching a point where a new spiral of the arms race becomes inevitable, with unpredictable political and military consequences.

Our major initiatives, which I have already mentioned, have evoked a broad response from the world public. But they have not met with due understanding on the part of the U.S. Administration.

The situation has worsened; once again there is growing anxiety around the world. I think it's no exaggeration to say— you yourselves are witnesses to it—that the world is in a state of turmoil. The world is in a state of turmoil, and it demands that the leaders of all countries, above all the major powers, primarily the Soviet Union and the United States, display political will and determination so that the dangerous trends can be halted.

So, something had to be done in order to overcome such a course of developments. We came to the conclusion that a new impetus was necessary, a powerful impetus to turning the process in the required direction. Such impetuses could be provided only by the leaders of the USSR and the United States of America. That is why, in replying to President Reagan's letter of July 25, I decided to invite him to a meeting to be held immediately. I wrote: The situation is such that we ought to put aside all affairs for a couple of days and meet without delay.

The letter was handed to the President by Comrade Shevardnadze.

Now, this extremely important meeting has been held. We believed that many things would depend on its outcome. And, naturally, we did not come to the meeting empty-handed.

What have we brought to Reykjavik? We have brought a whole package of major proposals which, if accepted, could within a brief period really bring about, I would say, a breakthrough in all directions of the struggle for limiting nuclear weapons and really eliminate the threat of nuclear war, and would make it possible to start moving toward a nuclear-free world.

I suggested to the President that we, right here in Reykjavik, give binding instructions to our foreign ministers and the departments concerned *to have three agreements drafted*, which the President and I could sign later during my visit to the United States of America.

The first concerned strategic arms; it should stipulate a 50 percent reduction of these arms, and no less, with a view to fully eliminating these deadliest of weapons already by the end of the century.

We acted on the belief that the world is waiting for really major steps, substantial reductions rather than some cosmetic steps intended merely to calm public opinion for a while. Really bold, responsible actions are now needed in the interests of the entire world, including the peoples of the Soviet Union and the United States of America.

Naturally, the Soviet and the U.S. delegations that would be assigned the job of drafting the agreement on strategic arms should work out a balanced reduction of their historically formed structure honestly and with care.

The point at issue is the very triad that was recognized way back when SALT-II was being drafted. But when I raised this question with the President, in response everything that features at the Geneva talks was brought up once again—levels and sublevels, in short, much arithmetic, and everything meant to confuse the essence of the matter. We then proposed the following for the sake of being more precise: that each component of the strategic offensive armaments—land-based strategic missiles, submarine-launched strategic missiles, and strategic bombers—be reduced by half.

The U.S. delegation agreed to that. Thus, we reached agreement on a very important issue.

I would like to draw your attention to the fact that we made substantial concessions here. You will remember, too, that when we made our 50-percent-cut proposal at Geneva, we counted medium-range missiles as strategic weapons since our territory is within their reach. Now we have dropped that demand, along with the question of forward-based systems. Agreement was thus reached in Reykjavik on cuts in strategic weapons thanks to these major concessions.

Our next proposal concerned medium-range missiles. We proposed that instructions be given to draw up an accord on weapons of that type too; the idea was to give up all the options, temporary or interim, that had been discussed so far, and to go back to the earlier American proposal on the total elimination of American and Soviet medium-range missiles in Europe. And what makes our new proposal different from our Geneva proposals is that we now left completely aside the nuclear potentials of France and Britain. You understand, of course, that this was a very large concession on our part. Indeed, those two countries are allies of the U.S.A. and they have nuclear potentials which continue to be built up and upgraded. And all of their military activities are closely coordinated within NATO. We know this for certain. Nevertheless, we removed that obstacle to agreement.

There was also concern about Asia. We offered a compromise there as well: let us sit down and start negotiations right away, air our complaints, and find a solution. We understood that the question of missiles with a range of less than 1,000 kilometers was bound to come up. So we made a proposal regarding that question: a freeze on those missiles and the holding of talks to decide what to do with them.

These are the large-scale measures we wanted to see carried out. I think that the Americans had not expected this from us, but they entered into the discussion and said frankly that they were not willing to remove their missiles from Europe. They again asked us to accept their interim option. We, however, insisted on completely ridding Europe of both Soviet and American medium-range missiles.

During the discussion on that question we called the U.S. President's attention to the fact that he seemed to be abandoning his brainchild, the "zero option," which at one time he was offering us with such insistence, even though we had now decided to take it up.

The discussion, and very heated discussion, continued into today. And we decided to make yet another constructive move: we said that if the American and Soviet missiles in Europe were eliminated we would agree to have 100 warheads left on our medium-range missiles in Asia while the Americans would have as many on theirs on U.S. territory. Eventually we reached an agreement on that type of nuclear weapons too, although, as I've already said, it was also a major concession on our part.

After all, a start has to be made somehow. I have pointed this out on more than one occasion. Bold, innovative solutions are needed! If we always turn to the past for advice and make use of what belongs to very different times, without considering where we are today and where we will be tomorrow, and that there may be no tomorrow at all if we act in this way, there will be no dialogue whatsoever. There must be some way of making a start. So we decided to take this step, although, I repeat, this was not easy for us.

In view of our readiness to make deep cuts in nuclear weapons, we put the question as follows: as soon as we enter the concrete phase of the elimination of nuclear weapons, we must be absolutely clear on the question of verification. Verification must now become stricter. The Soviet Union stands for triple verification, which would enable each side to feel perfectly confident that it would not be led into a trap. We reaffirmed our readiness for any form of verification. That question was solved, too, because of this stand of ours.

If we set about the practical abolition of nuclear weapons, another problem will arise: each side should have guarantees that during that time the other side will not be seeking military superiority. I think this is a perfectly fair and legitimate requirement both from a political and a military point of view.

Politically—if we were to begin reductions, we should see to it that all existing brakes on the development of new types of weapons are not only preserved, but also strengthened.

Militarily—steps should indeed be taken to preclude the following situation: both sides have been reducing their nuclear potentials, and while the reduction process is under way one of the sides secretly makes the necessary preparations and captures the initiative and attains military superiority. This is inadmissible. I apply this to the Soviet Union. And we have every right to demand the same of the American side.

That is why we raised this question: if we should enter the stage of a real, deep reduction, within ten years—and that's how things looked to us at the meeting—the nuclear potentials of the Soviet Union and the United States would have been eliminated; in that case, it would be necessary to ensure that during this period the mechanisms restraining the arms race, such as the ABM Treaty above all, are not weakened, but strengthened. Our proposal was thus reduced to the following: the sides should strengthen the ABM Treaty, a treaty of unlimited duration, by assuming equal commitments not to use the right to pull out of this Treaty within the ten-year period, the period during which the nuclear potentials would be reduced.

Is this proposition a correct one, is it logical? It is logical. Is it serious? It is serious. Does it meet the interests of both sides? It meets the interests of both sides. We also pointed out that all obligations under the ABM Treaty should be strictly fulfilled within these ten years, that only ABM research and testing in laboratory conditions should be allowed.

What did we mean by this? We realize the commitment of the U.S. Administration and the U.S. President to SDI. Our consent to the continuation of laboratory tests apparently grants the President the opportunity to perfect his ideas and eventually to clarify exactly what SDI is. But for many people, ourselves included, it is already clear as to what SDI is all about.

And it was at that point that a true battle began between two differing approaches to issues in world politics, including those of the termination of the arms race and a ban on nuclear weapons. The President insisted to the bitter end that America should have the right to conduct research and testing on every aspect of SDI both in and outside the laboratory, including in outer space. But who will agree to this?

We were on the verge of taking major and historic decisions, because until now the central issue in previous treaties—ABM, SALT-I, SALT-II—has always been arms limitations only, while today it has become considerable reductions. We have now been convinced one more time that the U.S. Administration, confident in American technological superiority, is hoping to obtain military superiority through SDI. And so it has gone so far as to bury the accords which had almost been achieved and on which we had already reached agreement. The instructions were to be given for drawing up the treaties, and the procedures were to be worked out for their actual implementation. They could be signed during my visit to Washington. But the American side torpedoed all of this.

I told the President that we were missing a historic chance. Our positions had never been so close. When saying goodbye, the President told me that he was disappointed and that I had arrived unwilling to reach agreements and accords. Why, he asked, do you, because of the one word SDI, display such a rigid approach to this issue and to that of testing? And I answered that it is not a matter of words, but rather of substance.

Herein lies the key to understanding what the U.S. Administration has in mind—the same thing as the U.S. military-industrial complex has in mind. The U.S. Administration is being held captive by this complex and thus the President is not free to take such a decision.

We took breaks, resumed debates and I noticed that the President was not supported. And that was why our meeting failed even though we were already near to producing historic results. That was the dramatic situation that developed at the meeting in Reykjavik. In spite of the very substantial concessions our side had made, we failed to reach an accord.

Although it was fraught with difficulties, our dialogue with the U.S.A. continued after Geneva. I expressed my opinion to the President as to what our meeting during my visit to the United States should be like. This is not a condition; it is my understanding of our responsibility, both my own and the President's. This responsibility requires precisely this approach to a future meeting in Washington.

We need a productive meeting. It should lead to tangible results and cardinal changes, especially on such vital issues as those of controlling nuclear arms, ending the arms race, and eliminating nuclear weapons. I told the President in my letters to him and again in person during our meeting: Mr. President, you and I must not allow our meeting in Washington to fail. That is why I called for a meeting without delay, which was held here in Reykjavik. We have constructive contributions to make so as to reach agreement in Washington; these are serious proposals and serious draft decisions.

I cannot allow myself even for a minute to consider the possibility of a meeting in Washington failing. What then, generally speaking, would people think in the Soviet Union, in the U.S.A. and all over the world? What sort of politicians are heading those two huge nations on which the fate of the entire world greatly depends? They meet with one another, exchange letters, and have already held their third meeting, but they cannot agree on anything. I think this would be simply a scandalous outcome with unpredictable consequences.

We just cannot allow this to happen. It would be disappointing not only for our own countries, but for the entire world. This is in fact an outline of a Washington meeting as it should be held and the results we should achieve. That was what prompted us to propose a working meeting here, in Reykjavik, so as to sort out everything in a businesslike manner, to listen to each other attentively and to try to find points of contact and common approaches that would meet the interests of our two countries, the interests of our allies and the interests of the peoples of all countries.

Regrettably, the Americans came to this meeting empty-handed, with the same old moth-eaten trash from which the Geneva talks are already choking. We tabled the proposals, which I have already spoken about, in order to overturn the situation developing, to clear the path, to bring negotiations up to a new level, and to make real decisions. And now you also know what happened.

What is to be done? The reality is that both the United States and the Soviet Union remain. A character in a novel by one of our Russian writers had planned "to close out" America. We are free of such syndromes. America is a reality. But it is not just the Soviet Union and the United States; the entire world is a reality, and today one cannot obtain authority or, what is more important, resolve any problems if one does not reckon with the realities of the modern world.

We felt that there was a definite lack of a new way of thinking at this meeting. And the ghost of pursuit for military superiority reemerged. This summer I met with Mr. Nixon, and he said to me then: I have grounds to say, on the basis of my vast political and life experience, that the search for that ghost of superiority has taken us too far. Now we do not know how to break away from the mounted stockpiles of nuclear weapons. All this is complicating and poisoning the situation in the world.

I think, nevertheless, that the entire meeting here was of major significance. We did, after all, come close to reaching agreements; only they have yet to be endorsed. We put our proposals forward in a package. I think you understand why this was done. The very path that we have traversed in reaching these agreements here in Iceland on major cuts in nuclear weapons has given us substantial experience and we have made considerable gains.

I think that both we and the U.S. President should reflect

upon the entire situation that ultimately arose here at this meeting, return once again to the issues under discussion, and try to step over the obstacles dividing us. We have agreed on many things already and have traversed a long path. The President most likely needs to consult with Congress, with political circles and with the American public.

Let America ponder all this. We will be waiting and will not withdraw the proposals we have made public. In fact, we have come near to reaching an agreement on these proposals. This is the first point.

Second, I think that all the realistic forces in the world must act now. All of us—those in the socialist world, in the capitalist world, and in the developing world—now have a unique chance: to really start, at last, work toward ending the arms race, banning nuclear weapons, eliminating these weapons, and removing the nuclear threat from mankind. In connection with this we submitted the following proposal to the U.S. President: let us agree that our representatives start talks on banning nuclear explosions immediately after the conclusion of our meeting in Reykjavik. Furthermore, we displayed a flexible approach and said that we regard this as a process during which we would also examine at some stage, perhaps even on a top-priority basis, the issue of ceilings on nuclear explosion yields, the issue of the number of nuclear explosions per year, and the fate of the 1974 and 1976 treaties. We would thus move further toward the elaboration of a comprehensive treaty banning all nuclear explosions.

We were close to establishing a formula on this issue as well. We told the American side that we do not demand that they introduce a moratorium. That is up to you. You will report to your Congress and to your people as to whether you will continue nuclear explosions or whether you will join our moratorium after the talks have started. That is up to you. But let us begin full-scale talks to work out an agreement that would ban nuclear explosions completely and finally.

Thus the positions drew closer together here. But the search was ended and all discussions halted when talks broke down on the issue of the ABM Treaty and we ended the meeting.

I think that we and the Americans should think about all of this, and that the world public should reflect upon the situation that has evolved in the world in regard to the principal issues of concern to the peoples of all countries—those of war and peace and of the nuclear threat. I do not think it is any exaggeration to say that everything we proposed to the President meets the interests of the American people and the peoples of all countries. If someone thinks that is not true, he should listen to the demands of the American people, the Soviet people, and the peoples of all countries.

Arriving here for this meeting, I said that it was time for action. The time to act really has arrived, and we must not waste it. And we will act. We will not give up our peace policy, our policy of fighting against the arms race and for the banning of nuclear weapons, our policy for eliminating nuclear weapons and the threat posed to the entire planet. And I am positive that we are not alone in this struggle.

This is what I wanted to tell you right now, immediately after the conclusion of the meeting. Perhaps I could say more if I had had more time to ponder everything that happened. It seems to me, however, that I expressed myself clearly and definitely on all issues.

We touched also on many other issues in the course of the meeting with the President. We discussed humanitarian issues and dealt with specific problems in that sphere. Two groups of experts were at work. You probably already know about that. One of them was headed from our side by Akhromeyev, Marshal of the Soviet Union and Chief of the General Staff, while the American side was headed by Paul Nitze. They worked practically the entire night.

The group on humanitarian issues was headed from our side by Bessmertnykh, Deputy Foreign Minister, and from the American side by Ms. Ridgway, Assistant Secretary of State.

There was an interesting exchange of opinions there as well, and certain aspects of the understandings reached could have become a component part of the final document. But because the meeting as a whole collapsed, the entire process came to a standstill.

As you see, this was an interesting, important, and promising meeting on the whole. But for the time being it has ended this way.

But let us not despair. I think that with this meeting we

have reached the very important stage of understanding where we are. And it has been shown that accords are possible. I am sure of this.

Thank you.

Do you really have questions after such a detailed speech? Well, let's have them. We will be here until dawn.

Question *(Czechoslovak Television):* Mikhail Sergeyevich, you said that a historic chance has been missed here, in Reykjavik. When, do you think, will a new chance emerge?

Answer: You know I would answer optimistically. Because much was accomplished before the meeting and at the meeting itself. If we think everything over again and if realism and responsibility reign—in the United States, in the White House, and in our Soviet leadership—then the chance will not be lost to resolve these issues.

Question *(The Japan Broadcasting Corporation):* Does this mean that the dialogue with the U.S.A. and with the Reagan Administration is continuing? Or you think that the possibilities for a productive dialogue with President Reagan are very slim?

Answer: I think that the need for dialogue at present is even greater, no matter how fraught with difficulties it might be.

Question *(the Soviet newspaper Pravda):* Mikhail Sergeyevich, why do you think the U.S. Administration decided to wreck the negotiations, to act so irresponsibly, and to ignore world public opinion?

Answer: It seems to me that America has yet to make up its mind. I don't think it has done this yet. This, we felt, reflected on the President's stand.

Question *(the Australian Radio Broadcasting Corporation):* You said that President Reagan is being held captive by the military-industrial complex. Does this mean that no progress will be made at all over the next two years? Do you have hopes that the next U.S. President will not be held captive by this complex?

Answer: Irrespective of what the military-industrial complex is at present and irrespective of the weight it carries in present-day America, let us not overestimate its potential. In any country the final say is with the people, and this includes the American people.

Question *(Icelandic Radio and Television):* After the meeting's poor outcome will the Soviet Union counter in some way the American SDI program and will it launch its space-arms program full blast?

Answer: I think that you have understood the essence of the Soviet position. If we have now approached a stage at which we will start cutting drastically nuclear weapons, both strategic and medium-range missiles (we have already come close to reaching an understanding with the Americans to do this within the next ten years), then we have the right to demand the guarantee that nothing unexpected and unforeseen will take place during this period. This also includes spheres such as that of the ABM system, and especially its space-based element.

I told the President that SDI does not worry us in military terms. In my opinion, there are only a few people even in America who believe that such a system can be created. Furthermore, if in the end America decides to do this, our reply will not be symmetrical. It's true, Mr. President, I told him, that I am allegedly your ally on the issue of SDI. He was surprised by this. And I told him it turns out that because I so sharply criticize SDI, you are supplied with a convincing argument that SDI is necessary. You put it simply: if Gorbachev is against it, then that means it's a good thing. And thus you earn applause and financing. True, cynics and skeptics have appeared who say: what if this is Gorbachev's crafty design—to stay out of SDI and thus ruin America. So you figure this one out yourself. But at any rate SDI does not scare us. I say this with confidence, for it is irresponsible to bluff in such matters. There will be a reply to the Strategic Defense Initiative. There will be one, though it will be asymmetrical. And it will not cost us much at that.

But what is the danger involved in SDI? For one thing, there is a political danger. Right away a situation is created which lends itself to uncertainty and stirs up mistrust and suspicion of one another. Then the reduction of nuclear weapons will be put aside. In short, a quite different situation is needed for us to seriously consider the question of reducing nuclear weapons. Second, we must not forget about the military side of the issue. SDI can lead to the appearance of new types of weapons. This we also can say with competence. It can bring about an entirely new stage of the arms race that can have very serious consequences.

It works out that, on the one hand, we agree to start reducing nuclear weapons—at present the most dangerous and dreadful—and, on the other, we are supposed to agree to research, and even carry it out to space, with the intention of creating novel weapons. This does not correspond to logic.

Question *(The Washington Post):* You have just held another meeting with President Reagan after two days of sessions. What is your impression of the President as a political figure? Do you believe that he shares your sense of responsibility for the destinies of the world?

Answer: My impression is that Mr. Reagan and I can continue the dialogue and search for ways to resolve major pressing problems, including those I have spoken about.

Question *(The Danish Broadcasting Corporation):* Do the unsatisfactory results of the meeting mean that no progress will be achieved on the banning of nuclear tests and on other problems which were discussed yesterday and today? Is this problem—the banning of nuclear tests—linked with other problems discussed at the sessions?

Answer: I have already answered this question. We do not believe that our contacts with Americans and with the President, much less international relations, have been severed as a result of the latest developments. The quest is under way, and it will be continued. All the more so, for the developments that took place here, in Iceland, make all people realize that they should join the common struggle for the normalization of the international situation, the quest for resolutions to dead-end situations, including those which were discussed in Reykjavik. In fact, one such dead-end situation arose here. However, I am an optimist.

Question *(GDR Television):* You said that the meeting had brought no results. Does this mean that it was useless? What do you think: has peace become more reliable since the Reykjavik meetings?

Answer: I believe you have thought your question out thoroughly. One thing I always like about our German friends is their concise manner of expression including the expression of thoughts. The fact that we concluded our meeting without having reached agreement on the problems to which we seemed to have found approaches —this, of course, is sad and disappointing. Nonetheless, I would not say the meeting was useless. On the contrary, it is a new stage in a complicated and difficult dialogue in the search for solutions. After all, these are difficult solutions to complex issues. Therefore, let us not spread panic throughout the world. But at the same time, the world should know all that is going on, and it should not feel like a passive bystander. The time has come for vigorous action from all quarters.

Question *(the American TV company ABC):* Mr. General Secretary, I do not understand why, when given an opportunity to achieve agreement with President Reagan on cuts in nuclear weapons, the Soviet side did not agree to SDI research. You yourself said in Geneva that you were willing to pay a high price for nuclear arms cuts. And now, when such an opportunity appeared, you dismissed it.

Answer: Your question contains an element of criticism, so I will answer it in some detail.

First, the U. S. President came to Reykjavik empty-handed. The American delegation, I would say, brought us trash from the Geneva talks. It was only thanks to the far-reaching proposals of the Soviet side that we came close to reaching some very major agreements (though they were not in fact formalized) on cuts in strategic offensive weapons and on medium-range missiles. We naturally hoped in that situation— and I think this is perfectly clear to a politician, a military man, and any normal person in general—that since we were signing such major agreements, we should make sure that nothing would happen that might thwart that difficult process toward which we had been moving for decades. I have already said what is meant here. I will add: the American side has long been burrowing under the ABM Treaty. It has already called into question SALT-II and would like now in Reykjavik to stage a funeral for the ABM Treaty, and with the participation of the Soviet Union and Gorbachev at that. This will not do. The whole world would fail to understand us. I am convinced in this.

If we begin to attack the ABM Treaty, too, the last mechanism which has contributed so much to constraining, in spite of everything, the process of the arms race, we are worthless politicians. But it is not enough to simply preserve it at a time when deep cuts in nuclear weapons are being initiated; it must be strengthened. And we have proposed a mechanism for strengthening it—not to use the right to pull out of the ABM Treaty for the ten years it will take to totally reduce and destroy the nuclear potentials of our countries.

At the same time, in order to ensure that neither the Soviet Union nor the United States seeks to overtake the other in space research and thus achieve military superiority, we said: we are for laboratory research and testing but against taking that research and the testing of components of space-based ABM defenses into outer space. Such is our demand. Thus, our demand, in this case also, was constructive and took into consideration our partner's positions. If it were to agree, the U. S. Administration would gain an opportunity to resolve its problems within the framework of continued laboratory research but without attempts to develop space ABM defenses. That's "an iron" logic, as children say, and sometimes we should take our lessons from them.

Now let us give the women the floor.

Question *(The Guardian):* Is the Soviet Union planning any new initiatives for Western Europe after what happened in Reykjavik?

Answer: I think Western Europe hears what I am saying and if it thinks our proposals over and studies them closely, it will find that they meet its interests. We are far from being indifferent to the interests of Western Europe, in whose soil the shoots of new thinking are taking root and where responsibility for the preservation and strengthening of our common European home is growing.

Question *(Newsweek):* What are your plans concerning a visit to Washington? You said that an agreement or two must be achieved before such a visit. Can such agreements be achieved before you come to Washington?

Answer: I think that in spite of the dramatic developments of today, we are not farther from Washington but closer to it. If the President and the U. S. Administration will listen to my proposal to continue reviewing everything we discussed here in Reykjavik and consult those circles whose counsel they deem essential, I do not think everything will be lost. There are opportunities, relying on what we had here in Reykjavik, to reach agreements that would make a meeting in Washington a real possibility which could produce results.

Question *(CNN):* Mr. Gorbachev, you said in your speech that President Reagan should think the situation over and keep counsel with Congress and the American people. Do you think that American public opinion will back the Soviet approach?

Answer: We will wait and see.

Question *(Rude Pravo):* I would like to ask you as a politician and a lawyer: How do you view human rights priorities in the nuclear-missile age and what role can the human factor play in resolving questions of war and peace?

Answer: You are a philosopher. I once studied philosophy myself and have now turned to it again. I think that when we discuss human rights, we should remember that today the question of safeguarding peace and freeing man from the nuclear threat is the main priority. If there is peace, there will be life—and we will sort out our problems one way or another. The number of educated people and educated nations in the world is constantly growing. Nations will sort things out. That is why in discussing human rights I would attach priority to man's right to live. This is first.

Second—as to the human factor—I believe that in the nuclear age (and I consider this a manifestation of a new way of thinking) the threat of nuclear war gives a new dimension to the role of the human factor in preventing this war. A nuclear war will affect everyone regardless of where it breaks out. It is only ill-wishers who see the hand of Moscow behind all anti-war movements, behind all those who work for peace. Today women, children, and men of all ages are rising up, joining hands, and demanding an end to the dangerous trend leading the world toward nuclear war. The role of the human factor in these conditions is growing immensely.

Queston *(Izvestia):* There has been much and frequent talk in the White House to the effect that Soviet ICBMs pose the main danger to America. We proposed in Reykjavik that this main danger to America be eliminated within ten years. What do you think? Why did the other side prove unwilling to eliminate this main danger, avert it from its country?

Answer: You are right to pose this question. For many years the following argument was used: the Soviet Union, they alleged, is not serious about disarmament and ending the arms race, inasmuch as it disregards America's concerns.

As you see, we proposed radical reductions. And we put the question very pointedly, at that. There is a triad of strategic weapons recognized by both us and the Americans. We suggested that the whole triad of strategic armed forces be cut by 50 percent over the first five years. This was a major step.

At the same time, however, we told the Americans that we had a concern of our own. A large part of the United States' strategic forces is deployed on submarines. This is close to 700 missiles with a total of nearly 6,000 independently targetable multiple warheads. And these submarines are known to be circulating in the seas and oceans around the Soviet Union. Where will they strike? This is no less dangerous than heavy land-based missiles.

In short, when they do not want to deal with certain questions, they look for problems and raise artificial obstacles. Here, however, in Reykjavik, we excluded the possibility of such fabricated obstacles. This is what's important. We undertook a very important step in removing stipulations with regard to medium-range missiles, which we consider to be strategic weapons. We also struck forward-based systems from the list. All this is a demonstration of our good will. Nevertheless, the Americans made no effort to meet us halfway.

The Americans think that they will achieve military superiority over us via outer space and thus realize the idea of one of their presidents, who said: he who will dominate outer space will dominate earth. This shows that we are forced to deal with imperial ambitions.

The world today is not what it once was, however. It does not want to be, and will not be, the private domain of either the United States of America or the Soviet Union. Every country has the right to choose, the right to its own ideology, to its own values. If we fail to recognize this, there will be no international relations. There will be only chaos and the law of the jungle. We will never agree to this.

America must long for the "good ole days," when it was strong and militarily superior to us, since we had emerged from the war economically weakened.

Apparently there is nostalgia for the past in America. Yet we would wish for our American partners to come to grips with today's realities. It is essential that they do so. Otherwise, that is if the Americans do not start thinking in today's terms and proceeding from today's realities, we all will not make progress in our search for the right solutions.

Question *(Bulgarian television):* I take it that the Geneva talks will not be stopped, and that the Soviet leadership will give instructions to the Soviet delegation to search for ways to resolve the problems which are yet unresolved.

Answer: You are correct.

Question: Do you think that after the Reykjavik meeting similar instructions will be given to the American delegation?

Answer: I hope so.

Question *(the Czechoslovak ČTK news agency):* In your opinion, how will the outcome of the Reykjavik meeting influence the all-European process?

Answer: I think that at this moment of responsibility the politicians and the peoples of Europe will measure up to the situation. Time requires actions, not just eloquent statements that are not followed up by anything concrete. The world is tired, fed up with empty talk; it needs real progress in the sphere of disarmament and the elimination of nuclear weapons. I believe that this trend will gain prominence. I am pinning particular hope on the wisdom and sense of responsibility of the politicians and peoples of Europe.

Question *(the American television company NBC):* As I understand, you are directly calling on other members of the world community to act as a kind of a lobby in order to influence the United States and make it change its mind?

Answer: We know how developed lobbyism is in your country, how the political process goes in America. Perhaps that is why it was difficult for the President to make a decision at this meeting. But when the matter at hand deals with consolidating peace and undertaking real steps to this end, when concerted efforts are needed—this concerns all, not just the United States and the Soviet Union—then, I think, one should speak not about lobbyism, but about the sense of responsibility, the common sense of peoples, about the appreciation of today's peace and the need to protect it. Therefore, it is insulting to accuse peoples or movements campaigning for peace of being lobbyists for the Soviet Union. The point is that people uphold their political and civic positions.

Question *(the Icelandic newspaper Morgunbladid):* I work as a newspaper publisher in Iceland. Was it difficult for you to decide to come to Reykjavik? After all, Iceland is a member of NATO. At the same time, as you know, our government proposed that the North be made a nuclear-free zone, and I would like to know your attitude toward this.

Answer: I wanted to conclude with this topic and will gladly take advantage of this question put by a representative of the Icelandic press to do so. I would like to remind everyone that it was the USSR who suggested Iceland as a possible venue for the meeting. That is why we had no difficulties whatsoever in deciding to come here.

I want to thank the government of Iceland and the people of Iceland for employing their entire potential—human, organizational, and material—toward resolving all problems involved in arranging this important meeting. We are grateful for this, and we have felt at ease here. I received much interesting information from Raisa Maximovna, who had many meetings in Iceland. They were all very interesting. We are pleased with the friendly atmosphere here and the great interest shown to our country. We thank Iceland and the Icelandic government for what they have done. We wish your people prosperity.

As to the latter part of your question concerning the intention of your country's government to make the North a nuclear-free zone—we welcome this.

Dear friends, thank you for your attention. I think that we have spent this time together usefully. I wish you all the best.

TELEVISED SPEECH

Report on the Meeting in Iceland with President Reagan

Moscow, October 14, 1986

Good evening, dear comrades.

As you know, my meeting in Iceland with the President of the United States, Ronald Reagan, concluded the day before yesterday, on Sunday. A press conference on its results has been televised. The text of my statement and my replies to journalists have been published.

Having returned home, I consider it my duty to tell you how the meeting went and how we assess what took place in Reykjavik.

The results of the meeting in the capital of Iceland have just been discussed at a meeting of the Politburo of the CPSU Central Committee. A report will be published tomorrow outlining the opinion our Party's leadership has formed about this major political event, the consequences of which, we are convinced, will be felt in international relations for a long time to come.

Before Reykjavik much was said and written about the forthcoming meeting. As is usually the case in such situations, there was a myriad of conjectures and views. This is normal. And in this case there was speculation as well.

Now that the meeting is over its results are in the center of attention of the world public. Everybody wants to know: What happened? What results did it produce? What will the world be like after it?

We strove to give the main questions of world politics— ending the arms race and nuclear disarmament—top priority at the meeting in Reykjavik. And that is how it was.

What are the motives for our persistence in this matter? One often hears conjectures abroad that the reason lies in our domestic difficulties. There is a thesis in Western calculations that the Soviet Union will ultimately be unable to endure the arms race economically, that it will break down and bow to the West. One need only squeeze the Soviet Union harder and step up the position of strength. Incidentally, the U.S. President made a remark to this effect in an address after our meeting.

I have said repeatedly that such plans are not only built on air; they are dangerous as they may result in fatal political decisions. We know our own problems better than anyone else. We do have problems which we openly discuss and resolve. We have our own plans and approaches on this score, and there is a common will of the Party and the people. In general, I would have to say that the Soviet Union's strength today lies in its unity, dynamism, and the political activity of its people. I think that these trends and, consequently, the strength of our society will be growing. The Soviet Union has the capacity to respond to any challenge, should the need arise. The Soviet people know this; the whole world should know this, too. But we are opposed to playing power games, for this is an extremely dangerous thing in the nuclear-missile age.

We are firmly convinced that the protracted feverish state of international relations harbors the threat of a sudden and fatal crisis. We must take practical steps away from the nuclear abyss. We need joint Soviet-American efforts, efforts on the part of the entire international community in order to radically improve international relations.

For the sake of these goals we, the Soviet leadership, carried out extensive preparatory work on the eve of the meeting, even before we received President Reagan's consent to attend it. Taking part in this work, in addition to the Politburo and the Secretariat of the CPSU Central Committee, were the Ministry of Foreign Affairs and the Defense Ministry, plus some other departments, representatives of science, military experts, and specialists from various branches of industry. The positions we worked out for the Reykjavik meeting were the result of wide-scale, repeated discussion with our friends, with the leadership of the socialist community countries. We sought to make the content of the meeting as meaningful as possible, putting forth far-reaching proposals.

Now about the meeting itself, how events developed there. This should be discussed not only in order to affirm the truth, which is already being distorted by our partners in the Reykjavik talks, but, more importantly, to inform you of what we plan to do next.

The first conversation with President Reagan started on Saturday, at 10:30 A.M. After the greetings necessary on such occasions and a brief conference with journalists, the two of us remained alone; only our interpreters were present. We exchanged views on the general situation, on the way the dialogue between our two countries was developing, and outlined the problems to be discussed.

Then I asked the President to listen to our concrete proposals on the main questions which prompted our meeting. I already spoke at length about them during the press conference. Still, I will recall them here in brief.

A whole *set of major measures* was submitted to the talks. These measures, if accepted, would usher in a new era in the life of mankind—a nuclear-free era. Herein lies the essence of the radical change in the world situation, the possibility of which was obvious and realistic. The talk was no longer about limiting nuclear arms, as was the case with the SALT-I, SALT-II and other treaties, but about the elimination of nuclear weapons within a comparatively short period of time.

The first proposal concerned strategic offensive weapons. I expressed our readiness to reduce them by 50 percent within the next five years. The strategic weapons on land, water, and in the air would be halved. In order to make it easier to reach accord, we agreed to a major concession by revoking our previous demand that the strategic equation include American medium-range missiles reaching our territory and American forward-based systems. We were also ready to take into account the U.S. concern over our heavy missiles. We regarded the proposal on strategic arms in the context of their total elimination, as we had suggested on January 15 this year.

Our second proposal concerned medium-range missiles. I suggested to the President that both Soviet and American missiles of this class in Europe be completely eliminated. Here, too, we were willing to make a substantial concession: we stated that, contrary to our previous stand, the nuclear-missile weapons of Britain and France need not be taken into account. We proceeded from the necessity to pave the way to detente in Europe, to free the European nations of the fear of a nuclear catastrophe, and then to move further—toward the elimination of all nuclear weapons. You will agree that this was another bold step on our part.

Anticipating the possible objections, we said we would agree to freeze missiles with a range of under 1,000 kilometers and immediately begin talks on what is to be done with them in the future. As for the medium-range missiles in the Asian part of our country—this issue was invariably present in President Reagan's "global version"—we suggested that talks be started immediately on this subject as well. As you see, here, too, our proposals were serious and far-reaching, facilitating a radical solution of this problem as well.

The third question I raised during my first talk with the President, one that formed an integral part of our proposal package, was the existing *Anti-Ballistic Missile (ABM) Treaty and the Nuclear Test Ban Treaty.* Our approach is as follows: Since we are entering a totally new situation which will witness the beginning of substantial reductions in nuclear weapons and their complete elimination in the foreseeable future, it is necessary to protect oneself from any unexpected developments. We are speaking of weapons which to this day make up the core of this country's defenses. Therefore it is necessary to exclude everything that could undermine equality in the process of disarmament, to preclude any chance of developing weapons of a new type that would ensure military superiority. We regard this stance as perfectly legitimate and logical.

This being the case, we have firmly stated the need for strict observance of the 1972 ABM Treaty of unlimited duration. Moreover, in order to consolidate its regime, we proposed to the President that a mutual pledge be taken by the U.S. and the Soviet Union to refrain from pulling out of the treaty for at least ten years, during which time strategic weapons would be abolished.

Taking into account the particular difficulties the Administration created for itself on this problem when the President personally committed himself to space weapons, to the so-called SDI, we did not demand termination of work in this field. The implication was, however, that all provisions of the ABM Treaty would be fully honored—that is, research and testing in this sphere would not go beyond laboratories. This restriction applies equally to the U.S.A. and to the USSR.

Listening to us, the President made remarks, asked for clarification on certain points. During the conversation, we presented the question of verification firmly and with resolve, linking it with the postnuclear situation. This situation demands special responsibility. I told the President that if both countries embark on nuclear disarmament, the Soviet Union will make its position on verification stricter. Verification must be plausible, comprehensive, and indisputable. It must create full confidence in reliable compliance with the agreement and include the right to on-site inspection.

I must tell you, comrades, that the President's initial reaction was not entirely negative. He even said: "What you have just stated is reassuring." But it did not escape our attention that our American interlocutors (George Shultz as well as Comrade Shevardnadze had joined the conversation on these issues by then) appeared to be somewhat confused. At the same time, immediate doubts and objections cropped up in their separate remarks. Straight away, the President and the Secretary of State started talking about divergencies and disagreement. In their words we clearly discerned the familiar old tones we had heard at the Geneva negotiations for many months: we were reminded of all sorts of sublevels on strategic nuclear armaments, the "interim proposal" on missiles in Europe, and that we, the Soviet Union, should join the SDI and should replace the existing ABM Treaty with some new agreement, and many other things in the same vein.

I expressed my surprise. How can this be? We propose to accept the American "zero option" in Europe and take up negotiations on medium-range missiles in Asia while you, Mr. President, are abandoning your previous stand. This is incomprehensible.

As for ABM, we propose to preserve and strengthen this fundamentally important agreement, and you want to give it up and even propose to replace it with some new treaty, and thereby—following renunciation of SALT-II—to wreck this mechanism standing guard over strategic stability. This, too, is incomprehensible.

We grasped the essence of the SDI plans as well, I said. If the United States creates a three-tiered ABM system in outer space, we shall respond to it. However, we are concerned about another problem: SDI would mean the transfer of weapons to a new medium, which would destabilize the strategic situation, make it even worse than it is today. If this is the United States' purpose, this should be stated plainly. But if you really want reliable security for your people and for the world in general, then the American stand is totally ungrounded.

I told the President directly: We have put forward major new proposals. However, what we are hearing from you now is precisely what everybody is fed up with and what can lead us nowhere. Mr. President, please, reexamine our proposals carefully and give us an answer point by point. I gave him an English translation of a draft of possible instructions that had been drawn up in Moscow and which, in the event that agreement is reached in principle, could be given to the Foreign Ministers and other departments to draw up *three draft agreements*. They could be signed later during my visit to the U.S.A.

In the afternoon we met again. The President announced the stand that had been drawn up during the break. As soon as he uttered the first phrases, it became clear that they were offering us the same old moth-eaten trash, as I put it at the press conference, from which the Geneva talks are already choking: all sorts of intermediate versions, figures, levels, sublevels, and so on. There was not a single new thought, fresh approach, or idea which would contain even a hint of a solution, of advance.

It was becoming clear, comrades, that the Americans had come to Reykjavik with nothing at all to offer. The impression was that they had come there empty-handed to gather fruits in their basket.

The situation was taking a dramatic turn.

The American President was not ready to take any radical decisions on questions of principle, to meet the Soviet side halfway so as to give a real impetus to productive and encouraging negotiations. This is precisely what I impressed upon the President in my letter, in which I put forward the idea that an urgent meeting be held in order to give a powerful impetus at the level of the top leaders of the two countries—an impetus to negotiations on nuclear disarmament.

Confident that our proposals were well-balanced and took

the partner's interests into account, we decided not to abandon our efforts to bring about a breakthrough at the meeting. A ray of hope on strategic armaments appeared, following many clarifying questions. Clinging to this we took one more great step in search of a compromise. I told the President: We both recognize that there is a triad of strategic offensive armaments—ground-based missiles, strategic submarines and strategic bombers. So let us make a 50-percent reduction in each part of the triad. And then there will be no need for all sorts of levels and sublevels, for all sorts of calculations.

After lengthy debate, we managed to reach mutual understanding on that issue.

Then the discussion turned to the problem of medium-range missiles. The Americans stubbornly stuck to the so-called interim proposal which provides for the preservation of a part of their missiles, including Pershing-2 missiles, in Europe, and, naturally, of our corresponding SS-20 missiles. We categorically opposed this, for reasons I have already described. Europe deserves to be free of nuclear weapons, to stop being held nuclear hostage. As for the President, it was difficult for him to fight his own "zero option," which he had promoted for so long. And still, we sensed the Americans' intention to thwart agreement under the guise of special concern for their allies in Asia.

The American side said much that was ungrounded. It is embarrassing to repeat it here. The talks began to move forward only when on this issue, too, we took one more step to meet the American side and agreed to the following formula: zero missiles in Europe, 100 warheads on medium-range missiles in the eastern part of our country and, accordingly, 100 warheads on medium-range missiles on U.S. territory. Most importantly, we managed to agree on eliminating nuclear weapons on the European continent.

Thus, accord was reached on the problem of medium-range missiles, too, and a major breakthrough was made in this direction of nuclear disarmament. The American Administration failed to hold out against our insistent striving to achieve positive results.

However, there still remained the ABM issue and the ban on nuclear explosions.

Two groups of experts, one from each side, worked through

the night before we met on Sunday for our third talk, which
was scheduled to be the concluding one. They thoroughly
analyzed what had been discussed at the two previous meetings with the President and reported the results of their night-
time debates respectively to the President and myself.

The result? *A possibility arose of undertaking to work out
agreements on strategic offensive armaments and on medium-
range missiles.*

The ABM Treaty in this situation acquired key significance;
its role was becoming even more important. Could one destroy, I asked, what has made it possible so far to somehow
restrain the arms race? If we now begin reducing strategic
and medium-range nuclear weapons, both sides should be
confident that during that time nobody will develop new
systems that would undermine stability and parity. Therefore, in my view, it would be perfectly logical to fix the time-
frame—the Americans mentioned seven years, and we proposed ten years—within which nuclear weapons must be
eliminated. We proposed ten years during which neither the
Soviet nor the American side may avail itself of the right—
and they have such a right—to withdraw from the ABM
Treaty, and during which research and tests may be conducted in laboratories only.

Thus, I think, you understand why we chose exactly ten
years? This was no random choice. The logic is plain and fair.
Fifty percent of strategic armaments is to be reduced in the
first five years, the other half in the next five years. This makes
ten years.

In connection with this I proposed that our high-ranking
representatives be instructed to start full-scale talks on the
discontinuation of nuclear explosions and thus in the end an
agreement could at last be worked out completely banning
explosions. In the course of working out the agreement—and
here again we displayed flexibility and assumed a constructive stand—specific issues connected with nuclear explosions could be resolved.

The reasoning President Reagan used in his response is a
familiar one to us in that we have come across it earlier both
in Geneva and in his public statements; SDI is a defense
system. If we begin eliminating nuclear weapons, how will we
protect ourselves from some madman who might get hold of

them? And Reagan is ready to share with us the results obtained within the research done on SDI. In answering this last remark, I said: Mr. President, I do not take this idea seriously, your idea about sharing with us the results of research on SDI. You do not even want to share with us oil equipment or equipment for the dairy industry, and still you expect us to believe your promise to share the research developments in the SDI project. That would be something like a "Second American Revolution," and revolutions do not occur that often. I told President Reagan that we should be realists and pragmatists. This is a more reliable approach, for the issues at hand are very serious.

By the way, when trying to justify his position on SDI yesterday, the President said that he needed this program to ensure that America and its allies remain invulnerable to a Soviet missile attack. As you see, he did not even make any mention of madmen. And the "Soviet threat" was again brought to light.

But this is nothing but a trick. We proposed that not only strategic armanents, but also all the nuclear armaments in the possession of the U.S. and the USSR, be eliminated under strict control.

How can there be a need to protect the "freedom of America" and its friends from Soviet nuclear missiles if these missiles no longer exist?

If there are no nuclear weapons, why should we need to protect ourselves from them? Thus the entire Star Wars undertaking is purely militaristic in nature and is directed at obtaining military superiority over the Soviet Union.

Let us return, however, to the talks. Although an agreement on strategic arms and medium-range missiles had been reached, it was premature to believe that everything had been completely settled as a result of the two first sessions. An entire day was ahead, nearly eight hours of nonstop and intense discussions in which these issues, which seemed to have been agreed upon already, were to be raised again and again.

The President sought to touch upon ideological issues as well in these discussions and in this way demonstrated, to put it mildly, total ignorance and the inability to understand both the socialist world and what is happening there. I rejected the attempts to link ideological differences to issues of ending the arms race. I persistently drew the President and the Secretary of State back to the subject that had brought us to Reykjavik. It was necessary to remind our interlocutors repeatedly about the third element of our package of proposals, without which it would be impossible to reach accord on the whole. I have in mind the need to comply strictly with the ABM Treaty, to consolidate the regime of this major treaty and to ban nuclear tests.

We had to draw attention again and again to things that seemed to be perfectly clear: having agreed to major reductions in nuclear arms, attempts—both in deed and in thought—to shake strategic stability and to circumvent the agreements should be made to be impossible. That is why we should have confidence in the preservation of the ABM Treaty, which has no time limit. You, Mr. President, I said, ought to agree that if we are beginning to reduce nuclear weapons, there should be the full assurance that the U.S. will not do anything behind the back of the USSR, while the Soviet Union will also not do anything to jeopardize U.S. security, to disvalue the agreement or to create difficulties.

Hence the key task to strengthen the ABM regime: to keep the results of the research under this program in the laboratory and prevent them from being applied in outer space. It is necessary that the right to pull out of the ABM Treaty is not used for ten years in order to create the confidence that in settling the issue of arms reduction at the same time we are ensuring security for both sides and for the world as a whole.

But the Americans obviously had other intentions. We saw that the U.S. actually wants to defeat the ABM Treaty, to revise it so as to develop a large-scale space-based ABM system for its own conceited ends. It would simply be irresponsible of me to agree to this.

As far as nuclear testing is concerned, it was perfectly clear here as well why the American side does not want to conduct serious talks on this issue. It would have preferred to carry these talks on endlessly and thus postpone the settlement of the issue of banning nuclear tests for decades. And once again we had to reject attempts to use the talks as a cover and to get a free hand in the field of nuclear explosions. I said bluntly that I was having doubts about the honesty of the U.S. position and questioned whether there wasn't something in it damaging for the Soviet Union. How can an agreement on the elimination of nuclear arms be reached if the United States continues to perfect these weapons? Still we were under the impression that SDI was the main snag. If it could have been removed it would have been possible to reach an accord on banning nuclear explosions as well.

At a certain point in the talks, when it became absolutely clear that to continue the discussion would be a waste of time, I reminded the other side that we had proposed a definite package of measures and asked them to consider it as such. If we have worked out a common position on the possibility of making major reductions in nuclear arms and at the same time have failed to reach agreement on the issue of ABM and nuclear testing, then everything we have tried to create here falls apart, I said.

The President and the Secretary of State reacted poorly to our firm position, but I could not pose the question in any other way. This is a matter concerning the security of our country, the security of the entire world, all peoples and all continents.

Our proposals were major, truly large-scale and clearly in the nature of compromise. We made concessions. But we did not see even the slightest desire on the American side to respond in kind or to meet us halfway. We were deadlocked. We began thinking about how to conclude the meeting. And nevertheless we continued our efforts to engage our partners in constructive dialogue.

During the conversation that was supposed to be the concluding one we ran out of time. Instead of going our separate ways—we to Moscow and they to Washington—yet another break was announced to allow the sides to think everything over and meet one more time after dinner. On returning to the house of the city's mayor after the break, we made yet another attempt to end the meeting successfully. We proposed the following text as the basis for summing up the positive results.

Here is the text:

"The Soviet Union and the United States will oblige themselves not to use their right to withdraw from the ABM Treaty, which has no time limit, for a period of ten years and during this period to ensure strict observance of all of its provisions. All testing on the space elements of the ABM defense in outer space will be prohibited excluding research and testing conducted in laboratories.

"In the first five years of this decade (until 1991 inclusive) the strategic offensive arms of both sides will be reduced by 50 percent.

"In the next five years of this period the remaining 50 percent of the strategic offensive arms of both sides will be eliminated.

"Thus, the strategic offensive arms of the USSR and the U.S.A. will be completely eliminated by the end of the year 1996."

Commenting on this text, I made an important addition in reference to the document which had been given to the President at the end of our first conversation. This document is basically a proposal to hold special negotiations after the ten years are up and nuclear weapons no longer exist in order to work out mutually acceptable decisions as to what should be done next.

But this time, too, our attempts to reach an agreement were to no avail. For four hours we again tried to make our interlocutors understand that our approach was well founded, that it was not at all threatening, and did not affect the interests of the genuine security of the United States. But with every hour it became more obvious that the Americans would not agree to keep SDI research and testing in the laboratories. They are bent on going into outer space with weapons.

I said firmly that we would never agree to help undermine the ABM Treaty with our own hands. We consider this an issue of principle, as well as a national security issue.

We were thus literally two or three steps from making possibly historic decisions for the entire nuclear-space era, but we were unable to make those last steps. A turning point in the world's history did not take place, even though, I will say again with full confidence, it could have.

Our conscience is clear, however, and we cannot be reproached. We did everything we could.

The scope of our partners' approach was not broad enough. They did not grasp the uniqueness of the moment and, ultimately, they did not have enough courage, sense of responsibility, or political resolve which are all so needed to settle key and pressing issues in world politics. They stuck to old positions which had already eroded with time and did not correspond to the realities of today.

Foreigners in Iceland, and my comrades here have asked me what, in my opinion, were the main reasons for the attitude of the American delegation at the Reykjavik meeting? There are a number of reasons, both subjective and objective, but the main one is that the leadership of that great country relies too heavily on the military-industrial complex, on the monopolistic groups which have turned the nuclear and other arms races into a business, into a way of making money, into the object of their existence and the meaning of their activities.

In my opinion, the Americans are making two serious mistakes in their assessment of the situation.

The first is a tactical mistake. They believe that sooner or later the Soviet Union will reconcile itself to the fact that the U.S. is attempting to revive its strategic diktat, that it will agree to the limitation and reduction of only Soviet weapons. It will do so because, so they think, the USSR is more interested in disarmament agreements than the U.S.A. But this is a grave delusion. The sooner the U.S. Administration overcomes it—I repeat perhaps for the hundredth time—the better it will be for them, for our relations and for the world situation in general.

The other mistake is a strategic one. The United States seeks to exhaust the Soviet Union economically with a buildup of sophisticated and costly space arms. It wants to impose hardships of all kinds on the Soviet leadership, to foil its plans, including those in the social sphere and those for improving our people's living standards, and thus spread among the people discontent in regard to their leaders and the country's leadership. Another aim is to restrict the Soviet Union's potential in its economic ties with developing countries which, in such a situation, would all be compelled to bow down before the United States. These are far-reaching designs. The strategic course of the current U.S. Administration also rests on delusions. Washington, it seems, does not wish to burden itself with a thorough analysis of the changes taking place in our country, does not wish to draw the appropriate practical conclusions for itself and for its course, but is rather busy with wishful thinking. It is building its policy toward the USSR on the basis of this delusion. It is, of course, difficult to predict all the long-term consequences of such a policy. One thing is clear to us already now: it will not and it cannot benefit anyone, including the United States.

Before addressing you, I read through the U.S. President's statement on Reykjavik. I noticed that the President gives himself all the credit for all the proposals discussed. Well, it seems as though these proposals are so attractive to the Americans and the peoples throughout the world that it's possible to resort to such a ruse. We are not consumed by vanity, but it is important that people get the true picture of what happened in Reykjavik.

So what is next? I already said at the press conference that the work done before the meeting and that done in Reykjavik was not in vain. We ourselves did a lot of thinking in connection with the meeting and reexamined a great deal. We have now better cleared the way to continue the fight for peace and disarmament. We freed ourselves from obstructions that had developed, from insignificant issues, and from stereotypes which hindered new approaches in the important area of our policies.

We know where we stand and see the possibilities available to us more clearly. The preparations for the Reykjavik meeting helped us to formulate a platform—a new, bold platform which promises greater chances for ultimate success. It meets the interests of our people and society at this new stage of socialist development. This platform also meets the interests of other countries and nations and thereby merits trust. We are confident that it will be received with understanding in many countries of the world and in the most differing political and public circles.

I think that many people around the world, including leaders vested with power, can and must draw weighty conclusions from the Reykjavik meeting. Everyone will have to think again and again about the essence of the matter, and about why such persistent efforts to achieve a breakthrough and start advancing toward a nonnuclear world and toward universal security have thus far failed to produce the needed result.

I would like to hope that the President also has a better insight now into our analysis, the intentions of the Soviet Union, and into the possibilities and limits for adjusting the Soviet stand. And I hope Mr. Reagan understands our analysis more fully and more precisely since receiving firsthand explanations of our constructive measures for stabilizing and improving the international situation.

The American leadership will obviously need some time. We are realists and we clearly understand that the issues that have remained unsettled for many years and even decades can hardly be settled at a single sitting. We have a great deal of experience in doing business with the United States. And we are aware that the domestic political climate can change there quickly and that the opponents of peace across the ocean are strong and influential. There is nothing new here for us.

If we do not despair, if we do not slam the door and give vent to our emotions—although there is more than enough reason for this—it is because we are sincerely convinced that new efforts are needed aimed at building normal interstate relations in the nuclear epoch. There is no other alternative.

And another thing: after Reykjavik, the infamous SDI became even more conspicuous as an epitome of obstructing peace, as a strong expression of militaristic designs, and an unwillingness to get rid of the nuclear threat looming over mankind. It is impossible to perceive this program in any other way. This is the most important lesson of the Reykjavik meeting.

In summing up these eventful days, I would like to say the following. The meeting was a major event. A reappraisal was made. A qualitatively new situation developed in that no one can continue to act as he acted before. The meeting was useful. It paved the way for a possible step forward, for a real positive shift, should the U.S.A. finally adopt realistic positions and abandon delusion in its appraisals.

The meeting has convinced us that the path we have chosen is correct and that a new mode of political thinking in the nuclear age is necessary and constructive.

We are energetic and determined. Having embarked on a program of reorganization, the country has already traversed a certain path. We have just started this process, but changes have already been made. Growth in industrial production over the past nine months reached 5.2 percent, labor productivity grew by 4.8 percent. National production income rose 4.3 percent as compared to the previous year.

This all is the strongest support for the Party's policies on the part of the people, for this is support by deed.

This shows that under new conditions the people's efforts are helping to accelerate the growth of the country's economic potential and are thus consolidating its defense capabilities.

The Soviet people and the Soviet leadership have unanimously agreed that the policy of socialism can and must be a policy of peace and disarmament. We shall not swerve from the course of the 27th CPSU Congress.

IV

TELEVISED SPEECH
The Impact of the Meeting in Iceland with President Reagan

Moscow, October 22, 1986

Good evening, dear comrades.

I speak with you again, and the subject is again the same—Reykjavik. This is a very serious issue. The outcome of the meeting with the U.S. President has stirred the entire world. A great deal of new data have come out over the past few days demanding assessments which I would like to share with you today.

You will remember that I said at the press conference in Reykjavik that we shall return again and again to this meeting between the leaders of the USSR and the U.S.

I am convinced that we have not yet realized the full significance of what happened. But we will reach this realization; if not today, then tomorrow. We will grasp the full significance of Reykjavik and will do justice to the accomplishments and gains, as well as to the missed opportunities and losses.

Dramatic as the course of the talks and their results were, the Reykjavik meeting greatly facilitated, perhaps for the first time in many decades, our search for a way to achieve nuclear disarmament.

I believe that as a result of the meeting we have now reached a higher level, not only in analyzing the situation, but also in determining the objectives and the framework of possible accords on nuclear disarmament.

Having found ourselves a few steps from an actual agreement on such a difficult and vitally important issue, we all grew to understand more fully the danger facing the world and the need for immediate solutions. And what is most important, we now know that it is both realistic and possible to avert the nuclear threat.

I would like to point out here that the Soviet program for eliminating nuclear arms by the year 2000 was until recently described by many "experts" in world politics as illusory and an unrealizable dream.

This is indeed the case when past experience is neither wealth nor counsel, but a burden that makes the search for solutions all the more difficult.

Reykjavik generated more than just hopes. Reykjavik also highlighted the difficulties encountered on the way to a nuclear-free world.

If this fact is not understood, it is impossible to assess correctly the results of the Icelandic meeting.

The forces opposed to disarmament are great. We felt that during the meeting and we feel this today. Reykjavik is being talked about a great deal.

Those who look realistically at the facts assess the meeting in Iceland as a major political event.

They welcome the fact that as a result of this meeting progress was made toward new qualitative levels in the fight against nuclear weapons. The results of Reykjavik, as they are viewed by the Soviet leadership, are encouraging to all who seek a change for the better.

Interesting assessments are being made in many countries at the state level, in public circles and in the scientific community. The opportunities that have been opened up are being characterized as corresponding to the aspirations of all mankind.

It is a common view that the meeting has raised both the Soviet-American dialogue and the East-West dialogue as a whole to a new level.

For the dialogue has been taken out of the plane of technical estimates and numerical comparisons and has been placed onto one with new parameters and dimensions.

From this height new prospects can be seen for the settlement of today's urgent issues. I am referring to security, nuclear disarmament, the prevention of new spirals in the arms race, and a new understanding of the opportunities that have opened up before humanity.

One could say that the debate over the results of the meeting has only just begun. I believe, I am even confident, that this debate will grow. And, we believe, the joint efforts of the people, of political figures and of public organizations will grow as well in an endeavor to take advantage of the opportunities that opened up in Reykjavik.

A course was outlined there for settling vitally important issues on which the very fate of humanity depends.

In the time that has passed since Reykjavik, however, something else has become clear.

Those groups linked with militarism and making profits from the arms race are obviously scared. They are doing their utmost to cope with the new situation and, coordinating their actions, are trying in every way possible to mislead the people, to control the sentiment of broad sections of the world public, to suppress the people's quest for peace, and to impede governments from taking a clear-cut position at this decisive moment in history.

These groups have at their disposal political power, economic leverage, and the powerful mass media. Of course, one should not overestimate their strength, but one should not underestimate it either. All indications are that the battle will be a difficult one.

Forces are being regrouped in the camp of the enemies of detente and disarmament. Feverish efforts are being made to create obstacles in order to stem the process started in Reykjavik.

Under these circumstances, I consider it necessary to return to the urgent issues which arose in connection with the meeting in Iceland.

Our point of view, which I made public one hour after the meeting, has not changed. I consider it necessary to state this not only in order to reiterate the appraisals made earlier.

I am doing this to draw your attention to the juggling with words and dissonance which we are observing. This might be the result of confusion or perplexity, but this also might be a preplanned campaign to fool the people.

The aims which were set before the meeting are explained differently. The initial negative reports of the Reykjavik meeting have quickly and concertedly become words of praise.

A hectic campaign has been started to misappropriate the other side's proposals.

The greatest efforts are being made to defend SDI, a project that was shown to be worthy of shame in Reykjavik. Generally speaking, Washington is now experiencing some hectic times.

But what is this? A preelection game that needs to depict Reykjavik as a success? Or are we dealing with a policy that will be unpredictable for years to come?

This needs to be studied carefully.

It certainly did catch our attention as to how and where certain political groupings are trying to steer the discussion of the results of the meeting.

The key elements of this campaign are worth mentioning. Efforts are being made in a bid to whitewash the destructive position of the U.S. Administration, which came to the meeting unprepared. They came, I would say one more time, with the same old baggage. But when the situation demanded definite answers, the U.S. side wrecked the chances for concluding the meeting with an accord.

A new situation has developed since Reykjavik, and meanwhile efforts are being made to force the USSR to return to the old approaches, to the unproductive numbers debates, and to walking in circles in a deadlock situation.

Evidently there are a great number of politicians in the West for whom the Geneva talks serve as a screen, and not as a forum for seeking accords.

What was once disguised thoroughly is now being disclosed: there are powerful forces in the ruling circles of the U.S. and Western Europe which are seeking to frustrate the process of nuclear disarmament. Certain people are once again beginning to claim that nuclear weapons are even a good thing.

A half-truth is the most dangerous lie, as a saying goes. It is extremely disquieting that not only have the mass media, leaning toward the right, taken such a stand, but so have leading figures in the U.S. Administration. And at times this stand is even one of downright deception.

I have already had the opportunity to report how things went in Reykjavik. We arrived at the meeting with constructive and the most radical arms-reduction proposals in the entire history of Soviet-U.S. negotiations. These proposals take into account the interests of both sides.

Upon arrival in Iceland, I spoke about this on the eve of the meeting in a conversation with the leaders of that country. The proposals had already been handed over to the President of the United States by the middle of my first conversation with him.

Far-reaching and interconnected, these proposals form *an integrated package* and are based on the program made public on January 15 for the elimination of nuclear weapons by the year 2000.

The *first* proposal is to reduce by half all strategic arms with no exceptions.

The *second* proposal is to eliminate completely Soviet and U.S. medium-range missiles in Europe and to start talks immediately on missiles of this type in Asia, as well as on missiles with a range of less than one thousand kilometers. We suggested that the number of such missiles be frozen immediately.

The *third* proposal is to consolidate the regime of the ABM Treaty and to start full-scale talks on a total nuclear test ban.

The discussions in Reykjavik, which I described in detail in my previous speeches, opened with the Soviet proposals.

Tremendous efforts and intense arguments resulted in the positions of the two sides drawing reassuringly closer together in two of the three areas.

The talks enabled the two sides to establish specific periods for the elimination of strategic offensive arms. We came to the agreement with President Ronald Reagan that the arms of this type belonging to the USSR and the U.S.A. can and must be completely eliminated by the year 1996.

An accord was also reached on the complete elimination of U.S. and Soviet medium-range missiles in Europe and on a radical cut in missiles of this type in Asia.

We attach great importance to these accords between the USSR and the United States: they prove that nuclear disarmament is possible.

This is the first half of the truth about the Reykjavik meeting. But there is still the other half and this is, as I have already said, that the U.S. side frustrated an agreement which, it seemed, was quite near at hand.

The U.S. Administration is now trying in every way possible to convince the people that the possibility of a major success in reaching definite agreements was not realized due to the Soviet Union's unyielding position on the issue of the so-called Strategic Defense Initiative (SDI).

It is even being asserted that we allegedly lured the President into a trap by putting forward "breathtaking" proposals on the reduction of strategic offensive arms and medium-range missiles and that later we ostensibly demanded, in the form of an ultimatum, that SDI be renounced.

But the essence of our position and proposals is as follows: we stand for the reduction and the eventual complete elimination of nuclear weapons and are absolutely against a new stage in the arms race and against its transfer to outer space.

Hence we are against SDI and for the consolidation of the ABM Treaty.

It is clear to every sober-minded person that if we start the process of radically cutting and then completely eliminating nuclear weapons, it is essential to rule out any possibility of either the Soviet or U.S. side gaining a unilateral military superiority.

It is precisely the extension of the arms race to a new sphere and the attempts to take offensive arms into outer space in order to achieve military superiority, that we perceive as the main danger of SDI.

SDI has become a barrier to ending the arms race, to getting rid of nuclear weapons, the main obstacle to a nuclear-free world.

When Mr. Shultz, U.S. Secretary of State, tells the American people that SDI is a sort of "insurance policy" for America, this, to say the least, is an attempt to mislead the American people.

In fact, SDI does not strengthen America's security but, by opening up a new stage of the arms race, destabilizes the military-political situation and thereby weakens both U.S. and universal security.

The Americans should know this.

They should also know that the U.S. stand on SDI announced in Reykjavik basically contradicts the ABM Treaty. Article XV of the Treaty does allow a party to withdraw from the Treaty, but only under certain circumstances, namely, "if it decides that extraordinary events related to the subject matter of this Treaty have jeopardized its (that party's) supreme interests." There have not been and are no such extraordinary events. It is clear that the elimination of nuclear weapons, if begun, would make the emergence of such extraordinary events even less likely. This is only logical.

Article XIII of the ABM Treaty, however, stipulates that the sides should "consider, as appropriate, possible proposals for further increasing the viability of this Treaty." The U.S., on the contrary, is seeking to depreciate the Treaty and deprive it of its meaning.

Each of these quotations is from the Treaty signed by the top representative of the United States.

Many stories have been invented to raise the prestige of SDI. One of them is that the Russians are terribly afraid of it. Another has it that SDI brought the Russians to the talks in Geneva and then to Reykjavik. A third is that only SDI will save America from the "Soviet threat." The fourth says that SDI will give the United States a great technological lead over the Soviet Union and other countries, and so on and so forth.

Understanding the problem, I can say now only one thing: continuing the SDI program will push the world into a new stage of the arms race and destabilize the strategic situation.

Everything else ascribed to SDI is in many respects rather dubious and is done in order to sell this suspicious and dangerous commodity in an attractive wrapping.

In upholding his position that prevented an agreement being reached in Reykjavik, the President asks the rhetorical questions: "Why are the Soviets so adamant that America remain forever vulnerable to Soviet rocket attack? Why does the Soviet Union insist that we remain defenseless forever?"

I must say I'm surprised by such questions. They give the impression that the American President has the opportunity of making his country invulnerable, of giving it secure protection against a nuclear strike.

As long as nuclear weapons exist and the arms race continues he has no such opportunity. Naturally, this also applies to ourselves.

If the President counts on SDI in this respect, it is futile. The system would be effective only if all missiles were eliminated. But then, one might ask, why an antimissile defense at all? Why build it? I won't even mention the money wasted, the system's cost, which, according to some estimates, will run into several trillion dollars.

So far, we have been trying to persuade America to give up this dangerous undertaking. We urge the American Administration to look for invulnerability and protection elsewhere—by totally eliminating nuclear weapons and establishing a comprehensive system of international security that would preclude all wars, nuclear or conventional.

The SDI program still remains an integral part of U.S. military doctrine.

The Fiscal 1984–1988 Defense Guidance now in force which the Pentagon produced at the beginning of Reagan's term in office, directly provides for the "prototype development of space-based weapons systems" including weapons to destroy Soviet satellites and accelerate the development of the system of the antimissile defense of U.S. territory with the possible U.S. pullout from the ABM Treaty.

The document says that the United States should develop weapons that "are difficult for the Soviets to counter, impose disproportionate costs, open up new areas of major military competition and obsolesce previous Soviet investment." Once again, as you can see, there is, as former President Nixon put it, a chase of the ghost; once again, there are plans to wear out the Soviet Union.

It is hard for the current administration to learn lessons.

Is this not the reason why its commitment to SDI is so stubborn? The plans for Star Wars have become the chief obstacle to an agreement on removing the nuclear threat. Washington's claim that we are now moving toward an agreement is of no use.

To eliminate nuclear weapons as a means of deterring American aggression, and, in return, be threatened from outer space can only be accepted by those who are politically naive. There are no such people in the Soviet leadership.

It is hard to reconcile oneself to the loss of the unique chance of saving mankind from the nuclear threat. With precisely this in mind, I said at the press conference in Reykjavik that we did not regard the dialogue as closed and hoped that President Reagan, on returning home, would consult the U.S. Congress and the American people, and adopt decisions logically necessitated by what had been achieved in Reykjavik.

Quite a different thing has happened. Aside from distorting the entire picture of the negotiations in Reykjavik—about which I will speak later—in recent days they have taken actions that, following such an important meeting between the two countries' top leaders, appear as simply wild to any normal point of view.

I am referring to the expulsion of another fifty-five Soviet Embassy and consular staff from the United States. We will, of course, take measures in response, very tough measures on an equal footing, so to speak. We are not going to put up with such outrageous practices. But now, I have this to say.

What kind of government is this, what can one expect from it in other affairs in the international arena? To what limits does the unpredictability of its actions go?

It turns out that it has no constructive proposals on key disarmament issues and that it does not even have a desire to maintain the kind of atmosphere essential for a normal continuation of the dialogue. It seems that Washington is not prepared for any of this.

The conclusion is obvious. It is confirmed by the considerable experience which has been accumulated. Every time a gleam of hope appears in the approaches to the major issues in Soviet-American relations and to a solution of questions involving the interests of the whole of mankind, a provocative action is immediately staged with the aim of frustrating the possibility of a positive outcome and poisoning the atmosphere.

Which is the real face of the U.S. Administration then? Is it looking for answers and solutions or does it want to finally destroy everything that may serve as a basis for headway and deliberately rule out any normalization?

Quite an unattractive portrait is emerging of the Administration of that great country—an Administration quick to take disruptive actions. Either the President is unable to cope with the entourage literally breathing hatred for the Soviet Union and for everything that may lead international affairs into calm waters or he himself is this way. In any event, there is no restraining the "hawks" in the White House, and this is very dangerous.

As for informing the American people about the meeting in

Reykjavik, the following has taken place, which is entirely in the spirit of what I have already mentioned: facts have been concealed from them. They were told the half-truth of which I spoke earlier. Things were portrayed so as to show that the United States, acting from a position of strength, virtually wrested consent from the Soviet Union to reach agreement on U.S. terms.

And the day is not far off when the United States will ostensibly attain its goal: it is essential, they say, not to slacken the pace of military preparations, to speed up the Star Wars program and to increase pressure in all directions.

These days have witnessed the drowning of a great cause in petty politicking and the sacrificing of the vital interests of the American people, allies, and international security as a whole to the arms manufacturers.

A good deal has been said about the openness of American society, about the freedom of information, the pluralism of opinions, and the fact that everyone there can see and hear what he pleases.

In Reykjavik, when pointing out the differences between our two systems, the President told me, and I quote: "We recognize freedom of the press and the right to hear any point of view." But how do things stand in reality?

Here is the latest fact.

It has been brought to my attention that a public organization of ours, the Novosti Press Agency, has published in English the text of my press conference in Reykjavik and of my speech on Soviet television and sent them out to many countries, including the United States.

Well, the fact is that the pamphlets with these texts have been detained at the U.S. customshouse for several days now. They are being prevented from reaching the American reader. There's the "right to hear any point of view" for you!

Or take, for example, the cinema. As I told the President when we were discussing humanitarian affairs, a great number of American films are shown on the Soviet screen. They give Soviet people an opportunity to become acquainted with both Americans' way of life and their way of thinking.

In "free America," on the other hand, Soviet films are practically not shown. The President avoided making any reply and, as usual in such cases, fell back on free enterprise, which lets everyone do whatever he wants.

I also told him about the publication of American books in this country as compared to that of our books in the United States: the ratio is approximately twenty to one.

I put the question of radio information before the President as well. I said that in this field, too, we are on an unequal footing. You have surrounded the Soviet Union with a network of radio transmitters and broadcast around the clock everything you like in many languages of the Soviet Union from the territories of other countries. America, availing itself of the fact that we are not its close neighbor, has isolated itself from our radio information by using the medium wave band—receivers in America are only of that kind. The President had nothing to say to that either.

Then I suggested to him that we take the following approach: we stop jamming the "Voice of America" broadcasts and you give us an opportunity to conduct radio broadcasts directed at the United States on your territory or somewhere nearby so that the broadcasts might reach the population of your country. The President promised to think about it.

It appears that the United States is becoming an increasingly closed society. People there are being isolated from objective information in a cunning and effective way. This is a dangerous process.

The American people should know the truth about what is going on in the Soviet Union, about the true content of Soviet foreign policy, about our real intentions, as well as the truth about the state of affairs in the world as a whole.

At the present stage, I would say, this is becoming extremely important.

Now a few words about how the outcome of the Reykjavik meeting is being portrayed in the United States. It took only several hours, or days at most, for everything discussed at Reykjavik to begin dispersing in the fog of inventions and fantasies. Attempts are being made to destroy the seedlings of trust before they take root.

The President stated recently that the only object of agreement had been ballistic missiles, and his assistants said plainly that bombers and all cruise missiles remained untouched.

The Secretary of State presented another version—that our accord dealt with all strategic arms. By the way, the latter was present during my talks with the President, as was our Minister of Foreign Affairs Eduard Shevardnadze.

Mr. Speakes, the White House spokesman, stated that possibly Mr. Reagan had been misunderstood and had actually never agreed to the elimination of all nuclear weapons.

Things got to the point of outright misrepresentation.

It is alleged, for example, that during the past meeting the U.S. President did not agree to the Soviet proposal on a *complete* elimination of *all* strategic offensive arms of the USSR and the U.S.A. by 1996, and that a common point of view on our proposal was never reached.

With all the responsibility of a participant in the talks I state: the President did, albeit without particular enthusiasm, consent to the elimination of all—I emphasize—not just certain individual ones, but all strategic offensive arms. And these are to be eliminated precisely within ten years, in two stages.

The interpretations of the discussion of the nuclear testing issue are a far cry from the truth, too. The United States' unilateral approach to this issue is pictured in such a way as to lead one to believe that the Soviet Union has given its full consent. This is not the case, nor could it be.

The issue of the elimination of medium-range missiles in Europe is also being presented in a distorted fashion, to say nothing of the fact that it is being withdrawn from the package proposed by the Soviet side.

But our consent to freeze the number of missiles with a range of under 1,000 kilometers is also being portrayed as the Soviet Union's "recognition" of the United States' "right" to deploy American missiles of the same class in Western Europe.

With such interpretations I myself will soon be in doubt as to what we really spoke about at Reykjavik: about removing the nuclear threat, reducing and eliminating nuclear arms? Or about how to keep this threat growing, how to diversify the nuclear arsenals and turn not just this entire planet, but outer space, the universe, too, into an arena of military confrontation? For this, comrades, is what is happening.

The prospects of reaching a mutual understanding between the Soviet and American sides so frightened certain people that they began erecting inconceivable obstacles ahead of time and inventing "preconditions."

An assistant to the President went so far as to say that before embarking on nuclear disarmament the U.S.A. must see some changes in the political climate in the Soviet Union.

All this is just not serious, not serious at all.

When similar claims were made seventy or forty years ago it was still possible to regard them as an inability to think things through, or as historical blindness. Nowadays they can only be the demonstration of a complete lack of understanding of reality.

The issue of conventional arms is also mentioned as one of the "preconditions." In and of itself it is serious enough.

To this day there is a well-worn thesis in the West concerning the "superiority" of the Soviet Union and other Warsaw Treaty states in conventional arms. It is this that is allegedly compelling NATO to continue building up its nuclear potential.

Of course, there is in fact no disbalance whatsoever. After Reykjavik this fact was publicly recognized for the first time by Mr. Shultz and Mr. Reagan. But the crux of the matter does not lie in the maintenance of parity. We do not want the arms race to move from the sphere of nuclear arms to the sphere of conventional ones.

Let me remind you that our January proposal on the elimination of nuclear weapons before the end of the century included also the provisions on the elimination of chemical weapons and on radical reductions in conventional armaments.

We have returned to that issue more than once since January. The proposals of the Warsaw Treaty countries were presented in greatest detail last summer in Budapest. We sent them to the other side, that is, the NATO countries.

So far we have received no answer.

Every day that has passed since Reykjavik has made it more

clear that the meeting in Iceland was that touchstone which determines the true value of the words and declarations of political figures.

So much has been said of the need to be free of the nuclear nightmare, of how we will be able to breathe more easily in a nuclear-free world. Let the USSR and the U.S.A. get things in motion.

But no sooner had a ray of hope appeared when many of those who had just been cursing nuclear weapons and pledging their allegiance to the idea of a nuclear-free world went back on their word.

Certain quarters in Western Europe even voiced their feeling that it was difficult to part with American nuclear weapons, with American missiles.

Evidently, the point is that the policy-makers in the West are thinking of nuclear weapons not in the terms of defense at all. Otherwise it would be difficult to explain why pretexts are now being sought for keeping the missiles in place or why support for the SDI program is being expressed at the government level.

Here is something for both us and the West European public to ponder.

In addition to direct attacks, subtle maneuvers are being made. Is it not possible to take from the negotiating table what is most advantageous, while ignoring that which is not to one's taste for one reason or another?

They say that difficulties at Reykjavik arose because we, the Soviet side, put forward our cardinal proposals in a package. But the package contains a balance of interests and concessions, a balance of withdrawn concerns and the interdependence of security interests. Here everything is as if on scales; the two pans must be balanced.

That is why, evidently, those in the West want to shatter this logically substantiated and just variant of an overall accord into pieces, doing nothing to restore the balance of compromises.

All the proposals we made at Reykjavik are objectively connected with central strategic-weapons systems. Our concessions are also a part of the package. No package, no concessions.

This is a reality of our national security. But such an approach ensures the security of the U.S.A. and all other countries as well.

That is why we attach such significance to strengthening the ABM Treaty. We are not endangering it in any way. On the contrary, we are opposed to having it revised, supplemented, or what not, and we are even more opposed to having it replaced with something else, as the President suggested at Reykjavik. Or maybe this was just a slip of the tongue.

Let me put it frankly: I was very much surprised when during the meeting he began persuading the Soviet side and me personally not to regard the ABM Treaty as gospel. What, then, should one's attitude to treaties be like? Should they be treated as mere slips of paper?

Without strict observance of the treaties, and especially such a fundamental one as this, it is impossible to ensure international order and basic stability. Otherwise the world would be subject to arbitrary rule and chaos.

Let me say once again: when SDI is given preference over nuclear disarmament, only one conclusion can be made—with the help of that military program efforts are being made to disprove the axiom of international relations of our epoch, an axiom laid out in simple, clear-cut words signed by the U.S. President and myself last year. These words read: nuclear war must not be fought and cannot be won.

Let me say in conclusion that the Soviet Union has put the maximum of goodwill into its proposals. We are not withdrawing these proposals; they still stand! Everything that has been said by way of their substantiation and development remains in force.

Good night, comrades. All the best.

V

THE 27TH PARTY CONGRESS

The Political Report of the
Central Committee of the CPSU
to the Party Congress of the CPSU

Moscow, February 25, 1986

Comrade Delegates,
Esteemed guests,

The 27th Congress of the CPSU has gathered at a crucial turning point in the life of the country and the contemporary world as a whole. We are beginning our work with a deep understanding of our responsibility to the Party and the Soviet people. It is our task to elaborate a broad conception, in the Leninist way, of the times we are living in, and to work out a realistic, well-thought-out program of action that would organically blend the grandeur of our aims with our real capabilities, and the Party's plans with the hopes and aspirations of every person. The resolutions of the 27th Congress will determine both the character and the rate of our movement toward a qualitatively new state of the Soviet socialist society for years and decades ahead.

The Congress is to discuss and adopt a new edition of the Program of the CPSU, amendments to the Party Rules, and Guidelines for Economic Development for the next five years and a longer term. I need hardly mention what enormous importance these documents have for our Party, our state, and our people. Not only do they contain an assessment of the past and a formulation of the urgent tasks, but also a glimpse into the future. They speak of what the Soviet Union will be like as it enters the 21st century, of the image of socialism and its positions in the international arena, of the future of humanity.

Soviet society has gone a long way in its development since the currently operative Party Program was adopted. In fact, we have built the whole country anew, have made tremendous headway in the economic, cultural, and social fields, and have raised generations of builders of the new society. We have blazed the trail into outer space for humanity. We have secured military strategic parity and have thereby substantially restricted imperialism's aggressive plans and capabilities to start a nuclear war. The positions of our Motherland and of world socialism in the international arena have grown considerably stronger.

The path traveled by the country, its economic, social and cultural achievements convincingly confirm the vitality of the Marxist-Leninist doctrine, and socialism's tremendous potential as embodied in the progress of Soviet society. We can be justly proud of everything that has been achieved in these years of intensive work and struggle.

While duly appraising our achievements, the leadership of the CPSU considers it its duty to tell the Party and the people honestly and frankly about the shortcomings in our political and practical activities, the unfavorable tendencies in the economy and the social and moral sphere, and about the reasons for them. For a number of years the deeds and actions of Party and Government bodies lagged behind the needs of the times and of life—not only because of objective factors, but also for reasons above all of a subjective nature. The problems in the country's development grew more rapidly than they were being solved. The inertness and rigidity of the forms and methods of management, the decline of dynamism in our work, and increased bureaucracy—all this was doing no small damage. Signs of stagnation had begun to surface in the life of society.

The situation called for change, but a peculiar psychology—how to improve things without changing anything—took the upper hand in the central bodies and, for that matter, at the local level as well. But that cannot be done, comrades. Stop for an instant, as they say, and you fall behind a mile. We must not evade the problems that have arisen. That sort of attitude is much too costly for the country, the state, and the Party. So let us say it loud and clear!

The top-priority task is to overcome the negative factors in society's socioeconomic development as rapidly as possible, to accelerate it and impart to it an essential dynamism, to learn from the lessons of the past to a maximum extent, so that the decisions we adopt for the future should be absolutely clear and responsible, and the concrete actions purposeful and effective.

The situation has reached a turning point not only in internal but also in *external* affairs. The changes in current world developments are so deep-going and significant that they require a reassessment and a comprehensive analysis of all factors. The situation created by the nuclear confrontation calls for new approaches, methods, and forms of relations between the different social systems, states, and regions.

Owing to the arms race started by imperialism, the 20th century, in the field of world politics, is coming to an end burdened with the question: will humanity be able to avert the nuclear danger, or will the policy of confrontation take the upper hand, thus increasing the probability of nuclear conflict. The capitalist world has not abandoned the ideology and policy of hegemonism, its rulers have not yet lost the hope of taking social revenge, and continue to indulge themselves with illusions of superior strength. A sober view of what is going on is hewing its way forward with great difficulty through a dense thicket of prejudices and preconceptions in the thinking of the ruling class. But the complexity and acuteness of this moment in history makes it increasingly vital to outlaw nuclear weapons, destroy them and other weapons of mass annihilation completely, and improve international relations.

The fact that the Party has deeply understood the fundamentally new situation inside the country and in the world arena, and that it appreciates its responsibility for the country's future, and has the will and resolve to carry out the requisite change, is borne out by the adoption at the April 1985 Plenary Meeting of the *decision to accelerate the socioeconomic development of our society.*

Formulating the long-term and fundamental tasks, the Central Committee has been consistently guided by Marxism-Leninism, the truly scientific theory of social development. It expresses the vital interests of the working people, and the ideals of social justice. It derives its vitality from its everlasting youthfulness, its constant capacity for development and creative generalization of the new facts and phenomena, and from its experience of revolutionary struggle and social reconstruction.

Any attempt to turn the theory by which we are guided into an assortment of rigid schemes and formulas which would be valid everywhere and in all contingencies is most definitely contrary to the essence and spirit of Marxism-Leninism. Lenin wrote back in 1917 that Marx and Engels rightly ridiculed the "mere memorizing and repetition of 'formulas,' that at best are capable only of marking out *general* tasks, which are necessarily modifiable by the *concrete* economic and political conditions of each particular *period* of the historical process." Those are the words, comrades, that everyone of us must ponder and act upon.

The *concrete* economic and political situation we are in, and the particular *period* of the historical process that Soviet society and the whole world are going through, require that the Party and its every member display their creativity, their capacity for innovation, and ability to transcend the limits of accustomed but already outdated notions.

A large-scale, frank, and constructive examination of all the crucial problems of our life and of Party policy has taken place during the discussion of the pre-Congress documents. We have come to the Congress enriched by the wisdom and experience of the whole Party, the whole people. We can now see more clearly what has to be done and in what order, and what levers we must set in motion so that our progress will be accelerated at a desired pace.

These days, many things, in fact everything, will depend on how effectively we will succeed in using the advantages and possibilities of the socialist system, its economic power and social potential, in updating the obsolescent social patterns and style and methods of work, in bringing them abreast of the changed conditions. That is the only way for us to increase the might of our country, to raise the material and spiritual life of the Soviet people to a qualitatively new level, and to enhance the positive influence of the example of socialism as a social system on world development.

We look to the future confidently, because we are clearly aware of our tasks and of the ways in which they should be carried out. We look to the future confidently, because we rely on the powerful support of the people. We look to the future confidently, because we are acting in the interests of the socialist Homeland, in the name of the great ideals to which the Communist Party has dedicated itself wholeheartedly.

I. THE CONTEMPORARY WORLD: ITS MAIN TENDENCIES AND CONTRADICTIONS

Comrades, the draft new edition of the Program of the Party contains a thorough analysis of the main trends and features of the development of the world today. It is not the purpose of the Program to anticipate the future with all its multiformity and concrete developments. That would be a futile exercise. But here is another, no-less-important point: if we want to follow a correct, science-based policy, we must clearly understand the key tendencies of the current reality. To penetrate deep into the dialectic of the events, into their objective logic, to draw the right conclusions that reflect the motion of the times, is no simple matter, but it is imperatively necessary.

In the days before the October Revolution, referring to the capitalist economy alone, Lenin noted that the sum total of the changes in all their ramifications could not have been grasped even by seventy Marxes. But, Lenin continued, Marxism has discovered "the *laws* . . . and the *objective* logic of these changes and of their historical development . . . in its chief and basic features."

The modern world is complicated, diverse and dynamic, and shot through with contending tendencies and contradictions. It is a world of the most difficult alternatives, anxieties, and hopes. Never before has our home on earth been exposed to such great political and physical stresses. Never before has man exacted so much tribute from nature, and never has he been so vulnerable to the forces he himself has created.

World developments confirm the fundamental Marxist-Leninist conclusion that the history of society is not a sum of fortuitous elements, that it is not a disorderly "Brownian motion," but a law-governed onward process. Not only are its contradictions a verdict on the old world, on everything that impedes the advance; they are also a source and motive force for social progress. This is progress which takes place in conditions of a struggle that is inevitable so long as exploitation and exploiting classes exist.

The liberation revolutions triggered by the Great October Revolution are determining the image of the 20th century. However considerable the achievements of science and technology, and however great the influence which rapid scientific and technological progress has on the life of society, nothing but the social and spiritual emancipation of man can make him truly free. And no matter what difficulties, objective and artificial, the old world may create, the course of history is irreversible.

The social changes of the century are altering the conditions for the further development of society. New economic, political, scientific, technical, internal, and international factors are beginning to operate. The interconnection between states and between peoples is increasing. And all this is setting new, especially exacting demands upon every state, whether it is a matter of foreign policy, economic and social activity, or the spiritual image of society.

The progress of our time is rightly identified with socialism. *World socialism* is a powerful international entity with a highly developed economy, substantial scientific resources, and a reliable military and political potential. It accounts for more than one-third of the world's population; it includes dozens of countries and peoples advancing along a path that reveals in every way the intellectual and moral wealth of man and society. A new way of life has taken shape, based on the principles of socialist justice, in which there are neither oppressors nor the oppressed, neither exploiters nor the exploited, in which power belongs to the people. Its distinctive features are collectivism and comradely mutual assistance, triumph of the ideas of freedom, unbreakable unity between the rights and duties of every member of society, the dignity of the individual, and true humanism. Socialism is a realistic option open to all humanity, an example projected into the future.

Socialism sprang up and was built in countries which were far from being economically and socially advanced at that time and which differed greatly from one another in mode of life and their historical and national traditions. Each one of them advanced to the new social system along its own way, confirming Marx's prediction about the "infinite variations and gradations" of the same economic basis in its concrete manifestations.

The way was neither smooth nor simple. It was exceedingly difficult to rehabilitate a backward or ruined economy, to teach millions of people to read and write, to provide them with a roof over their heads, with food and free medical aid. The very novelty of the social tasks, the ceaseless military, economic, political, and psychological pressure of imperialism, the need for tremendous efforts to ensure defense—all this could not but influence the course of events, their character, and the rate at which the socioeconomic programs and transformations were carried into effect. Nor were mistakes in politics and various subjectivist deviations avoided.

But such is life; it always manifests itself in diverse contradictions, sometimes quite unexpected ones. The other point is much more important: socialism has demonstrated its ability to resolve social problems on a fundamentally different basis than previously, namely a collectivist one; it has brought the countries to higher levels of development, and has given the working people a dignified and secure life.

Socialism is continuously improving social relations, multiplying its achievements purposefully, setting an example which is becoming more and more influential and attractive, and demonstrating the real humanism of the socialist way of life. By so doing, it is erecting an increasingly reliable barrier to the ideology and policy of war and militarism, reaction and force, to all forms of inhumanity, and is actively furthering social progress. It has grown into a powerful moral and material force, and has shown what opportunities are opening for modern civilization.

The course of social progress is closely linked with *anticolonial* revolutions, national liberation movements, the renascence of many countries, and the emergence of dozens of new ones. Having won political independence, they are working hard to overcome backwardness, poverty, and sometimes extreme privation—the entire painful legacy of their past enslavement. Formerly the victims of imperialist policy, deprived of all rights, they are now making history themselves.

Social progress is expressed in the development of the *international communist and working-class movement* and in the growth of the new massive democratic movement of our time, including the antiwar and antinuclear movement. It is apparent, too, in the polarization of the political forces of the capitalist world, notably in the U.S.A., the center of imperialism. Here, progressive tendencies are forcing their way forward through a system of monopolistic totalitarianism, and are exposed to the continuous pressure of organized reactionary forces, including their enormous propaganda machine which floods the world with stupefying misinformation.

Marx compared progress in exploitative society to "that hideous pagan idol, who would not drink the nectar but from the skulls of the slain." He went on: "In our days everything seems pregnant with its contrary. Machinery, gifted with the wonderful power of shortening and fructifying human labor, we behold starving and overworking it. The new-fangled sources of wealth, by some strange weird spell, are turned into sources of want. The victories of art seem bought by the loss of character. At the same pace that mankind masters nature, man seems to become enslaved to other men or to his own infamy. Even the pure light of science seems unable to shine but on the dark background of ignorance. All our invention and progress seem to result in endowing material forces with intellectual life, and in stultifying human life into a material force."

Marx's analysis is striking in its historical sweep, accuracy, and depth. It has, indeed, become still more relevant with regard to bourgeois reality of the 20th century than it was in the 19th century. On the one hand, the swift advance of science and technology has opened up unprecedented possibilities for mastering the forces of nature and improving the conditions of the life of man. On the other, the "enlightened" 20th century is going down in history as a time marked by such outgrowths of imperialism as the most devastating wars, an orgy of militarism and fascism, genocide, and the destitution of millions of people. Ignorance and obscurantism go hand in hand in the capitalist world with outstanding achievements of science and culture. That is the society we are compelled to be neighbors of, and we must look for ways of cooperation and mutual understanding. Such is the command of history.

The progress of humanity is also directly connected with the *scientific and technological revolution*. It matured slowly and gradually, and then, in the final quarter of the century, gave the start to a gigantic increase of man's material and spiritual possibilities. These are of a twofold nature. There is a qualitative leap in humanity's productive forces. But there is also a qualitative leap in means of destruction, in the military sphere, "endowing" man for the first time in history with the physical capacity for destroying all life on earth.

The facets and consequences of the scientific and technological revolution differ in different sociopolitical systems. Capitalism of the 1980s, the capitalism of the age of electronics and information science, computers and robots, is throwing more millions of people, including young and educated people, out of jobs. Wealth and power are being increasingly concentrated in the hands of a few. Militarism is thriving on the arms race greatly, and also strives gradually to gain control over the political levers of power. It is becoming the ugliest and the most dangerous monster of the 20th century. Because of its efforts, the most advanced scientific and technical ideas are being converted into weapons of mass destruction.

Before the developing countries the scientific and technological revolution is setting this most acute question: are they to enjoy the achievements of science and technology in full measure in order to gain strength for combating neocolonialism and imperialist exploitation, or will they remain on the periphery of world development? The scientific and technological revolution shows in bold relief that many socioeconomic problems impeding progress in that part of the world are unresolved.

Socialism has everything it needs to place modern science and technology at the service of the people. But it would be wrong to think that the scientific and technological revolution is creating no problems for socialist society. Experience shows that its advance involves improvement of social relations, a change of mentality, the forging of a new psychology, and the acceptance of dynamism as a way and rule of life. It calls insistently for a continuous reassessment and streamlining of the prevailing patterns of management. In other words, the scientific and technological revolution not only opens up prospects, but also sets higher demands on the entire organization of the internal life of countries and international relations. Certainly, scientific and technological progress cannot abolish the laws of social development or the social purpose and content of such development. But it exercises a tremendous influence on all the processes that are going on in the world, on its contradictions.

It is quite obvious that the two socioeconomic systems

differ substantially in their readiness and in their capacity to comprehend and resolve the problems that arise.

Such is the world we are living in on the threshold of the third millennium. It is a world full of hope, because people have never before been so amply equipped for the further development of civilization. But it is also a world overburdened with dangers and contradictions, which prompts the thought that this is perhaps the most alarming period in history.

The first and most important group of contradictions in terms of humanity's future is connected with the *relations between countries of the two systems, the two formations.* These contradictions have a long history. Since the Great October Revolution in Russia and the split of the world on the social-class principle, fundamental differences have emerged both in the assessment of current affairs and in the views concerning the world's social perspective.

Capitalism regarded the birth of socialism as an "error" of history which must be "rectified." It was to be rectified at any cost, by any means, irrespective of law and morality: by armed intervention, economic blockade, subversive activity, sanctions and "punishments," or rejection of all cooperation. But nothing could interfere with the consolidation of the new system and its historical right to live.

The difficulty that the ruling classes of the capitalist world have in understanding the realities, the recurrence of attempts at resolving by force the whole group of contradictions dividing the two worlds are, of course, anything but accidental. The intrinsic mainsprings and socioeconomic essence of imperialism prompt it to translate the competition of the two systems into the language of military confrontation. Owing to its social nature, imperialism ceaselessly gives rise to aggressive, adventurist policy.

Here we can speak of a whole complex of motives involved: the predatory appetites of the arms manufacturers and the influential military-bureaucratic groups, the selfish interest of the monopolies in sources of raw materials and markets for their goods, the bourgeoisie's fear of the ongoing changes, and, lastly, the attempts to resolve its own increasingly acute problems at socialism's expense.

Such attempts are especially typical of U.S. imperialism. It was nothing but imperial ideology and policy, the wish to create the most unfavorable external conditions for socialism and for the USSR that prompted the launching of the race of nuclear and other arms after 1945, just when the crushing defeat of fascism and militarism was, it would seem, offering a realistic opportunity for building a world without wars, and a mechanism of international cooperation—the United Nations—had been created for this purpose. But imperialism's nature asserted itself that time again.

Today, too, the right wing of the U.S. monopoly bourgeoisie regards the stoking up of international tensions as something that justifies military spending, claims to global supremacy, interference in the affairs of other states, and an offensive against the interests and the rights of the American working people. No small role seems to be played by the idea of using tensions to put pressure on the allies, to make them absolutely obedient, to subordinate them to Washington's dictation.

The policy of total contention, of military confrontation has no future. Flight into the past is no answer to the challenges of the future. It is rather an act of despair which, however, does not make this posture any less dangerous. By its deeds Washington will show when and to what extent it will understand this. We, for our part, are ready to do everything we can in order radically to improve the international situation. To achieve this, socialism need not renounce any of its principles or ideals. It has always stood for and continues to stand for the peaceful coexistence of states with different social systems.

As distinct from imperialism, which is trying to halt the course of history by force, to regain what it had in the past, socialism has never, of its own free will, related its future to any military solution of international problems. This was borne out at the very first big discussion that took place in our Party after the victory of the Great October Revolution. During that discussion, as we may recall, the views of the "Left Communists" and the Trotskyites, who championed the theory of "revolutionary war" which, they claimed, would carry socialism to other countries, were firmly rejected. This position, as Lenin emphasized in 1918, "would be completely at variance with Marxism, for Marxism has always been opposed to 'pushing' revolutions, which develop with the growing acuteness of the class antagonisms that engender revolutions." Today, too, we are firmly convinced that promoting revolutions from outside, and even more so by military means, is futile and inadmissible.

The problems and crises experienced by the capitalist world arise within its own system and are a natural result of the internal antagonistic contradictions of the old society. In this sense, capitalism negates itself as it develops. Unable to cope with the acute problems of the declining phase of capitalism's development, the ruling circles of the imperialist countries resort to means and methods that are obviously incapable of saving the society that history has doomed.

The myth of a Soviet or communist "threat" that is being circulated today, is meant to justify the arms race and the imperialist countries' own aggressiveness. But it is becoming increasingly clear that the path of war can yield no sensible solutions, either international or domestic. The clash and struggle of the opposite approaches to the perspectives of world development have become especially complex in nature. Now that the world has huge nuclear stockpiles and the only thing experts argue about is how many times or dozens of times humanity can be destroyed, it is high time to begin an effective withdrawal from the brink of war, from the equilibrium of fear, to normal, civilized forms of relations between the states of the two systems.

In the years to come, the struggle will evidently center on the actual content of the policy that can safeguard peace. It will be a hard and many-sided struggle, because we are dealing with a society whose ruling circles refuse to assess the realities of the world and its perspectives in sober terms, or to draw serious conclusions from their own experience and that of others. All this is an indication of the wear and tear suffered by its internal "systems of immunity," of its social senility, which reduces the probability of far-reaching changes in the policy of the dominant forces and augments its degree of recklessness.

That is why it is not easy at all, in the current circumstances, to predict the future of the relations between the socialist and the capitalist countries, the USSR and the U.S.A. The decisive factors here will be the correlation of forces on the world scene, the growth and activity of the peace potential, and its capability of effectively repulsing the threat of nuclear war. Much will depend, too, on the degree of realism that Western ruling circles will show in assessing the situation. But it is unfortunate when not only the eyesight but also the soul of politicians is blind. With nuclear war being totally unacceptable, peaceful coexistence rather than confrontation of the systems should be the rule in interstate relations.

The second group of contradictions consists of the *intrinsic contradictions of the capitalist world itself.* The past period has amply confirmed that the *general crisis of capitalism* is growing keener. The capitalism of today, whose exploitative nature has not changed, is in many ways different from what it was in the early and even the middle 20th century. Under the influence and against the background of the scientific and technological revolution, the conflict between the productive forces, which have grown to gigantic proportions, and the private-owner social relations, has become still more acute. Here there is growth of unemployment and deterioration of the entire set of social problems. Militarism, which has spread to all areas, is applied as the most promising means of enlivening the economy. The crisis of political institutions, of the entire spiritual sphere, is growing. Reaction is exerting fierce pressure all along the line—in domestic and foreign policy, economy and culture, and the use of the achievements of human genius. The traditional forms of conservatism are giving place to authoritarian tendencies.

Special mention should be made of such a dangerous manifestation of the crisis of capitalism as anticommunism and anti-Sovietism. This concerns not only foreign policy. In the present-day system of imperialism it is also a very important aspect of domestic policy, a means of exerting pressure on all the advanced and progressive elements that live and fight in the capitalist countries, in the nonsocialist part of the world.

True, the present stage of the general crisis does not lead to any absolute stagnation of capitalism and does not rule out the possibilities for economic growth, and the mastering of new scientific and technical fields. This stage "allows for" sustaining concrete economic, military, political, and other positions, and in some areas even the possibility for social revenge, for regaining what had been lost before. Because capitalism lacks positive aims and orientations, capable of expressing the interests of the working masses, it now has to cope with the unprecedented interlacement and mutual exacerbation of all of its contradictions. It faces more social and other impasses than it has ever known before in all the centuries of its development.

The contradictions *between labor and capital* are among the first to grow more acute. In the 1960s and 1970s, with the onset of a favorable economic situation, the working class and working people managed to secure a certain improvement of their condition. But from the mid-1970s on, the proliferating economic crises and another technological modernization of production changed the situation, and enabled capital to go on the counteroffensive, depriving the working people of a considerable part of their social gains. For a number of standard-of-living indicators, the working people were flung many years back. Unemployment has reached a postwar high. The condition of peasants and farmers is deteriorating visibly: some farms are going bankrupt, with their former owners joining the ranks of hired workers, while others become abjectly dependent on large agricultural monopolies and banks. The social stratification is growing deeper and increasingly striking. In the United States, for example, one percent of the wealthiest families own riches that exceed by nearly 50 percent the aggregate wealth of 80 percent of all American families, which make up the lower part of the property pyramid.

Imperialism's ruling circles are doubtlessly aware that such a situation is fraught with social explosions and political destabilization. But this is not making their policies more considered. On the contrary, the most irreconcilable reactionary groups of the ruling class have, by and large, taken the upper hand in recent years. This period is marked by an especially massive and brutal offensive by the monopolies on the rights of the working people.

The whole arsenal of means at capitalism's disposal is being put to use. The trade unions are persecuted and economically blackmailed. Antilabor laws are being enacted. The left and all other progressives are being persecuted. Continuous control or, to be more precise, surveillance of people's state of mind and behavior has become standard. The deliberate cultivation of individualism, of the principle that might makes right in the fight for survival, of immorality and hatred of all that is democratic—this is practiced on an unprecedented scale.

The future, the working people's fight for their rights, for social progress, will show how that basic contradiction between labor and capital will develop and what conclusions will be drawn from the prevailing situation. But mention must be made of the serious danger to international relations of any further substantial shift of policy, of the entire internal situation in some capitalist countries, to the right. The consequences of such a development are hard to predict, and we must not underrate their danger.

The last decades of the century are marked by new outbreaks of *interimperialist contradictions* and the appearance of their new forms and tendencies. This group of capitalist contradictions has not been eliminated either by class affinity, the interest in uniting forces, by military, economic, and political integration, or by the scientific and technological revolution. The latter has incontestably accelerated the internationalization of capitalist production, has given added impetus to the evening-up of levels as well as to the leaplike development of capitalist countries. The competition that has grown more acute under the impact of scientific and technological progress, is affecting those who have dropped behind ever more mercilessly. The considerable complication of the conditions of capitalist reproduction, the diversity of crisis processes, and the intensification of international competition have made imperialist rivalry especially acute and bitter. The commercial and economic struggle on the world market is witnessing ever greater reliance on the power of national state-monopoly capitalisms, with the role of the bourgeois state becoming increasingly aggressive and egoistic.

The *transnational monopoly capital* has gained strength rapidly. It is seizing control of, and monopolizing, whole branches or spheres of production both on the scale of individual countries and in the world economy as a whole. By the early 1980s, the transnational corporations accounted for more than one-third of industrial production, more than one half of foreign trade, and nearly 80 percent of the patents for new machinery and technology in the capitalist world.

The core of the transnational corporations consists of American firms. Their enterprises abroad use an additional army of wage and salary workers, whose number is half of those employed in manufacturing in the U.S.A. At present, they produce something like 1.5 trillion dollars worth of goods and services a year, or nearly 40 percent of gross U.S. output.

The size of the "second economy" of the United States is double or triple that of the economies of such leading West European powers as the FRG, France, and Britain, and second only to that of Japan. Today, the biggest U.S. transnational monopolies are empires whose scale of economic activity is comparable to the gross national product of an entire country.

A new knot of contradictions has appeared and is being swiftly tightened *between the transnational corporations and the nation-state form of society's political organization.* The transnational corporations are undermining the sovereignty both of developing and of developed capitalist countries. They make active use of state-monopoly regulation when it suits their interests, and come into sharp conflict with it when they see the slightest threat to their profits from the actions of bourgeois governments. But for all that, the U.S. transnational supermonopolies are, as a rule, active conductors of state hegemonism and the imperial ambitions of the country's ruling circles.

The relations between the three main centers of present-day imperialism—the U.S.A., Western Europe, and Japan—abound in visible and concealed contradictions. The economic, financial, and technological superiority which the U.S.A. enjoyed over its closest competitors until the end of the 1960s has been put to a serious trial. Western Europe and Japan managed to outdo their American patron in some things, and are also challenging the United States in such a traditional sphere of U.S. hegemony as that of the latest technology.

Washington is continuously calling on its allies not to waste their gunpowder on internecine strife. But how are the three centers of present-day imperialism to share one roof if the

Americans themselves, manipulating the dollar and the interest rates, are not loath to fatten their economy at the expense of Western Europe and Japan? Wherever the three imperialist centers manage to coordinate their positions, this is more often than not the effect of American pressure or outright dictation, and works in the interests and aims above all of the United States. This, in turn, sharpens, rather than blunts, the contradictions.

It appears that people are beginning to wonder about this cause-and-effect relationship. For the first time, governments of some West European countries, the social democratic and liberal parties, and the public at large have begun to discuss openly whether present U.S. policy coincides with Western Europe's notions about its own security and whether the United States is going too far in its claims to "leadership." The partners of the United States have had more than one occasion to see that someone else's spectacles cannot substitute for one's own eyes.

The clash of centrifugal and centripetal tendencies will, no doubt, continue as a result of changes in the correlation of forces within the imperialist system. Still, the existing complex of economic, politico-military, and other common interests of the three "centers of power" can hardly be expected to break up in the prevailing conditions of the present-day world. But within the framework of this complex, Washington should not expect unquestioning obedience to U.S. dictation on the part of its allies and competitors, and especially when this is to the detriment of their own interests.

The specificity of the interimperialist contradictions in the current period also includes the possibility for changes in their configuration in the coming decades, with new capitalist "centers of power" coming on the scene. This will doubtless lead to further growth of the bulk of contradictions, to their closer interlacement and aggravation.

A new, complex, and changing set of contradictions has taken shape between imperialism, on the one hand, and the developing countries and peoples, on the other. The liberation of former colonies and semicolonies was a strong political and ideological blow to the capitalist system. It has ceased to exist in the shape that it assumed in the 19th century and which extended into the first half of the 20th. A slow, arduous, but irreversible process of socioeconomic transformations is under way in the life of nations comprising the majority of mankind. This process, which has brought about not a few fundamental changes, has also encountered considerable difficulties.

By political maneuvering, blandishments, and blackmail, military threats and intimidation, and all too often by direct interference in the internal affairs of the newly free countries, capitalism has in many ways managed to sustain the earlier relationships of economic dependence. On this basis, imperialism managed to create and run the most refined system of neocolonialist exploitation, and to tighten its hold on a considerable number of newly free states.

The consequences of this are tragic. The developing countries with a population of more than two billion, have, in effect, become a region of wholesale poverty. In the early 1980s, the per capita income in the newly free countries was, on the whole, less than 10 percent that of the developed capitalist states. And in the past thirty years, far from shrinking, the gap has grown wider. Nor is it a question of just comparative poverty. There is illiteracy and ignorance, chronic undernourishment and hunger, appalling child mortality, and epidemics that afflict hundreds of millions of people.

This is a disgrace for civilized humanity! And its culprit is imperialism. Not only from the point of view of history, that is, of colonial plunder on entire continents which left behind a heritage of unbelievable backwardness, but equally in terms of present-day practices. In just the past ten years, the profits squeezed out of the developing countries by U.S. corporations exceeded their inputs fourfold. And in Latin America and the Caribbean, in the same period, the profits of U.S. monopolies were over eight times greater than their inputs.

It is no exaggeration to say that, to a large extent, the imperialist system still lives by plundering the developing countries, by mercilessly exploiting them. The forms and methods are changing, but the essence remains the same. In the United States, for example, a tangible portion of the national income comes from these very sources. The developing countries are being exploited by all the imperialist states, but, unquestionably, U.S. imperialism is doing it with the greatest impudence. Nonequivalent exchange, unequal trade, manipulations and arbitrary actions regarding interest rates, and the pump of the transnational corporations are being used to one and the same end. They are adding still more to the poverty and misery of some, and to the wealth of others, and increasing the polarization in the capitalist world economy.

The distressing condition of the developing countries is a major worldwide problem. This and nothing else is the true source of many of the conflicts in Asia, Africa, and Latin America. Such is the truth, however hard the ruling circles of the imperialist powers may invoke the "hand of Moscow" in order to vindicate their neocolonialist policy and global ambitions.

Take the problem of debts. Together with the profits shipped out yearly from the developing countries, the accumulated debt means just one thing: the prospects for their development have shrunk, and a further aggravation of the already grave social, economic, and other problems is inevitable.

In the existing circumstances, these countries will not, of course, be able to repay their debts. And if no fair solution is devised, the situation will be fraught with grave socioeconomic and political consequences on the international scene. It would be wrong to say that the imperialist ruling circles are blind to the underlying danger here. But all their concerns boil down to one thing—how to save the present system of enriching themselves through the exploitation and superexploitation of the peoples of the developing countries.

This other thing is certain as well: there is an irrefutable causal connection between the trillion-sized debt of these countries and the more than trillion-sized growth of U.S. military expenditures in the past ten years. The 200-odd billion dollars that are being annually pumped out of the developing countries and the practically equal size of the U.S. military budget in recent years are no coincidence. That is why militarism had a direct stake in maintaining and tightening the system of neocolonial superexploitation.

It is also obvious that with capitalism's contradictions growing sharper and its sphere of predominance shrinking, neocolonialism is becoming an increasingly important source of means that provide monopoly capital with the possibility for social maneuvering, reducing social tensions in the leading bourgeois states, and for bribing some sections of the working people. It is a truly extraordinary source, for a worker's hourly rate in the advanced capitalist states is higher, sometimes several times higher, than a day's earnings in the countries of Asia, Africa, and Latin America.

All this cannot go on forever. But, of course, no miracle can be expected: the situation is not going to straighten itself out on its own. The military force that the U.S.A. is counting on to maintain the status quo, to safeguard the interests of the monopolies and the military-industrial complex, and to prevent any further progressive change in the newly free countries, can only complicate the situation and precipitate new conflicts. The bags of money are liable to become kegs of gunpowder. Sooner or later, in this area too, capitalism will have to choose between the policy of force and shameless plunder, on the one hand, and the opportunity for cooperation on an equitable basis, on the other. The solutions must be radical—in the interests of the peoples of the developing states.

Analysis of yet another group of contradictions—those on a global scale, affecting the very foundations of the existence of civilization—leads to serious conclusions. This refers first of all to pollution of the environment, the air and oceans, and to the depletion of natural resources. The problems are aggravated not just by the excessive loads on the natural systems as a consequence of the scientific and technological revolution and the increasing extent of man's activity. Engels, in his time, foresaw the ill effects of subordinating the use of natural resources to the blind play of market forces. The need for effective international procedures and mechanisms, which would make for the rational use of the world's resources as an asset belonging to all humanity, is becoming increasingly apparent.

The global problems, affecting all humanity, cannot be resolved by one state or a group of states. This calls for cooperation on a worldwide scale, for close and constructive joint action by the majority of countries. This cooperation must be based on completely equal rights and a respect for the sovereignty of each state. It must be based on conscientious compliance with accepted commitments and with the standards of international law. Such is the main demand of the times in which we live.

Capitalism also causes an impoverishment of *culture*, an erosion of the spiritual values created over the centuries. Nothing elevates man more than knowledge. But in probably no other period of history has mankind experienced any stronger pressure of falsehood and deceit than it does now. Bourgeois propaganda foists cleverly doctored information on people all over the world, imposing thoughts and feelings, and inculcating a civic and social attitude advantageous to the ruling forces. What knowledge, what values and moral standards are implicit in the information dispensed to the people and in the system of education is, first and foremost, a political problem.

Life itself brings up the question of safeguarding culture, of protecting it from bourgeois corruption and vandalization. That is one of the most important worldwide tasks. We cannot afford to neglect the long-term psychological and moral consequences of imperialism's current practices in the sphere of culture. Its impoverishment under the onslaught of unbridled commercialism and the cult of force, the propaganda of racism, of lowly instincts, the ways of the criminal world and the "lower depths" of society, must be, and certainly will be, rejected by mankind.

The problems, as you see, comrades, are many, and they are large-scale and intricate. But it is clear that their comprehension is, on the whole, lagging behind the scope and depth of the current tasks. The imperative condition for success in resolving the pressing issues of international life is to reduce the time of search for political accords and to secure the swiftest possible constructive action.

We are perfectly well aware that not everything by far is within our power and that much will depend on the West, on its leaders' ability to see things in sober perspective at important crossroads of history. The U.S. President said once that if our planet were threatened by a landing from another planet, the USSR and the U.S.A. would quickly find a common language. But isn't a nuclear disaster a more tangible danger than a landing by extraterrestrials? Isn't the ecological threat big enough? Don't all countries have a common stake in finding a sensible and fair approach to the problems of the developing states and peoples?

Lastly, isn't all the experience accumulated by mankind enough to draw well-substantiated practical conclusions today rather than wait until some other crisis breaks out? What does the United States hope to win in the long term by producing doctrines that can no longer ensure U.S. security within the modest dimensions of our planet?

To keep in the saddle of history, imperialism is resorting to all possible means. But such a policy is costing the world dearly. The nations are compelled to pay an ever higher price for it, to pay both directly and indirectly. To pay with millions of human lives, with a depletion of national resources, with the waste of gigantic sums on the arms race. With the failure to solve numerous, increasingly difficult problems. And in the long run, perhaps, with the highest possible price that can be imagined.

The U.S. ruling circles are clearly losing their realistic bearings in this far-from-simple period of history. Aggressive international behavior, increasing militarization of politics and thinking, contempt for the interests of others—all this is leading to the inevitable moral and political isolation of U.S. imperialism, widening the abyss between it and the rest of humanity. It is as though the opponents of peace in that country are unaware that when nuclear weapons are at the ready, for civilization time and space lose their habitual contours, and mankind becomes the captive of an accident.

Will the ruling centers of the capitalist world manage to embark on the path of sober, constructive assessments of what is going on? The easiest thing is to say: maybe yes and maybe no. But history denies us the right to make such predictions. We cannot take "no" for an answer to the question: will mankind survive or not? We say: the progress of society, the life of civilization, must and will continue.

We say this not only by dint of the optimism that is usual for Communists, by dint of our faith in people's intelligence and common sense. We are realists and are perfectly well aware that the two worlds are divided by very many things, and deeply divided, too. But we also see clearly that the need to resolve the most vital problems affecting all humanity must prompt them toward interaction, awaken humanity's heretofore unseen powers of self-preservation. And here is the stimulus for solutions commensurate with the realities of our time.

The course of history, of social progress, requires ever more insistently that there should be *constructive and creative interaction between states and peoples on the scale of the entire world.* Not only does it so require, but it also creates the requisite political, social, and material premises for it.

Such interaction is essential in order to prevent nuclear catastrophe, in order that civilization can survive. It is essential in order that other worldwide problems that are growing more acute should also be resolved jointly in the interests of all concerned. The prevailing dialectics of present-day development consists in a combination of competition and confrontation between the two systems and in a growing tendency toward interdependence of the countries of the world community. This is precisely the way, through the struggle of opposites, through arduous effort, groping in the dark to some extent, as it were, that the controversial but *interdependent and in many ways integral world* is taking shape.

The Communists have always been aware of the intrinsic complexity and contradictoriness of the paths of social progress. But at the center of these processes—and this is the chief distinction of the communist world outlook—there unfailingly stands man, his interests and cares. Human life, the possibilities for its comprehensive development, as Lenin stressed, is of the greatest value; the interests of social development rank above all else. This is what guides the CPSU in its practical activity.

As we see it, the main trend of struggle in contemporary conditions consists in creating worthy, truly human material and spiritual conditions of life for all nations, ensuring that our planet should be habitable, and in cultivating a caring attitude toward its riches, especially to man himself—the greatest treasure, and all his potentials. And here we invite the capitalist system to compete with us under the conditions of a durable peace.

II. THE STRATEGIC COURSE: ACCELERATION OF THE COUNTRY'S SOCIOECONOMIC DEVELOPMENT

Comrades, by advancing the strategy of accelerating the country's socioeconomic development at the April Plenary Meeting, the Central Committee of the CPSU adopted a decision of historic significance. It won the wholehearted support of the Party, of the entire people, and is being submitted for discussion at the Congress.

What do we mean by acceleration? First of all, raising the rate of economic growth. But that is not all. In substance it means a new quality of growth: an all-out intensification of production on the basis of scientific and technological progress, a structural reconstruction of the economy, effective forms of management and of organizing and stimulating labor.

The policy of acceleration is not confined to changes in the economic field. It envisages an active social policy, a consistent emphasis on the principle of socialist justice. The strategy of acceleration presupposes an improvement of social relations, a renovation of the forms and methods of work of political and ideological institutions, a deepening of socialist democracy, and resolute overcoming of inertness, stagnation, and conservatism—of everything that is holding back social progress.

The main thing that will ensure us success is the living creativity of the masses, the maximum use of the tremendous potentials and advantages of the socialist system.

In short, comrades, acceleration of the country's socioeconomic development is the key to all our problems: immediate and long-term, economic and social, political and ideological, domestic and foreign. That is the only way a new qualitative condition of Soviet society can and must be achieved.

A. The Results of Socioeconomic Development and the Need for Its Acceleration

Comrades, the program tasks of the Party raised and discussed at our Congress necessitate a broad approach to the assessment of the results of the country's development. In the quarter of a century since the adoption of the Third CPSU Program, the Soviet Union has achieved impressive successes. The fixed production assets of our economy have increased seven times. Thousands of enterprises have been built and new industries created. The national income has gone up by nearly 300 percent, industrial production 400 percent and agricultural production 70 percent.

Before the war and in the early postwar years the level of the U.S. economy appeared to us hard to attain, whereas already in the 1970s we had come substantially closer to it in terms of our scientific, technical, and economic potential, and had even surpassed it in the output of certain key items.

These achievements are the result of tremendous effort by the people. They have enabled us to considerably enhance the well-being of Soviet citizens. In a quarter of a century real per capita incomes have gone up 160 percent, and the social consumption funds more than 400 percent. Fifty-four million flats have been built, which enabled us to improve the living conditions of the majority of families. The transition to universal secondary education has been completed. The number of people who finished higher educational establishments has increased fourfold. The successes of science, medicine, and culture are universally recognized. The panorama of achievements will not be complete if I say nothing about the deepgoing changes in social relations, the relations between nations, and the further development of democracy.

At the same time, difficulties began to build up in the economy in the 1970s, with the rates of economic growth declining visibly. As a result, the targets for economic development set in the CPSU Program, and even the lower targets of the 9th and 10th Five-Year-Plans, were not attained. Neither did we manage to carry out fully the social program charted for this period. A lag ensued in the material base of science and education, health protection, culture, and everyday services.

Certainly, the state of affairs was affected, among other things, by certain factors beyond our control. But they were not decisive. The main thing was that we had failed to produce a timely political assessment of the changed economic situation, that we failed to apprehend the acute and urgent need for converting the economy to intensive methods of development, and for the active use of the achievements of scientific and technological progress in the national economy. There were many appeals and a lot of talk on this score, but practically no headway was made.

By inertia, the economy continued to develop largely on an extensive basis, being oriented toward drawing additional labor and material resources into production. As a result, the rate of growth of labor productivity and certain other efficiency indicators dropped substantially. The attempts to rectify matters by undertaking new projects affected the problem of balance. The economy, despite the enormous resources at its disposal, ran into shortage of them. A gap appeared between the needs of society and the attained level of production, between the effective demand and the supply of goods.

And though efforts have been made of late, we have not succeeded in wholly remedying the situation. The output of most types of industrial and agricultural goods fell short of the targets set by the 26th Congress of the CPSU for the 11th Five-Year-Plan period. There are serious lags in engineering, the oil and coal industries, electrical engineering, in ferrous metals and chemical industries, and in capital construction. Neither have the targets been met for the main indicators of efficiency and the improvement of the people's standard of living.

And we, comrades, must draw the most serious lessons from all this.

The *first* of them may be described as the lesson of truth. A responsible analysis of the past clears the way to the future, whereas a half-truth which shamefully evades the sharp corners holds down the elaboration of realistic policy, and impedes our advance. "Our strength," Lenin said, "lies in stating the truth." That is precisely why the Central Committee deemed it essential to refer once more in the new edition of the Party Program to the negative processes that had surfaced in the 1970s and the early 1980s. That is why, too, we speak of them at the Congress today.

The *other lesson* concerns the sense of purpose and resolve in practical actions. The switchover to an intensive development of such an enormous economy as ours is no simple matter and calls for considerable effort, time, and the loftiest sense of responsibility. But once transformations are launched, we must not confine ourselves to half-hearted measures. We must act consistently and energetically, and must not hesitate to take the boldest of steps.

And *one more lesson*—the main one, I might say. The success of any undertaking depends to a decisive degree on how actively and consciously the masses take part in it. To convince broad sections of the working people that the chosen path is correct, to interest them *morally* and materially, and to restructure the psychology of the cadres—these are the crucial conditions for the acceleration of our growth. The advance will be all the more rapid, the tighter our discipline and organization will be, and the higher the responsibility of each for his job and its results.

Today, the prime task of the Party and the entire people is to reverse resolutely the unfavorable tendencies in the development of the economy, to impart to it the due dynamism and to give scope to the initiative and creativity of the masses, to truly revolutionary change.

There is no other way. In the absence of accelerated economic growth our social programs will remain wishful thinking, even though, comrades, they cannot be put off. Soviet people must within a short time feel the results of the common effort to resolve cardinally the food problem, to meet the need for high-quality goods and services, to improve the medical services, housing, the conditions of life, and environmental protection.

The acceleration of socioeconomic development will enable us to contribute considerably to the consolidation of world socialism, and will raise to a higher level our cooperation with fraternal countries. It will considerably expand our capacity for economic ties with the peoples of developing countries, and with countries of the capitalist world. In other words, implementation of the policy of acceleration will have far-reaching consequences for the destiny of our Motherland.

B. Economic Policy Guidelines

Comrades, the draft Program of the CPSU and the draft Guidelines define the main targets of our economic and social development. By the end of this century we intend to increase the national income nearly twofold while doubling the production potential and qualitatively transforming it. Labor productivity will go up by 2.3–2.5 times, energy consumption per ruble of national income will drop by 28.6 percent and metal consumption by nearly 50 percent. This will signify a sharp turn toward intensifying production, toward improving quality and effectiveness.

Subsequently, by intensifying these processes we intend to switch over to an economy having a higher level of organization and effectiveness, with comprehensively developed productive forces, mature socialist relations of production, and a smoothly functioning economic mechanism. That is our strategic line.

As was emphasized at the conference in the Central Committee of the CPSU in June 1985, the main factors behind this line are scientific and technological progress and a fundamental transformation of society's productive forces. It is impossible to effect cardinal changes with the previous material and technical foundation. The way out, as we see it, lies in thorough modernization of the national economy on the basis of the latest scientific and technological advances, breakthroughs on the leading avenues of scientific and technological progress, and restructuring of the economic mechanism and management system.

1. Modernization of the National Economy on the Basis of Scientific and Technological Progress

The CPSU has tremendous experience in carrying out major scientific-technological and socioeconomic transformations. However significant they are, the scale and complexity of the work we carried out in the past cannot be compared with what has to be done in the period ahead to modernize the national economy.

What do we need for this?

First of all, changing the structural and investment policy. The substance of the changes lies in shifting the center of attention from quantitative indices to quality and efficiency, from intermediate results to end results, from building up production assets to renewing them, from expanding fuel and raw material resources to making better use of them, and also to speeding up the development of research-intensive industries and of the production and social infrastructures.

A big step forward is to be made in this direction in the current five-year period. It is intended to allocate upwards of 200 billion rubles of capital investments—more than during the past ten years—for modernizing and technically reequipping production. Sizable though these amounts are, the planning and economic bodies will have to continue the search for additional resources for these purposes.

Large-scale integrated programs in the strategic areas have been drawn up, and their implementation has begun. The industries that play the key role in scientific and technological progress, that assure a quick economic return and the solution of urgent social problems, will move ahead more dynamically. Substantial funds and material, scientific and manpower resources are being concentrated to speed up their development.

It is clear that the effectiveness of modernization and also the economic growth rates depend to a crucial degree on *machine-building*. This is where the fundamental scientific and technological ideas are materialized, where new implements of labor and machine systems that determine progress in the other branches of the national economy are developed. Here the foundations are laid down for a broad advance to basically new, resource-saving technologies, higher productivity of labor and better quality of output.

The Congress delegates know that the CPSU Central Committee and the USSR Council of Ministers recently adopted a decision on the further development of machine-building. In substance, it is a national program for modernizing this essential sector of industry. A single management body has been set up in it. The machine-building complex has been set the goal of sharply raising the technical-economic level and quality of machines, equipment and instruments already by the end of the 12th Five-Year-Plan period. The capital investments allocated for modernizing this industry will be 80 percent greater than in the previous five years.

What, specifically, do we expect from the implementation of this program? The output of machinery and equipment is to increase by more than 40 percent, and their quality standards will be improved. The growing stream of machines of new generations will pave the way for a fundamental retooling of the national economy and a growth in its effectiveness. The resultant annual savings will amount to the labor of about 12 million people, more than 100 million tons of fuel, and many billions of rubles. Calculations show that the use of the Don-1500 harvester alone, for example, will lead to a considerable reduction in the number of grain harvesting machines, will release about 400,000 machine-operators, and will reduce grain losses by millions of tons.

Large-scale introduction of computers and comprehensive automation of production will tremendously influence the rate of technical modernization. Concrete targets in the development and large-scale application of modern computers and expansion of the manufacture of their components have been defined. The development of computer software and of management information systems is being put on an industrial footing. The Academy of Sciences of the USSR has set up an information science and computer technologies division to coordinate research and development.

Radical modernization of the fuel and energy complex is the keynote of the Energy Program. The Program puts the emphasis on energy-saving technologies, on the replacement of liquid fuel by natural gas and coal, and on more sophisticated methods of oil refining. Advanced technologies are also to be employed in the extraction industry: open-cast coal mining, the use of hydromonitors in coal extraction, the development of improved and more reliable oil extraction equipment and the universal introduction of automated systems. In the course of the current five-year period two and a half times more nuclear power plant generating capacities will be started up than in the previous five years, and outmoded units at thermal power stations will be replaced on a large scale.

A great deal will have to be done in the metal-making and chemical industries, in introducing more highly productive equipment there. The production of fundamentally new and improved structural and other advanced materials will accelerate the development of electronics, machine-building, construction, and other branches of the economy.

The Party attaches enormous importance to technical reequipment of the production infrastructure, in the first place, in transport and communications. Top priority will be given to the development of light industry and other industries that directly meet consumer demand. Advanced equipment for them is to be manufactured not only by specialized industries but also by other industries.

We will not be able to carry out technical modernization unless we radically improve capital construction. This calls for raising the entire building industry complex to a new industrial and organizational level, shortening the investment cycle by a minimum of 50 percent both in modernizing enterprises and in the construction of new facilities. We cannot reconcile ourselves any longer to slow construction rates that freeze enormous sums and retard scientific and technological progress in the national economy.

All these tasks, comrades, are gigantic in scale and significance. How they are carried out will, in the final analysis, determine the fulfilment of our plans and the rates of our growth. Each sector and each enterprise must have a clearcut program for the continuous modernization of production. The responsibility of the planning and economic bodies for the achievement of planned targets will increase accordingly. Party organizations should also direct their activities toward this.

It is especially important to prevent window dressing and the use of palliative instead of substantive measures. There are disquieting instances, and by no means solitary ones, of ministries and departments erecting new facilities under the guise of modernization, of stuffing them with outdated equipment, and of drawing up costly projects that do not assure the rise of production to higher technical-economic levels.

Here is an illustration of that approach. The Bryansk Engineering Works, which puts out motors for diesel locomotives, is now in the middle of a 140-million ruble retooling program. What results will this modernization of capacities yield? It turns out that the program does not provide for the introduction of advanced technologies, the number of workers has already been increased by nearly 1,000, and the return on the assets has dropped. The worst part of it is that they intend to use the new capacities to manufacture an outdated motor, although a more efficient model has been designed and tested.

What does the stance of the executives of the Ministry of the Heavy Machine-Building Industry and of the Ministry of Railways mean? Evidently some comrades have failed to grasp the profound importance of the tasks confronting them. Such facts deserve stern condemnation as undermining the Party's policy of modernization and of accelerated scientific and technological progress. Such cases should be examined with all severity.

The need for modernization poses new tasks for *scientific research*. The CPSU will consistently pursue a policy of strengthening the material and technical base of scientific research to the maximum, of providing scientists with the conditions for fruitful work. However, our country is entitled to expect, from its scientists, discoveries and inventions that will bring about genuinely revolutionary changes in the development of machinery and production methods.

Important measures to make the work of research establishments more effective have been outlined lately. They deal with incentives for scientists and new forms of interaction between science and production. A decision was recently adopted to set up intersectoral research-and-technological complexes, including the large institutes that are leaders in their respective fields, among them institutes under Academies of Sciences, design organizations and pilot plants.

Steps are also being taken to intensify the work of sectoral research institutes and to increase their contribution to speeding up scientific and technological progress. However, this process is going ahead at an impermissibly slow pace. Many institutes are still an appendage of ministry staffs; not infrequently they support departmental interests and are bogged down in red tape and paper work. The question of bringing science closer to production, of including sectoral research institutes into production and research-and-production associations, was forcefully raised at the June conference. We must ascertain who is opposing this, what stand the ministries and their Party committees take on this issue, and how they are reacting to life's demands.

The research potential of higher educational establishments must also be used more effectively. Upwards of 35 percent of our country's research and educational personnel, including about half of the holders of doctoral degrees, are concentrated there but they carry out no more than 10 percent of the research projects. The respective departments should draft and submit proposals for strengthening the links between university research and production. The proposals should also take into account the training of the next generation of researchers. Just as a forest cannot live on without undergrowth, a true scientist is inconceivable without students. This is a question of the future of science, and, therefore, of our country, too. Beginning with their freshman year, college and university students should be drawn into research work and into participation in applying research findings in production. This is the only way that real scientists and creatively thinking specialists can be trained.

In sum, comrades, the orientation of science toward the needs of the national economy should be carried out more energetically. However, it is equally important to orient production toward science, to make it maximally receptive to scientific and technological advances. Regrettably, no few scientific discoveries and major inventions fail to find practical application for years, and sometimes for decades. I shall cite a few examples.

The non-wear-and-tear effect, which Soviet scientists discovered three decades ago, led to the development of fundamentally new lubricants that greatly increase the service life of machine parts subjected to friction and sharply reduce labor outlays. This discovery, which may yield a saving of many millions of rubles, has not yet been applied on a broad scale because of the inertness of some high-ranking executives of the USSR Ministry of Petrochemical Industry and of a number of other ministries and departments.

The Ministry of the Motor Vehicle Industry and planning bodies are to blame for the fact that for about ten years now a newly invented antifriction bearing, which makes machines more reliable and failure-safe under the most rigorous operating conditions, has not been applied on a large scale. The Ministry of the Machine-Tool Industry has impermissibly held up the manufacture of unique hydraulic motors enabling extensive use of hydraulic techniques in mining and elsewhere, to increase labor productivity severalfold and to improve working conditions.

Unfortunately, this list could be continued. This kind of

attitude to new inventions is not infrequently based on the
ambitions of some groups of scientists, on departmental hostility toward inventions made "by others," and a lack of interest on the part of production managers in introducing them.
It is no secret that even the examination of invention applica-
tions is sometimes an ordeal that drags on for years.

We cannot reach our targets in accelerating scientific and
technological progress unless we find levers that will guarantee priority only to those research establishments and industrial enterprises whose work collectives actively introduce
whatever is new and progressive and seek ways and means of
manufacturing articles of high quality and effective yield.

We have already accumulated a definite amount of experience in improving the economic mechanism in the sphere of
science and its interaction with production. It must be thoroughly analyzed and then applied without delay, closely linking up material incentives for research collectives and individual researchers with their actual contribution to the
resolving of scientific and technological problems.

At all levels of economic management there should be a
new attitude to the introduction of new methods and technology. This also refers to the State Planning Committee of
the USSR, which should go over more boldly to all-inclusive
planning of scientific and technological progress, as well as to
the USSR State Committee for Science and Technology,
which is reorganizing its work too slowly. The Academy of
Sciences of the USSR, ministries and departments should pay
more attention to basic research and to applying its findings
in production. This is a sacred duty of every scientist, engineer, designer, and manager of an enterprise.

Our activity in the sphere of *foreign economic contacts* must
be tied up more closely with the new tasks. There should be a
large-scale, forward-looking approach to mutually advantageous economic relations. The member countries of the
Council for Mutual Economic Assistance have worked out a
policy of this kind. It presupposes a switchover in economic
relations among them from primarily trade relations to
deeper specialization and cooperation in production, above
all, in machine-building, and to the establishment of joint
associations and research-and-production complexes.

We have no few departments and organizations that are

responsible for separate spheres of foreign economic relations but they do not always coordinate their work. In setting the aim of actively using foreign economic contacts to speed up our development we have in mind a step-by-step restructuring of foreign trade, of making our exports and imports more effective.

2. Solving the Food Problem: A Top-Priority Task

Comrades, a problem we will have to solve in the shortest time possible is that of fully supplying our country with food. This is the aim of the Party's present agrarian policy, formulated in the decisions taken by the CPSU Central Committee at its May 1982 Plenary Meeting and in the Food Program of the USSR. In the period since their adoption a good deal has been done to expand the material and technical base of agriculture and of the related industries. The economy of the collective farms, state farms, interfarm enterprises and processing plants has become stronger; the productivity of crop-farming and livestock farming has risen.

There is progress, but the lag in agriculture is being overcome slowly. A decisive turn is needed in the agrarian sector to improve the food supply noticeably during the 12th Five-Year-Plan period. It is planned to more than double the growth rate of farm production and to ensure a substantial increase in the per capita consumption of meat, milk, vegetables, and fruit.

Can we do this? We can and we must. The Party has therefore worked out additional measures to raise the efficiency of all sectors of the agro-industrial complex. Their substance consists in changing the socioeconomic situation in the rural areas, in creating the conditions for greater intensification and guaranteed farm produce. The emphasis is put on economic methods of management, broader autonomy of collective farms and state farms and their higher responsibility for the results of their work.

In carrying out this policy we will have to make more effective use of the production potential in the agro-industrial complex and concentrate efforts and resources on the most important sectors providing the highest returns. It is a question, first and foremost, of increasing soil fertility and creating the conditions for stable farming. As the experience of recent years has shown, the key to success lies in large-scale application of intensive technologies. They have a tremendous effect. Their application made it possible to obtain, last year alone, an additional sixteen million tons of grain and a substantial amount of other produce.

Reducing losses of farm produce during harvesting, transportation, storage, and processing is the most immediate source of augmenting food stocks. We have no small potentialities in this respect; an increase in consumption resources could amount to as much as 20 percent, and in the case of some products to as much as 30 percent. Besides, eliminating the losses would cost two to three times less than supplying the same amount of produce.

The Central Committee and the Government have now defined major steps to reduce losses. Rapid expansion of agricultural machine-building will make it possible to equip the collective farms and state farms with highly productive machines capable of performing all the field jobs faster and better. We have also made additional outlays to increase the manufacture of machinery for the food industry and facilities for the processing and storage of food.

The Party and the state will persistently continue to strengthen the material and technical base of the agro-industrial complex. It is equally clear, however, that people will, as before, be the mainspring and inspiration of progress. Today, more than ever before, agriculture needs people who want to work actively, who have a high level of professional skill and a feeling for the new. Constant attention to the working and living conditions of the people in rural areas is the best guarantee of all our successes. All our plans are geared to this, and it is important that they should be carried out unswervingly.

All these are urgent measures, but the program of action is not confined to them. The switchover of the agrarian sector to new methods of administration and management has to be completed. The establishment, in the center and in the localities, of unified management bodies of the agro-industrial complex, called upon to carry out genuine and effective integration of agriculture and of the related industries, is undoubtedly a step of fundamental significance.

The establishment of this organizational framework is backed up by an effective economic mechanism. Proposals on this score have already been drafted. The main idea is to give broad scope to economic methods of management, to substantially broaden the autonomy of collective farms and state farms, to increase their interest in and responsibility for the end results. In substance, it is a question of creatively applying, in the conditions of today, Lenin's idea of the food tax.

It is intended to establish fixed plans for the purchase of produce from the collective farms and state farms for each year of the five-year period; these plans will not be altered. Simultaneously, the farms will be given the opportunity to use all the produce harvested over and above the plan, and in the case of fruit and potatoes and other vegetables a considerable part of the planned produce, as they see fit. The farms can sell it, additionally, to the state; can sell it, either fresh or processed, on the collective-farm market or through cooperative trade outlets; or use it for other needs, including the needs of personal subsidiary holdings. Additional allocations of material resources for which there is a heightened demand, and also other incentives, will encourage farms to sell grain to the state over and above the plan.

In future, the republics, territories, and regions will be given fixed quotas for the delivery of produce to centralized stocks; everything produced over and above that will be kept for the local supply system.

There is to be a transition to improved planning methods based on advanced standards. The role of cost accounting will be substantially increased. Past experience shows that neglect of the principles of self-support, material interest, and responsibility for performance led to a deterioration of the financial and economic position of collective farms and state farms and also to their considerable indebtedness. Genuine cost accounting, with the incomes of enterprises depending upon the end results, should become the rule for all links of the agro-industrial complex and, first and foremost, the collective farms and state farms. The contract and job-by-job systems of payment at the levels of teams, groups, and families to whom the means of production, including land, will be assigned for a period specified by contract, will become widespread.

There will be big opportunities for displaying initiative and resourcefulness. This also presupposes, however, a higher sense of responsibility for meeting the targets of the Food Program, for the results of the financial and economic activity of collective farms, state farms, interfarm enterprise, and organizations. A reliable barrier must be erected in the way of mismanagement and parasitism, and an end must be put to excuses such as "objective circumstances," which some collective farms and state farms have been using to cover up their ineptitude and sometimes a lack of desire to work better. The farms will have to use chiefly their own funds to develop production, increase profits and incomes, and provide incentives. The practice of providing bank loans will have to be substantially altered to stimulate a higher level of activity of collective farms and state farms.

As you see, comrades, conditions for rural economic management are undergoing a cardinal change. This calls for major changes in the style and methods of guidance of the agro-industrial complex. An end must be put to incompetent interference in production activity in rural areas. We expect the State Agro-Industrial Committee of the USSR and its local bodies to do everything so that our country receives weighty returns from the measures that are being taken.

3. Economic Management Must Measure Up to the New Demands

Comrades, the new economic tasks cannot be solved without an in-depth readjustment of the economic mechanism, without creating an integral, effective and flexible system of management that will make it possible to take fuller advantage of the possibilities of socialism.

It is obvious that economic management requires constant improvement. However, the situation today is such that we cannot limit ourselves to partial improvements. A radical reform is needed. Its meaning consists in truly subordinating the whole of our production to the requirements of society, to the satisfaction of people's needs, in orienting management toward raising efficiency and quality, accelerating scientific and technological progress, promoting a greater interest of people in the results of their work, initiative, and socialist enterprise in every link of the national economy, and, above all, in the work collectives.

The Central Committee of the CPSU and its Politburo have defined guidelines for reorganizing the economic mechanism. We set ourselves the aims of:

—heightening the efficiency of centralized guidance of the economy, strengthening the role of the center in implementing the main goals of the Party's economic strategy and in determining the rates and proportions of national economic growth, its balanced development. Simultaneously, the practice of interference by the center in the daily activities of the lower economic links must be overcome;

—resolutely enlarging the framework of the autonomy of associations and enterprises, increasing their responsibility for attaining the highest ultimate results. Toward this end, to transfer them to genuine cost accounting, self-support, and self-financing, and to make the income level of collectives directly dependent on the efficiency of their work;

—going over to economic methods of guidance at all levels of the national economy, for which purpose to reorganize the system of material and technical supply, improve the system of price formation, financing and crediting, and work out effective incentives to eliminate overexpenditure;

—introducing modern organizational management structures, taking into account the trends toward concentration, specialization, and cooperation of production. This is a question of setting up complexes of interconnected industries, research and technological intersectoral centers, various forms of economic associations and territorial-production associations;

—ensuring the best possible combination of sectoral and territorial economic management, integrated economic and social development of republics and regions, and the organization of rational intersectoral contacts;

—carrying out all-round democratization of management, heightening the part played in it by work collectives, strengthening control from below, and ensuring accountability and publicity in the work of economic bodies.

Comrades, we now unquestionably stand before the most thorough reorganization of the socialist economic mechanism. The reorganization has begun. The direction along which work is going ahead in the agro-industrial complex has been already spoken about. Management of the machine-building complex is being upgraded. Industrial enterprises are being transferred, in the main, to a two-level system of management. Beginning with the current year, new economic management methods which have gone through experimental testing have been introduced in enterprises and associations that turn out half of the total industrial output. Their introduction in the service sphere, in construction and in transport has begun. Collective forms of organizing work and providing incentives, and economic contract systems are being applied on an ever wider scale.

We are only at the beginning of the road, however. Time and energetic efforts are needed to reorganize the economic mechanism in our country with its vast and complex economy. Difficulties may arise, and we are not guaranteed against miscalculations either, but still the main thing now is to move ahead purposefully, step by step, along the direction we have chosen, supplementing and perfecting the economic mechanism on the basis of the accumulated experience and eliminating everything that has outlived itself or has failed to justify itself.

Success will depend largely on the *reorganization of the work of the central economic bodies; first and foremost the State Planning Committee of the USSR*. It must indeed become our country's genuine scientific and economic headquarters, freed from current economic matters. We have begun this work. New management bodies of the intersectoral complexes are being set up, and the major part of the day-to-day management functions is being delegated directly to the enterprises and associations. The State Planning Committee and other economic agencies must concentrate their efforts on long-term planning, on ensuring proportional and balanced economic development, on carrying out the structural policy, and on creating the economic conditions and incentives for attaining the best end results in each unit of the national economy. Considerable improvements are needed in the sphere of statistics.

Lately there has been a weakening of the *financial-credit influence on the economy*. The financial system does not sufficiently stimulate higher economic efficiency. The defective practice of income redistribution, with the losses of lagging enterprises, ministries, and regions covered at the expense of those that operate profitably, has reached a large scale. This undermines cost accounting, promotes parasitism, and prompts endless demands for assistance from the center. Crediting no longer serves its purpose.

"Any radical reforms," said Lenin, "will be doomed to failure unless our financial policy is successful." Accordingly, we must radically change the substance, organization, and methods of the work of the financial and credit bodies. Their chief aim is not to exercise petty control over the work of enterprises but to provide economic incentives and to consolidate money circulation and cost accounting, which is the best possible controller. Everything must be made dependent on the end result. The question of improving collection of the turnover tax, deductions from the profit and other budget revenues has obviously come on the agenda. Their size and the procedure for their payment should more effectively help reduce losses in production, raise quality of output and promote its sale.

Prices must become an active factor of economic and social policy. We shall have to carry out a planned readjustment of the price system as an integral whole in the interests of organizing effective cost accounting and in conformity with the aims of increasing the real incomes of the population. Prices must be made more flexible; price levels must be linked up not only with the outlays but also with the consumer properties of the goods, their effectiveness and the degree to which products meet the needs of society and consumer demand. Ceiling prices and contract prices are to be employed more widely.

The system of *material and technical supply* also needs thorough improvement. It must be turned into a flexible economic mechanism which helps the national economy to function rhythmically and steadily. It is the direct duty of the State Committee for Material and Technical Supply to contribute actively to the establishment of direct long-term relations betweeen producers and consumers on a contractual basis, and to improve the observance of the terms of delivery. Wholesale trade in the means of production should be developed.

In the final analysis, everything we are doing to improve management and planning and to readjust organization structures is aimed at creating conditions for the *effective functioning of the basic link of the economic system: the association or enterprise.*

As shown by analysis, the results of the experiments that have been carried out could have been much better, if, on the one hand, there had been a corresponding reorganization of the work of industrial ministries and central economic agencies, which continue their attempts to restrict the powers of enterprises, and, on the other hand, if the incentives for higher efficiency had been brought home to every section, work team and workplace. Special attention should be paid to this.

It is high time to put an end to the practice of ministries and departments exercising petty tutelage over enterprises. Ministries should concentrate their attention on technical policy, on intrasectoral proportions, and on meeting the requirements of the national economy in high-quality products put out by their respective industries. Enterprises and organizations should be given the right independently to sell to one another what they produce over and above the plan, as well as raw and other materials, equipment, etc., which they do not use. They should also be given the legal right to make such sales to the population. What sense is there in destroying or dumping onto waste heaps articles that could be useful in the household, in building homes, garages, or cottages or garden and vegetable plots?

It would be difficult to overestimate the role of economic *standards.* When the work collectives of enterprises know, ahead of time, specifics of the planned period—delivery targets, prices, deductions from profits to the budget, standards for forming wage funds and cost-accounting incentives funds—they can draw up creatively plans which provide for higher production growth rates and much higher efficiency without being afraid to reveal their as yet untapped potentialities. Moreover, enterprises should be given the possibility—following the example of the Volga Auto Works and the Sumy Engineering Works—themselves to earn the funds needed to expand and retool production.

It is especially important to give enterprises and organizations greater autonomy in the sphere of consumer goods manufacture and services. Their task is to react quickly to consumer demand. It is along these lines that we are reshaping the economic mechanism of light industry. The range of targets approved from above is being sharply limited for enterprises in this sphere; their plans will be drawn up chiefly on the basis of contracts with trade organizations, which, in turn, must see to it that their orders conform to the actual consumer demand. In other words, the quantity, range, and quality of goods, that is, just what people need, will be the main thing and not gross output. Besides, it is planned to establish intersectoral production and industrial-commercial associations for the manufacture and sale of light-industry goods and to open more retail outlets operated by them.

The time has also come to solve another problem. An enterprise's wage fund should be directly tied in with the returns from the sale of its products. This will help to exclude the manufacture and supply of low-grade goods for which there is no demand, or, as they say, production for the warehouse. Incidentally, that approach should be applied not only in light industry. We can no longer reconcile ourselves to a situation in which the personnel of enterprises producing worthless goods lead an untroubled life, drawing their full pay and receiving bonuses and other benefits. Indeed, why should we pay for work that produces goods nobody wants to buy? One way or another all this goes against us, comrades! We must not forget about this.

A well-thought-out approach must also be taken to the question of a rational combination of *large, medium, and small enterprises*. As experience shows, small, well-equipped plants have their own advantages in many cases. They can be quicker and more flexible in taking into account technological innovations and changes in demand, can faster meet the demand for small-batch and separate items, and can make better use of available manpower, especially in small towns.

Another substantial aspect of readjustment is consolidation of the territorial approach to planning and management. This is especially important for our vast and multinational country with its diverse features. The actions of ministries and departments that neglect the conditions in and the requirements of regions, with resulting economic imbalances, were rightly criticized at Party conferences and at congresses of the communist parties of constituent republics.

Some suggestions are also being received on this score. It is evidently worthwhile giving thought to enlarging the powers of republican and local bodies—following the example of the agro-industrial complex—in the management of construction, intersectoral production units, the social and production infrastructures, and many consumer goods factories. The work of the State Planning Committee of the USSR and of the ministries should get a broader territorial orientation. The question of national-economic management on the basis of large economic areas deserves study.

Our short- and long-term plans are linked, to a considerable degree, with the tapping of the natural wealth of Siberia and the Soviet Far East. This is a very important matter that requires a statesmanlike approach ensuring integrated regional development. Special attention should be paid to providing people there with the conditions for fruitful work and a full-blooded life. That is the main question today, and fulfillment of the set targets depends on how it is solved.

Attention should be drawn at our Congress to the problems involved in the further socioeconomic development of the Non-Black-Soil Zone of the Russian Federation. I will stress two points. The Central Committee of the CPSU and the Soviet Government have adopted special decisions for an upswing in the agriculture of the Non-Black-Soil Zone, and they must be carried out unswervingly and fully. That is in the first place. And in the second place, the local Party, government and economic bodies, and work collectives must pay much more attention to making effective use of the potential accumulated there, and of the allocated resources.

Consolidation of the territorial principle of management calls for a higher level of economic guidance in each republic, region, city, and district. Proposals that come from the localities are at times not thought out thoroughly, not dictated by the interests of the national economy but rather by a dependant's mentality, and sometimes even by self-seeking interests, which draw the economy into capital-intensive and low-productive projects. Due attention is not paid everywhere to raising the efficiency of production. In Kazakhstan, for example, the share of national income per unit of fixed production assets is a third less than the average for the Soviet economy. In Turkmenia, the productivity of social labor has not grown at all in 15 years. Thought should be given to how to tie in the resources allocated for social needs more closely with the efficiency of the regional economy.

Comrades, every readjustment of the economic mechanism begins, as you know, with a readjustment of thinking, with a rejection of old stereotypes of thought and actions, with a clear understanding of the new tasks. This refers primarily to the activity of our economic personnel, to the functionaries of the central links of administration. Most of them have a clear idea of the Party's initiatives, actively support them, boldly tackle complicated assignments, and seek and find the best ways of carrying them out. This attitude deserves utmost support. It is hard, however, to understand those who adopt a wait-and-see policy or who, like the Gogol character that thought up all kinds of fanciful ideas, do not actually do anything or change anything. There will be no reconciliation with the stand taken by functionaries of that kind. We will simply have to part ways with them. All the more so do we have to part ways with those who hope that everything will settle down and return to the old lines. That will not happen, comrades!

In our work on restructuring the economy and the economic mechanism it is more important than ever to rely on science. Life prompts us to take a new look at some theoretical ideas and concepts. This applies to such major problems as the interaction of the productive forces and the production relations, socialist ownership and its economic forms, commodity-money relations, the coordination of centralism with the autonomy of economic organizations, and so on.

Practice has revealed the insolvency of the ideas that under the conditions of socialism *the conformity of production relations to the nature of the productive forces* is ensured automatically, as it were. In real life, everything is more complicated. Indeed, the socialist production relations open up broad vistas for development of the productive forces. However, they must be constantly improved. And that means outdated economic management methods must be noticed in good time and replaced by new ones.

The forms of production relations and the economic management and guidance system now in operation took shape, basically, in the conditions of extensive economic development. These gradualy grew out of date, began to lose their stimulating effect and in some respects became a brake. We are now striving to change the thrust of the economic mechanism, to overcome its costliness and to orient it toward a higher level of quality and efficiency, acceleration of scientific and technological progress and enhancement of the human factor. This is the main thing that will, in practice, signify further improvement of the socialist production relations and will provide new scope for the growth of the productive forces.

In this work we must not be stopped by long-established ideas, let alone by prejudices. If, for example, it is necessary and justifiable to apply economic standards instead of targets that are sent down as directives, this does not mean a retreat from the principles of planned guidance but only a change in its methods. The same can be applied to the need to broaden the autonomy, initiative, and responsibility of associations and enterprises, and to enhance their role as socialist commodity producers.

Unfortunately, there is a widespread view that any change in the economic mechanism is regarded as practically being a retreat from the principles of socialism. In this connection I should like to emphasize the following: socioeconomic acceleration and the consolidation of socialism in practice should be.the supreme criterion in the improvement of management and of the entire system of the socialist production relations.

The *aspects of socialist property* as the foundation of our social system acquire great relevance. Socialist property has a rich content; it includes a multifaceted system of relations among people, collectives, industries, and regions of the country in the use of the means of production and its results, and a whole range of economic interests. This complex of relations requires a definite combination and constant regulation, especially since it is in motion. Unless we gain a deep understanding of these changes in theoretical terms we cannot arrive at correct practical decisions and consequently take prompt steps to mold a genuine sense of responsibility to socialist property.

We must provide the working people with greater incentives for putting the national riches to the best possible use and multiplying them. How can this be done? It would be naive to imagine that the feeling of ownership can be inculcated by words. A person's attitude toward property is shaped, first and foremost, by the actual conditions in which he has been put, by his possibilities of influencing the organization of production, and the distribution and use of the results of work. The problem is thus one of further intensifying socialist self-government in the economic sphere.

The role of work collectives in the use of social property must be raised decisively. It is important to carry out unswervingly the principle according to which enterprises and associations are wholly responsible for operating without losses, while the state does not bear any responsibility for their obligations. This is where the substance of cost accounting lies. You cannot be a master of your country if you are not a real master in your factory or collective farm, in your shop or livestock farm. It is the duty of the work collective to answer for everything, to multiply the social wealth. Multiplication of the social wealth, as well as losses, should affect the income level of every member of the collective. And, of course, a reliable barrier is needed against all attempts to extract unearned income from the social property. There are still "snatchers," persons who do not consider it a crime to steal from their plant everything that comes their way, and there are also sundry bribe-takers and grabbers who do not stop at using their position for selfish purposes. The full force of the law and of public condemnation should be applied to all of them.

Attention should also be paid to such a topical problem of regulating socialist property relations as ensuring unquestionable priority of the interests of the whole people over the interests of industries and regions. Ministries, departments, and territorial bodies are not the owners of means of production but merely institutions of state administration responsible to society for efficient use of the people's wealth. We cannot allow departmental and parochial interests to hinder realization of the advantages of socialist property.

We also stand for full clarity on the question of cooperative property. It has far from exhausted its possibilities in socialist production, in providing better satisfaction of people's needs. Many collective farms and other cooperative organizations are managed effectively. And wherever the need exists, utmost support should be given to the establishment and growth of cooperative enterprises and organizations. They should become widespread in the manufacture and processing of products, in housing construction and in construction on garden and vegetable allotments, and in the sphere of services and trade.

It is also time to overcome prejudices regarding *commodity-money* relations and underestimation of these relations in planned economic guidance. Refusal to recognize the importance of their active influence on people's interest in working better and on production efficiency leads to a weakening of the cost-accounting system and to other undesirable consequences. Conversely, sound commodity-money relations on a socialist basis can create a situation and economic conditions under which the results depend entirely on the standards of the work done by the collective and on the ability and initiative of the managers.

Thus, comrades, we are obliged to assess the situation again and again and to resolutely reorganize everything that has become out of date, that has outlived itself. A profound understanding of this task by Party activists and by all personnel, as well as its comprehension by the broad masses are indispensable for success, are the point of departure in the exceptionally important work of building up a new economic mechanism and management system.

4. *Putting Reserves of Economic Growth into Action*

Comrades, the Party has worked out a strategy of deepgoing transformations in the national economy and has begun to effect them. They will undoubtedly enable us to speed up economic growth. As was noted, however, this will require a good deal of time, but we must increase the growth rates at once, today. The specific feature of the 12th Five-Year-Plan period consists in retooling the national economy on a new scientific and technological basis while simultaneously stepping up the rates of our advance.

Hence the need to utilize all of our reserves to the maximum. It is more sensible to start with those that do not require big outlays but yield quick and tangible returns. This is a matter of economic-organizational and socio-psychological factors, of making better use of the production capabilities that have been built up, of making the incentives more effective, of improving the level of organization and tightening discipline, and of eliminating mismanagement. Our reserves are at hand, and with a dedicated approach plus good management they promise high returns.

Just look at the capacities in operation. The value of our country's fixed production assets exceeds 1.5 trillion rubles, but they are not all being used properly. This applies to a number of industries—to machine-building, heavy industry, the power industry, and agriculture. What is especially alarming is the fact that the most active assets—machinery, equipment, and machine-tools—often stand idle or else are operated at half capacity. In the engineering industry, for example, metal-cutting machine-tools are in use only slightly more than one shift a day. On the whole, our country annually loses billions of rubles' worth of industrial output because capacities are underloaded. Planning and economic bodies and work collectives at enterprises must do everything possible to ensure the operation of existing capacities at the designed level. In heavy industry alone, this would nearly double the output growth rates.

Failure to meet component delivery obligations is another hindrance. A violation of this kind in one place has a ripple effect throughout the national economy and lowers its efficiency. Jerky production also does tangible damage. It is no secret that at the beginning of the month many plants stand idle longer than they function. But at the end of the month they begin a headlong rush, as a result of which output quality is low. This chronic disease must be eradicated. Strict observance of component delivery obligations is the duty of work collectives and also of management at all levels. We will not be able to achieve our aims unless we bring order into planning and supply, create the necessary stocks, and impose higher financial liability at all levels for failure to meet obligations and for spoilage.

There are also great reserves in the use of manpower. Some economic managers complain of a manpower shortage. I think the complaints are groundless in most cases. If you look into the matter more closely you will see that there is no shortage of labor. But there is a low level of labor productivity, inadequate work organization and ineffective incentive schemes. Add to this the creation of superfluous jobs by planning and economic bodies. It is a well-known fact that some of our enterprises, design offices and research institutes have considerably larger staffs than their counterparts abroad with the same work load.

Once people at enterprises get down in earnest to improving work organization and incentives, to tightening discipline, and setting higher demands, reserves that had never been thought to exist previously are brought to light. Application of the Shchokino method and the certification of work places convincingly confirm this. When Byelorussian railwaymen went over to a new pay system, with one person doing two or more different jobs, about 12,000 workers were soon freed for jobs in other sectors.

Of course, more attention must also be paid to production mechanization and automation. In tackling this problem one does not have to wait for machines and devices to be designed and made somewhere else. A great deal can be accomplished by using one's own capabilities. For instance, efforts in this direction in Zaporozhye Region led, in three years, to a 9 percent reduction in the number of workers employed in manual jobs in industry and a 15 percent reduction in the number of those in similar jobs in the building trades. I think that other regions, territories, and republics have no fewer possibilities. The important thing is to put persistent and dedicated effort into this, showing consideration for the people who have to perform manual operations, and striving to reduce production outlays.

Generally speaking, comrades, there are enormous economic reserves. We have not yet really begun to use many of them. The mentality of a substantial section of the managerial personnel at various levels took shape against the background of an abundance of resources. Many were spoiled by these riches, and that led to wastefulness. However, the situation changed long ago. The former influx of manpower has dwindled, and we have begun to pay a heavy price for every ton of oil, ore, and coal we extract and deliver. We cannot close our eyes to these facts; we must reckon with them. We must economize everywhere and always: on the job and at home. We must not ignore mismanagement and wastefulness. Nearly the whole of this year's growth in the national income is to come from raising labor productivity and lowering materials and energy consumption.

That is not simple, but wholly feasible. All the more so since our country has accumulated experience in making thrifty use of resources; but it is not being spread fast enough. Party, YCL, and trade union organizations should constantly promote thrift and encourage those who make economical and rational use of raw materials, electrical energy, and fuel. We must make it a firm rule that overexpenditure of resources is disadvantageous and savings are tangibly rewarded.

I would like to put special emphasis on the problem of *output quality standards*. This is more than our immediate and major reserve. Accelerated scientific and technological progress is impossible today without high quality standards. We are sustaining great material and moral losses because of flaws in design, deviations from technology, the use of low-grade materials and poor finishing. This affects the precision and reliability of machines and instruments and hinders satisfaction of consumer demand for goods and services. Last year millions of meters of fabrics, millions of pairs of leather footwear, and many other consumer items were returned to factories or marked down as inferior-grade goods. The losses are significant: wasted raw materials and the wasted labor of hundreds of thousands of workers. Radical measures must be taken to rule out the manufacture of defective or low-grade goods. The full force of pecuniary and administrative influence and legislation must be applied for this purpose. There is also evidently a need to adopt a special law on the quality of output.

Recently the Central Committee of the CPSU called upon Party committees, government and economic bodies, trade union and YCL organizations and all working people to make maximum efforts to radically improve the quality of goods. This must be a matter of concern for every Communist, for every Soviet citizen, for all who respect their own work, for all who cherish the honor of their enterprise, their industry, and the honor of our country.

A great deal of important and intensive work lies ahead of us. The first year of the five-year-plan period is a year of persistent work, a year of tests for every manager and work collective. We must pass this test, draw all the reserves of the economy into production, and consolidate the foundation for further transformations.

The industry and talent of Soviet citizens are the key to attaining the goal that has been set. It is now up to efficient organization and precise direction of this great force. The part to be played by socialist emulation in this effort cannot be overestimated. It should be spearheaded at raising the standards of work, economizing and thriftiness, and reaching the targets set before each collective and at each workplace. Enthusiasm and growing skills have been and, we are confident, will continue to be our reliable support.

C. The Basic Guidelines of Social Policy

Comrades, questions of social policy, concern for man's welfare, have always stood at the center of our Party's attention.

The social sphere encompasses the interests of classes and social groups, nations and nationalities, the relationship between society and individual, the conditions of work and life, health and leisure. *It is the sphere in which the results of economic activity affecting the vital interests of the working people are realized, and the loftiest aims of socialism are carried into effect. It is the sphere in which the humanism of the socialist system, its qualitative difference from capitalism, is seen most distinctly and graphically.*

Socialism has eliminated the main source of social injustice—the exploitation of man by man, and inequality in relation to the means of production. Social justice reigns in all areas of socialist social relations. It is embodied in the real power of the people and the equality of all citizens before the law, the actual equality of nations, respect for the individual, and conditions for the all-round development of the person-ality. It is also embodied in broad social guarantees—employ-ment, access to education, culture, medical care, and housing, concern for people in old age, and mother-and-child welfare. Strict observance in life of the principle of social justice is an important condition for the unity of the people, society's political stability, and dynamic development.

But life, as they say, does not stand still. So we must look at the further development of the social sphere with new eyes, and appreciate the full measure of its increasing significance. We are obliged to do so in keeping with the general course worked out by the Party for the acceleration of socioeconomic development, and with the program aim of our Party, that of achieving the complete well-being and a free all-round de-velopment of all members of society.

Lessons of the past, too, require that we pay greater atten-tion to social issues. The Party's Central Committee holds that central and local bodies had underestimated relevant prob-lems concerning the material base of the country's social and cultural sphere. As a result, a residual principle had actually taken shape governing allocation of resources for its develop-ment. There was a certain overemphasis on technocratic ap-proaches, blunting attention to the social aspect of produc-tion, to everyday life and leisure; this could not but reduce the interest of the working people in the results of their work, slacken discipline, and lead to other negative developments.

We are not at all indifferent to what ways and means are used to improve the material and spiritual aspects of life and what social consequences this entails. If private-owner para-sitic sentiments, and leveling tendencies begin to surface, this means that something is wrong about the choice of ways and means in our work, and has got to be rectified. During the discussion of the pre-Congress documents, Party members and nonmembers spoke with concern of the slackening of control over the measure of labor and consumption, of in-fringements of socialist justice, and of the need for stepping up the fight against unearned incomes. The gravity and im-portance of these questions is more than obvious.

In short, the attained level of development and the magni-tude of the new tasks call for a long-term, deeply considered, integral, and strong social policy that would extend to all aspects of the life of society. It is essential for the planning and management bodies, for central and local economic organizations to deal resolutely with the needs of the social sphere.

The objectives of social policy are thoroughly characterized in the drafts of the Party Program and the Guidelines. Allow me to dwell on some issues related to its implementation.

1. Steady Improvement of the People's Standard of Living, Consistent Application of Social Justice

The long-term plans for the country's social and economic development envisage *raising the people's well-being to a qualitatively new level*. In the coming fifteen years, the volume of resources allocated for the improvement of the conditions of life is to be doubled. Real per capita incomes are to go up 60 to 80 percent. The rise in incomes in the 12th five-year period is to cover millions of people. Huge funds are being earmarked for increasing the construction of homes and social and cultural facilities. Those are the plans. But we must mention the main thing: these plans will become reality only if every Soviet person works hard and efficiently. This applies to every person wherever he may work and whatever post he may occupy. What we accomplish is what we are going to have, and how we are going to live.

Socialist transformations have radically changed both the purpose of work and the attitude to work of the mass of workers and peasants. This is vividly reflected in the massive growth of socialist emulation. Relying on its wealth of experience, the Party intends to continue promoting these traditions, and to cultivate a conscious and creative attitude to work as the prime duty to society.

At election meetings and conferences, Communists have rightly raised the question of not only improving the forms of moral incentives, but also of greatly increasing material incentives and establishing due order in this important matter. It was rightly pointed out that the so-called "figure juggling," payment of unearned money and unmerited bonuses, and setting "guaranteed" pay rates unrelated to the worker's contributed work, are impermissible. It should be said quite emphatically on this score that when equal payments are fixed for the work of a good employee and that of a negligent one this is a gross violation of our principles. And first of all it is an intolerable distortion of socialism's basic principle: "From each according to his ability, to each according to his work," which expresses the substance of the social justice of the new social system.

It is essential that the government's wage policy should ensure that incomes strictly correspond to the quantity and quality of work done. Proceeding from this, the increase of wage rates and basic salaries of factory and office workers in productive fields envisaged in the 12th five-year period will be enacted for the first time essentially at the expense and within the limits of the sums earned by the enterprises themselves. This procedure will make a more active impact on the acceleration of technical progress and on heightening the efficiency of production.

Rates and salaries in the nonproductive sphere will go up, drawing on centralized sources. A phased increase of the salaries of doctors and other medical workers was started last year. The increase of the rates and salaries of those employed in public education is to be completed in 1987, and a start is to be made that year in raising the salaries of cultural workers. Measures are being taken to extend the wage and salary advantages of factory and office workers in certain regions of Eastern Siberia and the Soviet Far East.

Many proposals made by working people refer to the role of social consumption funds in enforcing the principle of justice. These funds already account for nearly one-third of the consumed material goods and services. We hold that they are in no way charity. They play an important role in providing equal access for members of society to education and culture, equalizing conditions for the raising of children, and easing the life of those who may, for one reason or another, need a grant or continuous assistance. At the same time, it is a means of encouraging and stimulating qualified, conscientious work. The Party intends to continue promoting the further growth and more effective use of these social funds. In the 12th five-year period they are to go up by 20 to 23 percent.

Combating unearned incomes is an important function of the socialist state. We must admit today that owing to a slackening of control and for a number of other reasons groups of people have appeared with a distinct proprietary mentality and a scornful attitude to the interests of society.

Working people have legitimately raised the question of rooting out such things. The Central Committee agrees completely with these demands. It is considered necessary, already in the immediate future, to carry out additional measures against parasites, plunderers of socialist property, bribe-takers, and all those who embarked on a path alien to the work-oriented nature of our system. We should also give thought to proposals about perfecting our tax policy, including the introduction of a progressive inheritance tax.

But while combating unearned incomes, we must not permit any shadow to fall on those who do honest work to earn a supplementary income. What is more, the state will promote various forms of satisfying popular demand and providing services. We must attentively examine proposals for regulating individual labor. It stands to reason that such labor must be in full conformity with socialist economic principles, and rest on either cooperative principles or on contracts with socialist enterprises. Society, the population only stand to gain from this.

All the efforts to perfect the distributive relations will have little effect and the objective of enhancing the people's well-being will not be attained if we fail to *saturate the market with diverse goods and services*. That, indeed, is the purpose of the Comprehensive Program for the Development of the Production of Consumer Goods and Services.

In the current five years it is planned to secure higher growth rates for output of consumer goods and retail trade, and to considerably improve the organization of trade and public catering. Heavy industry has been instructed to involve all enterprises in the production of manufactured goods and to ensure output of high-quality materials and equipment for light industry and the food industry.

We must build up an up-to-date services industry as quickly as possible. That is the job of central organizations, but also—no less, and perhaps even more—of the Councils of Ministers of Union Republics, and all bodies of local government. Resolute measures must be taken to eliminate the glaring disproportions between the supply and demand of services. This applies first of all to services that lighten domestic work and those connected with the improvement and renovation of flats, with tourism, and the servicing of cars, the demand for which is increasing at an especially swift rate. Responding to the proposals of the working people, we are promoting broad expansion of collective gardening and vegetable growing. This has got off the ground; but the work must be continued and all artificial obstacles must be removed.

The social importance and acuteness of the *housing problem* have predetermined our serious attitude to it. To provide every family with a separate flat or house by the year 2000 is, in itself, a tremendous but feasible undertaking. In the current five years, and especially in the five-year periods to follow, the scale of house-building and of modernizing available housing will increase. The building of cooperative and individual housing should be encouraged in every way. There are great reserves here for expanding the building of homes. Those who are backing the construction of youth complexes are doing the right thing. The motivation and energy of young people can do a lot in this respect.

Much is being said about the need for seriously improving the practice of distributing housing. These questions must be settled on a broad democratic basis and put under continuous public control. Proposals for fair changes in the system of house rents by gearing them to the size and quality of all the occupied living space merit attention. There have been many complaints about the low quality of house-building. It is essential to work out measures that would stimulate a substantial improvement of quality, and also an improvement of the layout, the amenities, and architecture of our towns and villages.

Comrades, the qualitative changes in the social sphere are impossible without *deep-going changes in the content of labor*. The main role here is to be played by the technical reconstruction of the economy: mechanization, automation, computerization and robotization which, as I want to stress specially, must have an explicitly clear social orientation. Already in the current five years it is planned to sharply reduce the share of manual labor, and by the year 2000 to bring it down in the productive sphere to 15–20 percent, relieving millions of people of manual operations. The further change of labor in the context of the scientific and technological revolution sets high demands on education and the professional training of people. In substance, the task of *establishing a single system of continuous education* is now on the agenda.

In recent years, the Central Committee has taken important steps in that direction. A reform has been launched of the *general and vocational school.* It should be said that the rate and extent of the measures taken under the reform are not satisfactory as yet. A more profound approach is required to the study of the scientific basis of contemporary production and of the leading trends of its intensification. And what is especially urgent is that all pupils should learn the use of computers. In sum, it is essential that the Leninist principle of combining education with productive labor should be implemented more fully, that the effectiveness of education should be considerably raised, and that radical improvements should be carried out in the training of young people for independent life and labor and in bringing up politically conscious builders of the new society.

The Party is setting the task of *restructuring higher and specialized secondary education.* In recent years the growing output of specialists was not accompanied by the requisite improvement in the quality of their training. The material base of the higher school is lagging behind gravely. The use of engineers and technicians must be considerably improved.

At present, proposals have been drawn up to alter the prevailing situation. It is in the interests of society to raise the prestige of the work of engineers. The structure of higher and specialized secondary education is to be revised, so that the training of specialists will be abreast of the times and they will acquire substantial theoretical knowledge and practical skills. The relationship of higher educational institutions and specialized secondary schools with various branches of the economy should evidently follow new lines, and their mutual interest in raising the level of training and retraining of cadres, in cardinally improving their use in production, should be enhanced.

Nothing is more valuable to every person and, for that matter, to society than health. *The protection and improvement of the health of people* is a matter of cardinal importance. We must consider the problems of health from broad social positions. Health depends above all on the conditions of work and life, and on the standard of living. It stands to reason, of course, that the public health service is also of tremendous importance. We must meet the needs of the population in high-quality medical treatment, health protection, and pharmaceuticals as quickly as possible and, moreover, everywhere. All this puts the question of the material and technical base of the health service in a new way, calling for the solution of many urgent scientific, organizational, and personnel problems. Considerable funds will be needed, of course, and we must see to it that they are made available.

It has long since been noted, and most aptly, that health cannot be bought in a pharmacy. The main thing is a person's way of life and, among other things, how sensibly and wholesomely a person uses his or her spare time. The opportunities for this are at hand, but the organizational side of the matter is very poorly run. Much depends on the initiative of the public, on people's avocational activity. But in towns and villages, and within work collectives, they often wait for instructions and count on assistance from above. Why do we make poor use of what is already at our disposal—of palaces, clubs, stadiums, parks, and many other facilities? Why don't the Soviets, the trade unions, and the Komsomol tackle these questions properly? Why not start a movement for more active building of simple playgrounds and gymnasiums on the residential principle? And finally, why not organize sports, tourist, and other clubs on a cooperative basis?

A fight has been mounted across the country against hard drinking and alcoholism. In the name of the health of society and of the individual we have taken resolute measures and started a battle against traditions that were shaped and cultivated over the centuries. While we should have no illusions about what has been accomplished, we can safely say that incidents of drunkenness on the job and in public places have become fewer. The situation with families is improving, the number of industrial injuries has gone down, and discipline has been tightened. But extensive, persevering, and varied efforts are still needed to secure a final break with prevailing habits. There must be no indulgence here!

We face the acute task of ensuring the *protection of nature and rational use of its resources*. Socialism, with its plan-governed organization of production and humane world outlook, is quite capable of creating a harmonious balance between society and nature. A system of measures to that effect has already been implemented in our country, and quite considerable funds are being allocated for this purpose. There are also practical results.

Still, in a number of regions the state of the environment is alarming. And the public, notably our writers, are quite right in calling for a more careful treatment of land and its riches, of lakes, rivers, and the plant and animal world.

Scientific and technical achievements are being introduced much too slowly in nature protection. The projects of new and the reconstruction of operating enterprises are still being based on outdated notions, with wasteless and low-waste production techniques being introduced on too small a scale. During the processing of minerals, most of the extracted mass goes to waste, polluting the environment. More resolute economic, legal, and educational measures are required here. All of us living today are accountable to our descendants and to history for the environment.

2. Improvement of Social-Class Relations and Relations Among the Peoples of the USSR

Comrades, analyzing problems involved in *interrelationship of classes and social groups* is of vital importance for a Marxist-Leninist party. By carefully taking into account both the community and the specific nature of their interests in its policy, the Communist Party ensures society's strong unity and successful fulfillment of its most important and complex tasks.

The working class holds a vanguard place in Soviet society. Owing to its position in the socialist production system, its political experience, high political awareness, good organization, labor and political activity, the working class unites our society and plays the leading role in improving socialism, in communist construction. Constant concern for the consolidation of the alliance of the working class, the peasantry, and the intelligentsia is the cornerstone of the policy pursued by the Communist Party of the Soviet Union. It is precisely this which enables us to muster forces for the speedy solution of the economic and social tasks we have set ourselves.

The unity of socialist society by no means implies a leveling of public life. Socialism encourages diversity of people's interests, requirements, and abilities, and vigorously supports the initiative of social organizations that express this diversity. Moreover, socialism needs this diversity, which it regards as an essential condition for the further promotion of people's creative activity and initiative, and the competition of minds and talents, without which the socialist way of life and the movement forward would be inconceivable.

Generally speaking, the problem is as follows: unless we elevate emulation to a new, incomparably higher level in production, in the economy, as well as in the fields of science and the arts, we shall not be able to cope with the task of accelerating the country's socioeconomic progress. To improve the socialist way of life is to ensure the maximum opportunities for fostering collectivism, the cohesion of society, and the individual's activity.

The *problems of consolidating the family* are attracting public attention. Our achievements in cultivating the new, socialist type of family are indisputable. Socialism has emancipated women from economic and social oppression, securing for them the opportunity to work, obtain an education, and participate in public life on an equal footing with men. The socialist family is based on the full equality of men and women, and their equal responsibility for the family.

Yet the formation of the new type of family is no simple matter. It is a complicated process that involves many problems. In particular, although the divorce rate has dropped in the past few years, it is still high. There is still a large number of unhappy families. All this has a negative effect, above all on the upbringing of children, as well as on the morale of men and women, on their labor and public activity. It stands to reason that society cannot be indifferent to such phenomena. The strong family is one of its principal pillars.

Young families need special care. Young people must be well prepared for family life. More thought should be given to the system of material assistance to newlyweds, above all in solving their housing and everyday problems. It would apparently be a good thing to consider the proposals for improving relevant legislation with a view to heightening the citizens' responsibility for consolidating the family. But that is not all.

It is necessary to organize the practical work of state and public organizations so that it will promote in every way a strengthening of the family and its moral foundations. This means the creation of conditions for family participation in public festivities and in cultural and sports events, and for family recreation. Families in which successive generations work in the same profession should be widely honored; good family traditions should be given every support and young people should be brought up on the basis of the experience of older generations. Here a big contribution can be made by the mass information media: television, literature, cinema, and the theater.

Securing living and working conditions for women that would enable them to successfully combine their maternal duties with active involvement in labor and public activity is a prerequisite for solving many family problems. In the 12th five-year period we are planning to extend the practice of letting women work a shorter day or week, or to work at home. Mothers will have paid leaves until their babies are eighteen months old. The number of paid days off granted to mothers to care for sick children will be increased. Lower-income families with children of up to twelve years of age will receive child allowances. We intend to fully satisfy the people's need for preschool children's institutions within the next few years.

Thought should also be given to appropriate organizational forms. Why not reinstate women's councils within work collectives or residentially, integrating them in a single system with the Soviet Women's Committee at its head? Women's councils could help to resolve a wide range of social problems arising in the life of our society.

Concern for the older generation, for war and labor veterans, should rank as one of the top priorities. The Party and the Soviet Government will do everything possible for the pensioners' well-being to rise with the growth of society's prosperity. In the 12th five-year period it is planned to increase the minimum old-age, disability, and loss-of-breadwinner pensions paid to factory and office workers, and to raise the previously fixed pensions of collective farmers. But man lives not by bread alone, as the saying goes. According to the information reaching the Central Committee, many retired veterans feel left out of things. Apparently, additional measures should be taken by government and public organizations, centrally and locally, to assist the veterans in becoming more actively involved in production and sociopolitical life. After all, more than fifty million Soviet people are veterans.

The setting up of a national mass organization of war and labor veterans could be a new step in this direction. It could be instrumental in involving highly experienced people in social and political affairs, and first of all in educating the rising generation. The pensioners' involvement, both on a cooperative and on an individual family basis, in the services or trade, producing consumer goods or turning out farm produce could be highly useful. The new organization could be helpful in improving everyday and medical services for pensioners and expanding their leisure opportunities. As we see it, it will certainly have a lot of work to do.

Comrades, of tremendous importance for the multinational Soviet state is *development of relations among the peoples of the USSR*. The foundation for solving the nationalities problem in our country was laid by the Great October Socialist Revolution. Relying on Lenin's doctrine and on the gains of socialism, the Communist Party has done enormous transformative work in this area. Its results are an outstanding achievement of socialism that has enriched world civilization. National oppression and inequality of all types and forms have been done away with once and for all. The indissoluble friendship among nations and respect for national cultures and for the dignity of all peoples have been established and have taken firm root in the minds of tens of millions of people. The Soviet people are a qualitatively new social and international community, cemented by the same economic interests, ideology, and political goals.

However, our achievements must not create the impression that there are no problems in the national processes. Contradictions are inherent in any kind of development, and are unavoidable in this sphere as well. The main thing is to see their emergent aspects and facets, to search for and give prompt and correct answers to questions posed by life. This is all the more important because the tendency toward national isolation, localism, and parasitism still persist and make themselves felt quite painfully at times.

In elaborating guidelines for a long-term nationalities policy, it is especially important to see to it that the republics' contribution to the development of an integrated national economic complex should match their mature economic and spiritual potential. It is in the supreme interests of our multinational state, and each of the republics, to promote cooperation in production, collaboration, and mutual assistance among the republics. It is the task of Party organizations and the Soviets to make the fullest possible use of available potentialities in the common interests and to persistently overcome all signs of localism.

We are legitimately proud of the achievements of the multinational Soviet socialist culture. By drawing on the wealth of national forms and characteristics, it is developing into a unique phenomenon in world culture. However, the healthy interest in all that is valuable in each national culture must by no means degenerate into attempts to isolate oneself from the objective process by which national cultures interact and come closer together. This applies, among other things, to certain works of literature and art and scholarly writings in which, under the guise of national originality, attempts are made to depict in idyllic tones reactionary nationalist and religious survivals contrary to our ideology, the socialist way of life, and our scientific world outlook.

Our Party's tradition, traceable to Lenin, of being particularly circumspect and tactful in all that concerns the nationalities policy and the interests of every nation or nationality and national feelings, calls at the same time for resolute struggle against national narrow-mindedness and arrogance, nationalism and chauvinism, no matter what their guise may be. We Communists must unswervingly follow Lenin's wise teachings, must creatively apply them to the new conditions, and be extremely heedful and principled as regards relations among peoples in the name of the further consolidation of fraternal friendship among all the peoples of the USSR.

The social policy elaborated by the Party has many aspects to it and is quite feasible. However, its success will largely hinge on the social orientation of the cadres, on persistence and initiative in carrying out our plans. Concern for people's needs and interests must be an object of unflagging attention on the part of the Party, government, and economic organizations, of trade unions and of each executive. If we succeed in securing a decisive switch to the social sphere, many of the problems that face us today and will face us tomorrow will be solved far more quickly and much more effectively than has so far been the case.

III. FURTHER DEMOCRATIZATION OF SOCIETY AND PROMOTION OF THE PEOPLE'S SOCIALIST SELF-GOVERNMENT

Comrades, Lenin regarded democracy, the creative initiative of working people, as the principal force behind the development of the new system. Unmatched in his faith in the people, he showed concern for raising the level of the political activity and culture of the masses, stressing that illiterate people were outside politics. Nearly seventy years have elapsed since then. The general educational and cultural level of Soviet people has risen immeasurably and their sociopolitical experience has grown richer. This means that the possibility and need of every citizen to participate in managing the affairs of the state and society have grown enormously.

Democracy is the wholesome and pure air without which a socialist public organism cannot live a full-blooded life. Hence, when we say that socialism's great potential is not being used to the full in our country, we also mean that the *acceleration of society's development is inconceivable and impossible without a further development of all the aspects and manifestations of socialist democracy.*

Bearing that in mind, the Party and its Central Committee are taking measures aimed at deepening the democratic character of the socialist system. Among them are steps to heighten the activities of the Soviets, the trade unions, the Komsomol, the work collectives, and the people's control bodies, and to promote publicity. But all that has been and is being done should be assessed in terms of the scale and complexity of our new tasks, rather than by yesterday's standards. As stressed in the new edition of the Party Program, these tasks call for consistent and unswerving development of the *people's socialist self-government.*

In socialist society, particularly under the present circumstances, government should not be the privilege of a narrow circle of professionals. We know from theory and from our extensive experience that the socialist system can develop successfully only when the people really run their own affairs, when millions of people are involved in political life. This is what the working people's self-government amounts to, as Lenin saw it. It is the essence of Soviet power. The elements of self-government develop within rather than outside our statehood, increasingly penetrating all aspects of state and public life, enriching the content of democratic centralism and strengthening its socialist character.

The Party is the guiding force and the principal guarantor of the development of socialist self-government. Playing the leading role in society, the Party is itself the highest form of a self-governing sociopolitical organization. By promoting inner-Party democracy and intensifying the activity of Communists at all levels of the political system, the CPSU sets the right direction for the process of furthering the people's socialist self-government and broadening the participation of the masses and of each person in the affairs of the country.

The result of the revolutionary creativity of the working people, the *Soviets of People's Deputies* have stood the test of time, displaying their viability and vast potentialities in securing full power for the people, in uniting and mobilizing the masses. The very logic of the development of socialist democracy shows the urgent need for making the maximum use of these potentialities of Soviet representative bodies.

The fact that the Supreme Soviet of the USSR and the Supreme Soviets of the Union and the Autonomous Republics are becoming increasingly businesslike and effective in their activity with each passing year is most welcome. It is their duty to consistently improve legislation, supervise law enforcement and check on the actual outcome of the work done by each state body and each executive. At their sessions, the Supreme Soviets should place greater emphasis on discussing proposals submitted by trade unions, the Komsomol, and other public organizations, the reports of administrative bodies, the situation in different branches of the economy, and the development of the various regions.

I should like to draw the special attention of Congress delegates to the activity of *local Soviets*. Today they can and must serve as one of the most effective means of mobilizing the masses for the effort to accelerate the country's socioeconomic development. As they receive the electoral mandate, local government bodies undertake responsibility for all aspects of life on their territory. If someone may be allowed to say, "This is none of my business," this approach is certainly unacceptable to the Soviets. Housing and education, public health and consumer goods, trade and services, public transport and the protection of nature are principal concerns of the Soviets. Whenever we hear complaints from working people on these subjects, which is still fairly often, it means that the Soviets lack efficiency and initiative, and that their control is slack. But while making legitimate demands on the Soviets, we should not be blind to the fact that for the time being their ability to tackle many of the local problems is limited; there exists excessive centralization in matters that are not always clearly visible from the center and can be much better solved locally.

That is why we resolutely follow a course of promoting the autonomy and activity of local government bodies. Proposals to this effect are currently being worked out by the CPSU Central Committee, the Presidium of the Supreme Soviet and the USSR Council of Ministers. Their goal is to make each Soviet a complete and responsible master in all things concerning the satisfaction of people's everyday needs and requirements; in using the allocated funds, the local potentialities and reserves; in coordinating and supervising the work of all organizations involved in servicing the population. In this connection, we must make a thorough examination of the relationship between Soviets and the centrally managed enterprises in their territories, and increase the local governing bodies' interest in the results of their work.

The sessions of Soviets should be conducted far more effectively, the analytical and supervisory activity of standing committees should be more thorough, and the practice of deputies' enquiries should be improved. The committees' recommendations and the deputies' proposals and observations should be carefully considered and taken into account by the executive bodies.

While mapping out further improvements of the work of the Soviets, we should remember that none of them will yield the desired results unless backed by the deputies' initiative. The Party will continue to see to it that deputies are elected from among the worthiest people who are capable of effectively running staff affairs, and that the composition of the Soviets is systematically renewed. In this connection, it is apparently time to make necessary corrections in our election procedures as well. There are quite a number of outstanding problems here awaiting solution.

The Party has always deemed it its duty to heighten the authority of the people's representatives, and, at the same time, to enhance their responsibility to the electorate in every way possible. The title of a deputy is not just something that goes with one's office; it is not an honorary privilege; it means a lot of hard work at the Soviet and among the population. And we must do all we can for the strict observance of the law on the status of deputies, and see to it that each deputy should be afforded every opportunity to exercise his or her authority.

The development of the people's self-government calls for *a further strengthening of democratic principles in administration*, in the activity of the Soviets' executive committees, of their apparatus, and of all other government bodies. Most of the people working in them are competent and take what they do close to heart. However, one should always remember that, even if its executives are masterminds, no apparatus will ever get what it wants unless it relies on the working people's motivated support and participation in government. The times are making increasingly exacting demands on the work of the apparatus. And there are quite a few shortcomings here; one often encounters departmental approach and localism, irresponsibility, red tape, and formal indifference to people. One of the main reasons for this is the slackening of control over the activity of the apparatus by the working people, the Soviets themselves, and public organizations.

Bearing all this in mind, the Party has set itself the task of putting to use all the instruments that actually enable every citizen to actively influence administrative decision-making, verify the fulfilment of decisions, and receive necessary information about the activity of the apparatus. This should be the purpose of a system of regular reports to work collectives and general meetings by all administrative bodies. Much can be done in this area by people's control committees, groups and teams, by voluntary trade union inspectors, and the mass media.

The elective bodies themselves should be more exacting and strict toward their own apparatus. One cannot overlook the fact that executives who remain in office for long periods tend to lose their feel for the new, to shut themselves off from the people by instructions they have concocted themselves, and sometimes even hold back the work of elective bodies. Apparently it is time to work out a procedure that would enable Soviets, as well as all public bodies, to evaluate and certify the work of the responsible executives of their apparatus after each election, making desirable personnel changes.

Our time demands ever more active involvement on the part of *public organizations* in governing the country. When the work of our public organizations is considered from this angle, however, it becomes clear that many of them are lacking in initiative. Some of them try to operate above all through their regular staff, in a bureaucratic way, and lean only a little on the masses. In other words, the popular, creative, independent nature of public organizations is far from being fully realized.

In our country, the trade unions are the largest mass organizations. On the whole, they do a lot to satisfy the requirements of factory and office workers and collective farmers, to promote emulation, tighten discipline, and heighten labor productivity. Still, trade union committees are in many cases lacking in militancy and resolve when it comes to defending the working people's legitimate interests, ensuring labor protection and safety, and constructing and running health-building, sports, and cultural facilities. Understandably, such passivity suits those managers for whom production sometimes obscures the people. The trade unions, however, should always give priority to social policy objectives, to promoting the working people's interests. Properly speaking, this is the basic purpose of their activity. The All-Union Central Council of Trade Unions and other trade union bodies enjoy extensive rights and control considerable funds, both the state's and their own. It is up to them, therefore, to make extensive and confident use of them, instead of waiting for somebody else to fulfill the tasks they are charged with.

Comrades, our future largely depends on the kind of young

people we are bringing up today. That is the task of the whole Party, of all the people. It is the most important and fundamental task of the *Leninist Young Communist League*. Our young people are hardworking, ready for exploits and self-sacrifice, and devoted to socialism. Nonetheless, it is the duty of the older generations to do everything they can for those who will replace them to be still more intelligent, more capable and better educated, worthy of taking the baton and carrying into the future the ideals of justice and freedom bequeathed to us by the Great October Revolution.

As Lenin said, it is impossible to master communism through books alone, it is impossible to cultivate a sense of responsibility without charging people with responsible tasks. The young people of the 1980s are broad-minded, well-educated, and vigorous. I should say, they are ready for action and look for a chance to show their worth in all areas of public life. So, the YCL must make every effort to support their drive in all areas—the national economy, science and engineering, in achieving high levels of knowledge and culture, in political life, and in defending the Motherland. This effort, more than any other, should be of a questing nature, interesting and appealing to young people, and closely linked to the needs of the young in production, study, home life, and leisure.

Together with the YCL, the Party, government, and economic bodies should consistently seek to promote deserving young people to leadership positions in management, production, science, and culture. We say: in our country, all roads are open to young people. That is true. But persistent efforts are needed for these words not to lose luster and the road for young people to be really wide.

By and large, the CPSU Central Committee deems it advisable to take further steps to increase the role of the trade unions, the YCL, the unions of creative workers, and voluntary societies in the system of the people's socialist self-government. In particular, it is planned to extend the range of questions that governmental bodies can settle only with the participation or prior agreement of trade union, YCL, or women's organizations and to grant these organizations the right to suspend, in some cases, the implementation of administrative decisions.

Our Party Program aims at the most effective exercise of all forms of *direct democracy*, of direct participation by the popular masses in the elaboration, adoption, and execution of governmental and other decisions. An enormous role is played here by the *work collectives* operating in all spheres of the life of society, and chiefly in the national economy. The granting of broader powers to enterprises, the introduction of cost accounting, and promotion of the spirit of socialist enterprise will become truly effective only if the working man himself displays greater activity. We cannot put up with instances which still exist, where workers do not know the programs of their own enterprises, where their suggestions do not receive due attention and are not taken into account. These instances show that in some places the force of inertia determines the state of affairs, hinders the involvement of factory and office workers in management, and impedes the process of fostering among them the feeling that they are full-fledged masters of production.

The Law on Work Collectives adopted two years ago has indisputably stimulated initiatives by work collectives. But we cannot yet say this Law is producing the results we expected. This is evident from the CPSU Central Committee's examination of its application at the Minsk Motor Works and elsewhere. Our conclusion is unambiguous: it is necessary to radically improve the mechanism that enables us to make the democratic principles and norms of the Law operative in everyday practice. Step by step we must extend the range of issues on which the work collective's decisions are final, enhance the role of the general meetings of factory and office workers and raise responsibility for implementing their decisions. There has arisen an idea of having a council, say, of the work collective made up of representatives of the management, Party, trade union and YCL organizations, team councils, rank-and-file workers, and specialists function, in the period between general meetings, both at the level of teams and the enterprise as a whole.

Today the advanced teams which apply the cost-accounting principle are already becoming primary self-government units with elected managers. Life shows the viability of this practice. It has confirmed that in developing democratic economic management principles it is advisable to extend the principle of electiveness to all team leaders and then gradually to some other categories of managerial personnel—foremen, shift, sector, or shop superintendents, and state-farm department managers. Long years of experience testify that this is the direction in which we must look for modern forms of combining centralism and democracy, of combining one-man management and the principle of electiveness in running the national economy.

Undeviating observance of the democratic principles of guiding collective farms and other cooperative organizations, including observance of their rules, is a matter that receives our constant attention. In recent times our efforts in this sphere have somehow relaxed, and too many organizations have been interfering in the activities of cooperative societies. Party and government bodies must see to it that collective-farm or cooperative self-government is exercised unfailingly, that any attempts to resort to pressure or to practice armchair management are thwarted.

Our Constitution provides for nationwide discussions and referendums on major issues of our country's life and for discussions on decisions to be passed by local Soviets. We must expedite the drafting of a law on this highly important question. We must make better use of such reliable channels for the development of direct democracy as citizens' meetings, constitutents' mandates, letters from people, the press, radio, TV, and all other means of eliciting public opinion and of quickly and sensitively responding to the people's needs and mood.

Broader publicity is a matter of principle to us. It is a political issue. Without publicity there is not, nor can there be, democracy, political creativity of the citizens and participation by the citizens in administration and management. This is an earnest, if you like, of a responsible statesmanlike attitude to the common cause on the part of millions upon millions of factory workers, collective farmers, and members of the intelligentsia, and a point of departure in the psychological reorientation of our cadres.

When the subject of publicity comes up, calls are sometimes made for exercising greater caution when speaking about the shortcomings, omissions, and difficulties that are inevitable in any ongoing effort. There can only be one answer to this, a Leninist answer: Communists want the truth, always and under all circumstances. The experience of the past year has shown how forcefully Soviet people support an uncompromising appraisal of everything that impedes our advance. But those who have grown used to doing slipshod work, to practicing deception, indeed feel really awkward in the glare of publicity, when everything done in the state and in society is under the people's control and is in full public view. Therefore we must make publicity an unfailingly operative system. It is needed in the center and, no less, perhaps much more, in the localities, wherever people live and work. The citizen wants to know, and should know, not only decisions taken on a nationwide scale but also decisions taken locally by Party and government bodies, factory managements and trade unions.

The whole range of the *Soviet citizen's sociopolitical and personal rights and freedoms* should promote the broadening and further development of socialist democracy. The Party and the state regard the deepening of these rights and freedoms and the strengthening of their guarantees as their primary duty. But the gist of socialism is that the rights of citizens do not, and cannot, exist outside their duties, just as there cannot be duties without corresponding rights.

It is essential to stimulate the activity of our citizens, of one and all, in constructive work, in eliminating shortcomings, abuses, and all other unhealthy phenomena, all departures from our legal and moral standards. Democracy was and remains a major lever for *strengthening socialist legality*, and stable legality was and remains an inseparable part of our democracy.

A good deal of work has been done lately to strengthen law and order in all spheres of the life of society. But the efforts in this direction must not be slackened in any way. We must continue to improve Soviet legislation. Our legislation—the civil, labor, financial, administrative, economic, and criminal laws—must help more vigorously in introducing economically viable management methods, in exercising effective control over the measure of labor and consumption and in translating the principles of social justice into reality.

We must persistently increase the responsibility of the law-enforcement and other bodies, and strengthen the legal service in the Soviets and in the national economy, and state arbitration, and also improve the legal education of the population. As before, full use must be made of Soviet legislation in combating crime and other breaches of the law, so that the people in towns and villages know that the state is concerned about their peace and personal inviolability, and that not a single wrongdoer evades the punishment he deserves.

We must very strictly observe the democratic principles of justice, the equality of citizens before the law and other guarantees that protect the interests of the state and of every citizen. In this context it is necessary to take vigorous steps to enhance the role of the procurators' supervision, to improve the functioning of courts of law and the bar, and to complete, in the very near future, the drafting of a law, as provided for by the Constitution, on the procedure of filing appeals in court against unlawful actions by officials that infringe upon the rights of citizens. Naturally, the more vigorously Party and government bodies, trade unions, the YCL, work collectives, and volunteer public-order squads, and the public at large are involved in such effort, the more fully legality and law and order will be ensured.

In the context of the growing subversive activity by imperialist special services against the Soviet Union and other socialist countries, greater responsibility devolves upon the *state security bodies*. Under the Party's leadership, and scrupulously observing Soviet laws, these bodies are conducting extensive work to expose enemy intrigues, to frustrate all kinds of subversion and to protect our country's sacred frontiers. We are convinced that Soviet security forces and border guards will always meet the demands made of them, will always display vigilance, self-control, and tenacity in the struggle against any encroachment on our political and social system.

Taking into account the complicated international situation and the growing aggressiveness of the reactionary imperialist quarters, the CPSU Central Committee and its Politburo pay unflagging attention *to our country's defense capability, to the combat might of the Armed Forces of the USSR*, to the tightening of military discipline. The Soviet Army and Navy have modern arms and equipment, well-trained servicemen and skilled officers and political cadres who are completely dedicated to the people. They acquit themselves with honor in the most complicated, and at times rigorous, situations. Today we can declare with all responsibility that the defense capability of the USSR is maintained on a level that makes it possible to protect reliably the peaceful life and labor of the Soviet people.

The Party and the government have always been striving to ensure that the Soviet soldier and officer are constantly aware of our society's care and attention while performing their arduous duties, and that our Armed Forces are a school of civic responsibility, fortitude, and patriotism.

It is clear, comrades, that here, at this Congress, we are merely charting the general framework and the main outlines for perfecting our democracy, statehood, and the entire Soviet political system. Implementation of the Congress decisions undoubtedly will bring about fresh manifestations of the people's initiative and new forms of mass social and political creative activity.

IV. BASIC AIMS AND DIRECTIONS OF THE PARTY'S FOREIGN POLICY STRATEGY

Comrades,

The tasks underlying the country's economic and social development also determine the CPSU's strategy in the world arena. Its main aim is crystal clear—to provide the Soviet people with the possibility of working under conditions of lasting peace and freedom. Such, in essence, is the Party's primary program requirement of our foreign policy. To fulfil it in the present situation means, above all, to terminate the material preparations for nuclear war.

After having weighed all the aspects of the situation that has taken shape, the CPSU has put forward a coherent program for total abolition of weapons of mass destruction before the end of this century, a program that is historic in terms of its dimensions and significance. Its realization would open for mankind a fundamentally new period of development and provide an opportunity to concentrate entirely on constructive labor.

As you know, we have addressed our proposals not only through the traditional diplomatic channels but also directly to world public opinion, to the peoples. The time has come to realize thoroughly the harsh realities of our day: nuclear weapons harbor a hurricane which is capable of sweeping the human race from the face of the earth. Our address further underscores the open, honest, Leninist character of the CPSU's foreign policy strategy.

Socialism unconditionally rejects war as a means of settling political and economic contradictions and ideological disputes among states. Our ideal is a world without weapons and violence, a world in which each people freely chooses its path of development, its way of life. This is an expression of the humanism of communist ideology, of its moral values. That is why for the future as well the *struggle against the nuclear threat, against the arms race, for the preservation and strengthening of universal peace* remains the fundamental direction of the Party's activities in the international arena.

There is no alternative to this policy. This is all the more true in periods of tension in international affairs. It seems that never in the decades since the war has the situation in the world been so explosive, and consequently complex and uncongenial as in the first half of the 1980s. The right-wing group that came to power in the U.S.A. and its main NATO fellow travellers made a steep turn from detente to a policy of military strength. They have adopted doctrines that reject good-neighborly relations and cooperation as principles of world development, as a political philosophy of international relations. The Washington administration remained deaf to our calls for an end to the arms race and an improvement of the situation.

Perhaps it may not be worth churning up the past? Especially today when in Soviet-U.S. relations there seem to be signs of change for the better, and realistic trends can now be detected in the actions and attitudes of the leadership of some NATO nations. We feel that it is worthwhile, for the drastic frosting of the international climate in the first half of the 1980s was a further reminder that nothing comes of itself: peace has to be fought for, and this has to be a persevering and purposeful fight. We have to look for, find, and use even the smallest opportunity in order—while this is still possible—to reverse the trend toward an escalation of the threat of war. Realizing this, the Central Committee of the CPSU at its

April Plenary Meeting once again analyzed the character and dimensions of the nuclear threat and defined the practical steps that could lead to an improvement of the situation. We were guided by the following considerations of principle.

First, the character of present-day weapons leaves any country no hope of safeguarding itself solely with military and technical means, for example, by building up a defense system, even the most powerful one. The task of ensuring security is increasingly seen as a political problem, and it can only be resolved by political means. In order to progress along the road of disarmament what is needed is, above all, the will. Security cannot be built endlessly on fear of retaliation, in other words, on the doctrines of "containment" or "deterrence." Apart from the absurdity and amorality of a situation in which the whole world becomes a nuclear hostage, these doctrines encourage an arms race that may sooner or later go out of control.

Second, in the context of the relations between the USSR and the U.S.A., security can only be mutual, and if we take international relations as a whole it can only be universal. The highest wisdom is not in caring exclusively for oneself, especially to the detriment of the other side. It is vital that all should feel equally secure, for the fears and anxieties of the nuclear age generate unpredictability in politics and concrete actions. It is becoming extremely important to take the critical significance of the time factor into account. The appearance of new systems of weapons of mass destruction steadily shortens time and narrows down the possibilities for adopting political decisions on questions of war and peace in crisis situations.

Third, the U.S.A., its military-industrial machine remains the locomotive of militarism, for so far it has no intention of slowing down. This has to be taken into consideration, of course. But we are well aware that the interests and aims of the military-industrial complex are not at all the same as the interests and aims of the American people, as the actual national interests of that great country.

Naturally, the world is much larger than the U.S.A. and its occupation bases on foreign soil. And in world politics one cannot confine oneself to relations with only one, even a very important, country. As we know from experience, this only promotes the arrogance of strength. Needless to say, we attach considerable significance to the state and character of the relations between the Soviet Union and the U.S.A. Our countries coincide on quite a few points, and there is the objective need to live in peace with each other, to cooperate on a basis of equality and mutual benefit, and on this basis alone.

Fourth, the world is in a process of swift changes, and it is not within anybody's power to maintain a perpetual status quo in it. It consists of many dozens of countries, each having perfectly legitimate interests. All without exception face a task of fundamental significance: without neglecting social, political, and ideological differences all have to master the science and art of restraint and circumspection on the international scene, to live in a civilized manner, in other words, under conditions of civil international intercourse and cooperation. But to give this cooperation wide scope there has to be an all-embracing system of international economic security that would in equal measure protect every nation against discrimination, sanctions, and other attributes of imperialist, neocolonialist policy. Alongside disarmament such a system can become a dependable pillar of international security in general.

In short, the modern world has become much too small and fragile for wars and a policy of strength. It cannot be saved and preserved if the way of thinking and actions built up over the centuries on the acceptability and permissibility of wars and armed conflicts are not shed once and for all, resolutely and irrevocably.

This means the realization that it is no longer possible to win an arms race, or nuclear war for that matter. The continuation of this race on earth, let alone its spread to outer space, will accelerate the already critically high rate of stockpiling and perfecting nuclear weapons. The situation in the world may assume such a character that it will no longer depend upon the intelligence or will of political leaders. It may become captive to technology, to technocratic military logic. Consequently, not only nuclear war itself but also the preparations for it, in other words, the arms race, *the aspiration to win military superiority can, speaking in objective terms, bring no political gain to anybody.*

Further, this means understanding that the present level of the balance of the nuclear potentials of the opposite sides is much too high. For the time being it ensures *equal danger* to each of them. But only for the time being. Continuation of the nuclear arms race will inevitably heighten this equal threat and may bring it to a point where even parity will cease to be a factor of military-political deterrence. Consequently, it is vital, in the first place, greatly to reduce the level of military confrontation. In our age, genuine equal security is guaranteed not by the highest possible, but by the lowest possible level of strategic parity, from which nuclear and other types of weapons of mass destruction must be totally excluded.

Lastly, this means realizing that in the present situation there is no alternative to cooperation and interaction between all countries. Thus, the objective—I emphasize, objective— conditions have taken shape in which confrontation between capitalism and socialism can proceed *only and exclusively in forms of peaceful competition and peaceful contest.*

For us peaceful coexistence is a political course which the USSR intends to go on following unswervingly, ensuring the continuity of its foreign policy strategy. The CPSU will pursue a vigorous international policy stemming from the realities of the world we live in. Of course, the problem of international security cannot be resolved by one or two, even very intensive, peace campaigns. Success can only be achieved by consistent, methodical, and persevering effort.

Continuity in foreign policy has nothing in common with a simple repetition of what has been done, especially in tackling the problems that have piled up. What is needed is a high degree of accuracy in assessing one's own possibilities, restraint, and an exceptionally high sense of responsibility when decisions are made. What is wanted is firmness in upholding principles and stands, tactical flexibility, a readiness for mutually acceptable compromises, and an orientation on dialogue and mutual understanding rather than on confrontation.

As you know, we have made a series of unilateral steps—we put a moratorium on the deployment of intermediate-range missiles in Europe, cut back the number of these missiles, and stopped all nuclear explosions. In Moscow and abroad there have been talks with leaders and members of the governments of many countries. The Soviet-Indian, Soviet-French, and Soviet-U.S. summits were necessary and useful steps.

The Soviet Union has made energetic efforts to give a fresh impetus to the negotiations in Geneva, Stockholm, and Vienna, the purpose of which is to curb the arms race and strengthen confidence between states. Negotiations are always a delicate and complex matter. Of cardinal importance here is to make an effort to achieve a mutually acceptable balance of interests. To turn weapons of mass destruction into an object of political scheming is, to say the least, immoral, while in political terms this is irresponsible.

Lastly, concerning our Statement of January 15 of this year. Taken as a whole, our program is essentially an alloy of the philosophy of shaping a safe world in the nuclear-space age with a platform of concrete actions. The Soviet Union offers approaching the problems of disarmament in their totality, for in terms of security they are linked with one another. I am not speaking of rigid linkages or attempts at "giving way" in one direction in order to erect barricades in another. What I have in mind is a plan of concrete actions strictly measured out in terms of time. The USSR intends to work perseveringly for its realization, regarding it as the *central direction of its foreign policy for the coming years.*

The Soviet military doctrine is also entirely in keeping with the letter and spirit of the initiatives we have put forward. Its orientation is unequivocally defensive. In the military sphere we intend to act in such a way as to give nobody grounds for fears, even imagined ones, about their security. But to an equal extent we and our allies want to be rid of the feeling that we are threatened. The USSR undertook the obligation not to be the first to use nuclear weapons and it will abide strictly by that obligation. But it is no secret that scenarios for a nuclear strike against us do exist. We have no right to overlook this. The Soviet Union is a staunch adversary of nuclear war in any variant. Our country stands for removing weapons of mass destruction from use, for limiting the military potential to reasonable adequacy. But the character and level of this ceiling continue to be restricted by the attitudes and actions of the U.S.A. and its partners in the blocs. Under these conditions we repeat again and again: *the Soviet Union lays no claim to more security, but it will not settle for less.*

I should like to draw attention to the problem of verification, to which we attach special significance. We have declared on several occasions that the USSR is open to verification, that we are interested in it as much as anybody else. All-embracing, strictest verification is perhaps the key element of the disarmament process. The essence of the matter, in our opinion, is that *there can be no disarmament without verification and that verification without disarmament makes no sense.*

There is yet another matter of principle. We have stated our attitude to Star Wars quite substantively. The U.S.A. has already drawn many of its allies into this program. There is the danger that this state of things may become irreversible. Before it is too late, it is imperative to find a realistic solution *guaranteeing that the arms race does not spread to outer space.* The Star Wars program cannot be permitted to be used as a stimulus for a further arms race or as a roadblock to radical disarmament. Tangible progress in what concerns a drastic reduction of nuclear potentials can be of much help in surmounting this obstacle. For that reason the Soviet Union is ready to make a substantial step in that direction, to resolve the question of intermediate-range missiles in the European zone separately—without linking it to problems of strategic armaments and outer space.

The Soviet program has touched the hearts of millions of people, and among political leaders and public personalities interest in it continues to grow. The times today are such that it is hard to brush it off. The attempts to sow doubt in the Soviet Union's constructive commitment to accelerate the solution of the pressing problem of our day—the destruction of nuclear weapons—and to tackle it in practical terms are becoming less and less convincing. Nuclear disarmament should not be the exclusive domain of political leaders. The whole world is now pondering over this, for it is a question of life itself.

But, also, it is necessary to take into account the reaction of the centers of power that hold in their hands the keys to the success or failure of disarmament negotiations. Of course, the U.S. ruling class, to be more exact its most egoistical groups linked to the military-industrial complex, have other aims that are clearly opposite to ours. For them disarmament spells out a loss of profits and a political risk, for us it is a blessing in all respects—economically, politically, and morally.

We know our principal opponents and have accumulated a complex and extensive experience in our relations and talks with them. The day before yesterday, we received President Reagan's reply to our Statement of January 15. The U.S. side began to set forth its considerations in greater detail at the talks in Geneva. To be sure, we shall closely examine everything the U.S. side has to say on these matters. However, since the reply was received literally on the eve of the Congress, the U.S. Administration apparently expects, as we understand it, that our attitude to the U.S. stand will be made known to the world from this rostrum.

What I can say right away is that the President's letter does not give grounds for amending in any way the assessment of the international situation as had been set forth in the report before the reply was received. The report says that the elimination of nuclear arms is the goal all the nuclear powers should strive for. In his letter the President agrees in general with some or other Soviet proposals and intentions as regards the issues of disarmament and security. In other words, the reply seems to contain some reassuring opinions and statements.

However, these positive pronouncements are drowning in various reservations, "linkages," and "conditions" which in fact block the solution of radical problems of disarmament. Reduction in the strategic nuclear arsenals is made conditional on our consent to the Star Wars program and reductions, unilateral, by the way, in the Soviet conventional arms. Linked to this are also problems of regional conflicts and bilateral relations. The elimination of nuclear arms in Europe is blocked by the references to the stand taken by Great Britain and France and the demand to weaken our defenses in the eastern part of the country, while the U.S. military forces in that region remain as they are. The refusal to stop nuclear tests is justified by arguments to the effect that nuclear weapons serve as a factor of "containment." This is in direct contradiction with the purpose reaffirmed in the letter—the need to do away with nuclear weapons. The reluctance of the U.S.A. and its ruling circles to embark on the path of nuclear disarmanent manifests itself most clearly in their attitude to nuclear explosions, the termination of which is the demand of the whole world.

To put it in a nutshell, it is hard to detect in the letter we have just received any serious readiness by the U.S. Administration to get down to solving the cardinal problems involved in eliminating the nuclear threat. It looks as if some people in Washington and elsewhere, for that matter, have got used to living side by side with nuclear weapons, linking with them their plans in the international arena. However, whether they want it or not, the Western politicians will have to answer the question: are they prepared to part with nuclear weapons at all?

In accordance with an understanding reached in Geneva there will be another meeting with the U.S. President. The significance that we attach to it is that it ought to produce practical results in key areas of limiting and reducing armaments. There are at least two matters on which an understanding could be reached: the cessation of nuclear tests and the abolition of U.S. and Soviet intermediate-range missiles in the European zone. And then, as a matter of fact, if there is readiness to seek agreement, the question of the date of the meeting would be resolved of itself: we will accept any suggestion on this count. But there is no sense in empty talks. And we shall not remain indifferent if the Soviet-U.S. dialogue that has started and inspired some not unfounded hopes of a possibility for changes for the better is used to continue the arms race and the material preparations for war. It is the firm intention of the Soviet Union to justify the hopes of the peoples of our two countries and of the whole world, who are expecting from the leaders of the USSR and the U.S.A. concrete steps, practical actions, and tangible agreements on how to curb the arms race. We are prepared for this.

Naturally, like any other country, we attach considerable importance to the security of our frontiers, on land and at sea. We have many neighbors, and they are different. We have no territorial claims on any of them. We threaten none of them. But as experience has shown time and again, there are quite a few persons who, in disregard of the national interests of either our country or those of countries neighboring upon us, are endeavoring to aggravate the situation on the frontiers of the Soviet Union.

For instance, counterrevolution and imperialism have turned Afghanistan into a bleeding wound. The USSR supports that country's efforts to defend its sovereignty. We should like, in the nearest future, to withdraw the Soviet troops stationed in Afghanistan at the request of its government. Moreover, we have agreed with the Afghan side on the schedule for their phased withdrawal as soon as a political settlement is reached that will ensure an actual cessation and dependably guarantee the nonresumption of foreign armed interference in the international affairs of the Democratic Republic of Afghanistan. It is in our vital, national interest that the USSR should always have good and peaceful relations with all its neighbors. This is a vitally important objective of our foreign policy.

The CPSU regards the *European direction* as one of the main directions of its international activity. Europe's historic opportunity and its future lie in peaceful cooperation among the nations of that continent. And it is important, while preserving the assets that have already been accumulated, to move further: from the initial to a more lasting phase of detente, to mature detente, and then to the building of dependable security on the basis of the Helsinki process and a radical reduction of nuclear and conventional weapons.

The significance of the *Asian and Pacific direction* is growing. In that vast region there are many tangled knots of contradictions and, besides, the political situation in some places is unstable. Here it is necessary, without postponement, to search for the relevant solutions and paths. Evidently, it is expedient to begin with the coordination and then the pooling of efforts in the interests of a political settlement of painful problems so as, in parallel, on that basis to at least take the edge off the military confrontation in various parts of Asia and stabilize the situation there.

This is made all the more urgent by the fact that in Asia and other continents the *flash points of military danger* are not being extinguished. We are in favor of vitalizing collective quests for ways of defusing conflict situations in the Middle East, Central America, Southern Africa, in all of the planet's turbulent points. This is imperatively demanded by the interests of general security.

Crises and conflicts are fertile soil also for international terrorism. Undeclared wars, the export of counterrevolution in all forms, political assassinations, the taking of hostages, the highjacking of aircraft, and bomb explosions in streets, airports, and railway stations—such is the hideous face of terrorism, which its instigators try to mask with all sorts of cynical inventions. The USSR rejects terrorism in principle and is prepared to cooperate actively with other states in order to uproot it. The Soviet Union will resolutely safeguard its citizens against acts of violence and do everything to defend their lives, honor, and dignity.

Looking back over the past year one will see that, by all the evidence, the prerequisites for improving the international situation are beginning to form. But prerequisites for a turn are not the turn itself. The arms race continues and the threat of nuclear war remains. However, international reactionary forces are by no means omnipotent. The development of the world revolutionary process and the growth of mass democratic and antiwar movements have significantly enlarged and strengthened the *huge potential of peace, reason, and good will*. This is a powerful counterbalance to imperialism's aggressive policy.

The destinies of peace and social progress are now linked more closely than ever before with the dynamic character of the *socialist world system's economic and political development*. The need for this dynamism is dictated by concern for the welfare of the peoples. But for the socialist world it is necessary also from the standpoint of counteraction to the military threat. Lastly, it helps demonstrate the potentialities of the socialist way of life. We are watched by both friends and foes. We are watched by the huge and heterogeneous world of developing nations. It is looking for its choice, for its road, and what this choice will be depends to a large extent on socialism's successes, on the credibility of its answers to the challenges of time.

We are convinced that socialism can resolve the most difficult problems confronting it. Of vital significance for this is the increasingly vigorous interaction whose effect is not merely the adding up but the multiplication of our potentials and which serves as a stimulus for common advancement. This is reflected also in joint documents of countries of the socialist community.

Interaction between governing communist parties remains the heart and soul of the *political cooperation* among these countries. During the past year there has been practically no fraternal country with whose leaders we have not had meetings and detailed talks. The forms of such cooperation are themselves being updated. A new and perhaps key element, the multilateral working meetings of leaders of fraternal countries, is being established. These meetings allow for prompt and friendly consultations on the entire spectrum of problems of socialist construction, on its internal and external aspects.

In the difficult international situation the prolongation of the *Warsaw Treaty* by a unanimous decision of its signatories was of great significance. This Treaty saw its second birth, so to speak, and today it is hard to picture world politics as a whole without it. Take the Sofia Conference of the Treaty's Political Consultative Committee. It was a kind of threshold of the Geneva dialogue.

In the *economic sphere* there is now the Comprehensive Program of Scientific and Technological Progress. Its importance lies in the transition of the CMEA countries to a coordinated policy in science and technology. In our view, changes are also required in the work of the very headquarters of socialist integration—the Council for Mutual Economic Assistance. But the main thing is that in carrying out this program there is less armchair administration and fewer committees and commissions of all sorts, that more attention is given to economic levers, initiative, and socialist enterprise, and that work collectives are drawn into this process. This would indeed be a Party approach to such an extraordinary undertaking.

Vitality, efficiency, and initiative—all these qualities meet the requirements of the times, and we shall strive to have them spread throughout the system of relations between fraternal parties. The CPSU attaches growing significance to live and broad communication between citizens of socialist countries, between people of different professions and different generations. This is a source of mutual intellectual enrichment, a channel for exchanges of views, ideas, and the *experience of socialist construction*. Today it is especially important to analyze the character of the socialist way of life and understand the processes of perfecting democracy, management methods and personnel policy on the basis of the development of several countries rather than of one country. A considerate and respectful attitude to each other's experience and the employment of this experience in practice are a huge potential of the socialist world.

Generally speaking, one of socialism's advantages is its ability to learn: to learn to resolve the problems posed by life; to learn to forestall the crisis situations that our class adversary tries to create and utilize; to learn to counter the attempts to divide the socialist world and play off some countries against others; to learn to prevent collisions of the interests of different socialist countries, harmonize them by mutual effort, and find mutually acceptable solutions even to the most intricate problems.

It seems to us that it is worth taking a close look also at the relations in the socialist world as a whole. We do not see the community as being separated by some barrier from other socialist countries. The CPSU stands for honest, aboveboard relations with all communist parties and all countries of the world socialist system, for comradely exchanges of opinion between them. Above all, we endeavor to see what unites the socialist world. For that reason the Soviet Communists are gladdened by every step toward closer relations among all socialist states, by every positive advance in these relations.

One can say with gratification that there has been a measure of improvement of the Soviet Union's relations with its great neighbor—*socialist China*. The distinctions in attitudes, in particular to a number of international problems, remain. But we also note something else—that in many cases we can work jointly, cooperate on an equal and principled basis, without prejudice to third countries.

There is no need to explain the significance of this. The Chinese Communists called the victory of the USSR and the forces of progress in the Second World War a prologue to the triumph of the people's revolution in China. In turn, the formation of People's China helped to reinforce socialism's positions in the world and disrupt many of imperialism's designs and actions in the difficult postwar years. In thinking of the future, it may be said that the potentialities for cooperation between the USSR and China are enormous. They are great because such cooperation is in accordance with the interests of both countries; because what is dearest to our peoples—socialism and peace—is indivisible.

The CPSU is an inalienable component of the international communist movement. We the Soviet Communists are well aware that every advance we make in building socialism is an advance of the entire movement. For that reason the CPSU sees its primary internationalist duty in ensuring our country's successful progress along the road opened and blazed by the October Revolution.

The communist movement in the nonsocialist part of the world remains the principal target of political pressure and persecution by reactionary circles of the bourgeoisie. All the fraternal parties are constantly under fire from anticommunist propaganda, which does not scruple to use the most despicable means and methods. Many parties operate underground, in a situation of unmitigated persecution and repressions. Every step the Communists take calls for struggle and personal courage. Permit me, comrades, on behalf of the 27th Congress, on behalf of the Soviet Communists to express sincere admiration for the dedicated struggle of our comrades, and profound fraternal solidarity with them.

In recent years the communist movement has come face to face with many new realities, tasks, and problems. There are all indications that it has entered upon a qualitatively new phase of development. The international conditions of the work of Communists are changing rapidly and profoundly. A substantial restructuring is taking place in the social pattern of bourgeois society, including the composition of the working class. The problems facing our friends in the newly independent states are not simple. The scientific and technological revolution is exercising a contradictory influence on the material condition and consciousness of working people in the nonsocialist world. All this requires the ability to do a lot of reappraising and demands a bold and creative approach to the new realities on the basis of the immortal theory of Marx, Engels, and Lenin. The CPSU knows this well from its own experience.

The communist movement's immense diversity and the tasks that it encounters are likewise a reality. In some cases this leads to disagreements and divergences. The CPSU is not dramatizing the fact that complete unanimity among communist parties does not always exist and not in everything. Evidently, there generally cannot be an identity of views on all issues without exception. The communist movement came into being when the working class entered the international scene as an independent and powerful political force. The parties that comprise it have grown on national soil and pursue common end objectives—peace and socialism. This is the main determining thing that unites them.

We do not see the diversity of our movement as a synonym for disunity, much as unity has nothing in common with uniformity, hierarchy, interference by some parties in the affairs of others, or the striving of any party to have a monopoly over what is right. The communist movement can and should be strong by virtue of its class solidarity, of equal cooperation among all the fraternal parties in the struggle for common aims. This is how the CPSU understands unity and it intends to do everything to foster it.

The trend toward strengthening the potential of peace, reason, and good will is enduring and in principle irreversible. At the back of it is the desire of people, of all nations to live in concord and to cooperate. However, one should look at things realistically: the balance of strength in the struggle against war is taking shape in the course of an acute and dynamic confrontation between progress and reaction. An immutable factor is the CPSU's solidarity with the forces of national liberation and social emancipation, and our course toward close interaction with socialist-oriented countries, with revolutionary-democratic parties, and with the Non-Aligned Movement. The Soviet public is prepared to go on promoting links with noncommunist movements and organizations, including religious organizations that are against war.

This is also the angle from which the CPSU regards its relations with the *social democratic movement*. It is a fact that the ideological differences between the Communists and the Social Democrats are deep, and that their achievements and experience are dissimilar and nonequivalent. However, an unbiased look at the standpoints and views of each other is unquestionably useful to both the Communists and the Social Democrats, useful in the first place for furthering the struggle for peace and international security.

We are living in a world of realities and are building our international policy in keeping with the specific features of the present phase of international development. A creative analysis of this phase and vision of prospects have led us to a conclusion that is highly significant. Now, as never before, it is important to find ways for closer and more productive cooperation with governments, parties, and mass organizations and movements that are genuinely concerned about the destinies of peace on earth, with all peoples, in order to *build an all-embracing system of international security.*

We see the Fundamental Principles of this system in the following:

1. *In the military sphere:*

—renunciation by the nuclear powers of war—both nuclear and conventional—against each other or against third countries;

—prevention of an arms race in outer space, cessation of all nuclear weapons tests and the total destruction of such weapons, a ban on and the destruction of chemical weapons, and renunciation of the development of other means of mass annihilation;

—a strictly controlled lowering of the levels of military capabilities of countries to limits of reasonable adequacy;

—disbandment of military alliances, and as a stage toward this—renunciation of their enlargement and of the formation of news ones;

—balanced and proportionate reduction of military budgets.

2. *In the political sphere:*

—strict respect in international practice for the right of each people to choose the ways and forms of its development independently;

—a just political settlement of international crises and regional conflicts;

—elaboration of a set of measures aimed at building confidence between states and the creation of effective guarantees against attack from without and of the inviolability of their frontiers;

—elaboration of effective methods of preventing international terrorism, including those ensuring the safety of international land, air, and sea communications.

3. *In the economic sphere:*
—exclusion of all forms of discrimination from international practice; renunciation of the policy of economic blockades and sanctions if this is not directly envisaged in the recommendations of the world community;

—joint quest for ways for a just settlement of the problem of debts;

—establishment of a new world economic order guaranteeing equal economic security to all countries;

—elaboration of principles for utilizing parts of the funds released as a result of a reduction of military budgets for the good of the world community, of developing nations in the first place;

—the pooling of efforts in exploring and making peaceful use of outer space and in resolving global problems on which the destinies of civilization depend.

4. *In the humanitarian sphere:*
—cooperation in the dissemination of the ideas of peace, disarmament, and international security; greater flow of general objective information and broader contact between peoples for the purpose of learning about one another; reinforcement of the spirit of mutual understanding and concord in relations between them;

—extirpation of genocide, apartheid, advocacy of fascism and every other form of racial, national, or religious exclusiveness, and also of discrimination against people on this basis;

—extension—while respecting the laws of each country—of international cooperation in the implementation of the political, social, and personal rights of people;

—deciding in a humane and positive spirit of questions related to the reuniting of families, marriage, and the promotion of contacts between people and between organizations;

—strengthening of and quests for new forms of cooperation in culture, art, science, education, and medicine.

These Principles stem logically from the provisions of the Program of the CPSU. They are entirely in keeping with our concrete foreign policy initiatives. Guided by them it would be possible to make peaceful coexistence the highest universal principle of relations between states. In our view, these Principles could become the point of departure and a sort of guideline for a direct and systematic dialogue—both bilateral and multilateral—among leaders of countries of the world community.

And since this concerns the destinies of peace, such a dialogue is particularly important among the permanent members of the Security Council—the five nuclear powers. They bear the main burden of responsibility for the destinies of humankind. I emphasize—not a privilege, not a foundation for claims to "leadership" in world affairs, but responsibility, about which nobody has the right to forget. Why then should their leaders not gather at a *round table* and discuss what could and should be done to strengthen peace?

As we see it, the entire existing mechanism of arms-limitation negotiations should also start to function most effectively. We must not "grow accustomed" to the fact that for years these talks have been proceeding on a parallel course, so to speak, with a simultaneous buildup of armaments.

The USSR is giving considerable attention to a joint examination, at international forums as well as within the framework of the Helsinki process, of the world economy's problems and prospects, the interdependence between disarmament and development, and the expansion of trade and scientific and technological cooperation. We feel that in the future it would be important to convene a *World Congress on Problems of Economic Security* at which it would be possible to discuss as a package everything that encumbers world economic relations.

We are prepared to consider seriously any other proposal aimed in the same direction.

Under all circumstances success must be achieved in the battle to prevent war. This would be an epoch-making victory of the whole of humanity, of every person on earth. The CPSU sees active participation in this battle as the essence of its foreign policy strategy.

V. THE PARTY

Comrades,

The magnitude and novelty of what we have to do make exceptionally high demands on the character of the political, ideological, and organizational work conducted by the CPSU, which today has more than nineteen million members welded together by unity of purpose, will, and discipline.

The Party's strength is that it has a feel for the time, that it feels the pulse of life, and always works among the people. Whenever the country faces new problems the Party finds ways of resolving them, restructures and remolds leadership methods, demonstrating its ability to measure up to its historic responsibility for the country's destiny, for the cause of socialism and communism.

Life constantly verifies our potentialities. Last year was special in this respect. As never before there was a need for unity in the Party ranks and unity in the Central Committee. We saw clearly that it was no longer possible to evade pressing issues of society's development, to remain reconciled to irresponsibility, laxity, and inertness. Under these conditions the Politburo, the Secretariat of the Central Committee, and the Central Committee itself decided that the cardinal issues dictated by the times had to be resolved. An important landmark on this road was the April Plenary Meeting of the Central Committee. We told the people frankly about the difficulties and omissions in our work and about the plans for the immediate future and the long term. Today, at this Congress, we can state with confidence that the course set by the April Plenary Meeting received the active support of the Communists, of millions of working people.

The present stage, which is one of society's qualitative transformation, requires the Party and each of its organizations to make new efforts, to be principled in assessing their own work, and to show efficiency and dedication. The draft new edition of the Party Program and the draft amendments in the Party Rules presented to the Congress proceed from the premise that the task of mobilizing all the factors of acceleration can only be carried out by a Party that has the interests of the people at heart, a Party having a scientifically substantiated perspective, asserting by its labor the confidence that the set targets would be attained.

The Party can resolve new problems successfully if it is itself in uninterrupted development, free of the "infallibility" complex, critically assesses the results that have been attained, and clearly sees what has to be done. The new requirements being made of cadres, of the entire style, methods, and character of work are dictated by the magnitude and complexity of the problems and the need to draw lessons from the past without compromise or reservations.

At present, comrades, we have to focus on the practical organization of our work and the placing and education of cadres, of the body of Party activists, and to take a fresh look at our entire work from the Party's point of view—at all levels, in all echelons. In this context, I should like to remind you of Lenin's words: "When the situation has changed and different problems have to be solved, we cannot look back and attempt to solve them by yesterday's methods. Don't try—you won't succeed!"

A. To Work in a New Way, to Enhance the Role and Responsibility of Party Organizations

The purpose of restructuring Party work is that each Party organization—from republican to primary—should vigorously implement the course set by the April Plenary Meeting and live in an atmosphere of quest, of renewal of the forms and methods of its activity. This can only be done through the efforts of all the Communists, the utmost promotion of democracy within the Party itself, the application of the principle of collective leadership at all levels, the promotion of criticism and self-criticism, control, and a responsible attitude to the work at hand. It is only then that the spirit of novelty is generated, that inertness and stagnation become intolerable.

We feel just indignation about all sorts of shortcomings and those responsible for them—people who neglect their duties and are indifferent to society's interests: hack worker and idler, grabber and writer of anonymous letters, petty bureaucrat and bribe-taker. But they live and work in a concrete collective, town, or village, in a given organization and not some place away from us. Then who but the collective and the Communists should openly declare that in our working society each person is obliged to work conscientiously and abide strictly by the norms of socialist human association, which are the same for everybody? What and who prevents this?

This is where the task of enhancing the role of the Party

organization rises to its full stature. It does not become us, the Communists, to put the blame on somebody else. If a Party organization lives a full-blooded life founded on relations of principle, if Communists are engaged in concrete matters and not in a chit-chat on general subjects, success is assured. It is not enough to see shortcomings and defects, to stigmatize them. It is necessary to do everything so that they should not exist. *There is no such thing as Communists' vanguard role in general: it is expressed in practical deeds.*

Party life that is healthy, businesslike, multiform in its concrete manifestations and concerns, characterized by openness and publicity of plans and decisions, by the humaneness and modesty of Communists—that is what we need today. We, the Communists, are looked upon as a model in everything—in work and behavior. We have to live and work in such a way that the working person can say: "Yes, this is a real Communist." And the brighter and cleaner life is within the Party, the sooner we shall cope with the complex problems which are typical of the present time of change.

Guided by the decisions of the April and subsequent Plenary Meetings of the Central Committee and working boldly and perseveringly, many Party organizations have achieved good results. In defining the ways for advancement, the CPSU Central Committee relies chiefly on that experience, striving to make it common property. For example, the decisions on accelerating scientific and technological progress are based to a large extent on the innovative approach to these matters in the Leningrad Party organization, and its experience underlies the drafting of the programs for the intensification and integration of science and production, and socioeconomic planning. Party organizations in the Ukraine should be commended for creating scientific and technological complexes and engineering centers and for their productive work in effectively utilizing recycled resources. The measures to form a unified agroindustrial complex in the country underwent a preliminary trial in Georgia and Estonia.

Many examples could be given of a modern approach to work. A feel for the new, and active restructuring in accordance with the changing conditions are a characteristic of the Byelorussian, Latvian, Sverdlovsk, Chelyabinsk, Krasnodar, Omsk, Ulyanovsk, and other Party organizations. Evidence of this is also provided by many election meetings, conferences, and republican congresses. They were notable for their businesslike formulation of issues, the commitment of Communists to seeking untapped resources and ways of speeding up our progress, and exactingness in assessing the work of elective bodies.

But not everybody can see the need for restructuring, and not everywhere. There still are many organizations, as is also confirmed by the election campaign, in which one does not feel the proper frame of mind for a serious, self-critical analysis, for drawing practical conclusions. This is the effect of adherence to the old, the absence of a feel for the time, a propensity for excessive organization, the habit of speaking vaguely, and the fear of revealing the real state of affairs.

We shall not be able to move a single step forward if we do not learn to work in a new way, do not put an end to inertness and conservatism in any of their forms, if we lose the courage to assess the situation realistically and see it as it actually is. To make irresponsibility recede into the past, we have to make a rule of calling things by their names, of judging everything openly. It is about time to stop exercises in misplaced tact where there should be exactingness and honesty, a Party conscience. Nobody has the right to forget Lenin's stern warning: "False rhetoric and false boastfulness spell moral ruin and lead unfailingly to political extinction."

The consistent implementation of the *principle of collectivism* is a key condition for a healthy life in every Party organization. But in some organizations the role of Plenary Meetings and of the bureaus as collegiate bodies was downgraded, and the joint drafting of decisions was replaced by instructions issued by one individual, and this often led to gross errors. Such sidetracking from the norms of Party life was tolerated in the Central Committee of the Communist Party of Kirghizia. A principled assessment was given at the Congress of the Republic's Communist Party of the activities not only of the former First Secretary but also of those who connived at unscrupulousness and servility.

It is only strict compliance with and the utmost strengthening of the principle of collective leadership that can be a barrier to subjectivist excesses and create the conditions for the adoption of considered and substantiated decisions. A leader who understands this clearly has the right to count on long and productive work.

More urgently than before there is now the *need to promote criticism and self-criticism and step up the efforts to combat window-dressing.* From the recent past we know that where criticism and self-criticism are smothered, where talk about successes is substituted for a Party analysis of the actual situation, all Party activity is deformed and a situation of complacency, permissiveness, and impunity arises that leads to the most serious consequences. In the localities and even in the center there appeared quite a few officials who are over-sensitive to critical remarks leveled at them and who go so far as to harass people who come up with criticism.

The labor achievements of the people of Moscow are widely known. But one can say confidently that these accomplishments would have been much greater had the city Party organization not lost, since some time ago, the spirit of self-criticism and a healthy dissatisfaction with what had been achieved, had complacency not surfaced. As was noted at a city Party conference, the leadership of the City Committee had evaded decisions on complex problems while parading its successes. This is what generated complacency and was an impediment to making a principled evaluation of serious shortcomings.

Perhaps in their most glaring form negative processes stemming from an absence of criticism and self-criticism manifested themselves in Uzbekistan. Having lost touch with life the republic's former top leadership made it a rule to speak only of successes, paper over shortcomings, and respond irritably to any criticism. In the republican Party organization discipline slackened, and persons for whom the sole principle was lack of principles, their own well-being, and careerist considerations were in favor. Toadyism and unbridled laudation of those "senior in rank" became widespread. All this could not but affect the state of affairs. The situation in the economy and in the social sphere deteriorated markedly, machinations, embezzlement, and bribery thrived, and socialist legality was grossly transgressed.

It required intervention by the CPSU Central Committee to normalize the situation. The republic was given all-sided assistance. Many sectors of Party, governmental, and economic work were reinforced with cadres. These measures won the approval and active support of the Communists and the working people of Uzbekistan.

There is something else that causes concern. The shortcomings in the republic did not appear overnight, they piled up over the years, growing from small to big. Officials from all-Union bodies, including the Central Committee, went to Uzbekistan on many occasions and they must have noticed what was happening. Working people of the republic wrote indignant letters to the central bodies about the malpractices. But these signals were not duly investigated.

The reason for this is that at some stage some republics, territories, regions, and cities were placed out of bounds to criticism. As a result, in the localities there began to appear districts, collective farms, state farms, industrial facilities, and so on that enjoyed a kind of immunity. From this we have to draw the firm conclusion that *in the Party there neither are nor should be organizations outside the pale of control and closed to criticism, there neither are nor should be leaders fenced off from Party responsibility.*

This applies equally to ministries, departments, and any enterprises and organizations. The CPSU Central Committee considers that the role of Party committees of ministries and departments must be enhanced significantly, that their role in restructuring the work of the management apparatus and of industries as a whole must be raised. An examination of the reports of the Party committees of some ministries in the Central Committee shows that they are still using their right of control very timidly and warily, that they are not catalysts of the new, of the struggle against departmentalism, paperwork, and red tape.

The Party provides political leadership and defines the general prospect for development. It formulates the main tasks in socioeconomic and intellectual life, selects and places cadres, and exercises general control. As regards the ways and means of resolving specific economic and sociocultural problems, wide freedom of choice is given to each management body and work collective, and managerial personnel.

In improving the forms and methods of leadership, the Party is emphatically against confusing the functions of Party committees with those of governmental and public bodies.

This is not a simple question. In life it is sometimes hard to see the boundary beyond which Party control and the organization of the fulfillment of practical tasks become petty tutelage or even substitution for governmental and economic bodies. Needless to say, each situation requires a specific approach, and here much is determined by the political culture and maturity of leaders. The Party will endeavor to organize work so that everyone on his job will act professionally and energetically, unafraid to shoulder responsibility. Such is the principled Leninist decision on this question and we should abide strictly by it at all levels of Party activity.

1. For the Purity and Integrity of the Image of the Party Member, for a Principled Personnel Policy

Comrades,

The more consistently we draw the Party's huge creative potential into the efforts to accelerate the development of Soviet society, the more tangible becomes the profound substantiation of the conclusion drawn by the April Plenary Meeting *about the necessity of enhancing the initiative and responsibility of cadres and about the importance of an untiring struggle for the purity and integrity of the image of the Party member.*

The Communist Party is the political and moral vanguard. During the past five years it has admitted nearly 1,600,000 new members. Its roots in the working class, in all strata of society are growing increasingly stronger. In terms of per hundred new members there are 59 workers and 26 trained specialists working in various branches of the economy, while four-fifths of all those admitted are young people.

By and large, the Party's composition is formed and its ranks grow in accordance with the Rules, but as in any matter the process of admittance to the Party requires further improvement. Some organizations hasten the growth of the Party ranks to the detriment of their quality, and do not set high standards for new members. Our task is to show tireless concern for the purity of the Party ranks and dependably close the Party to uncommitted people, to those who join it out of careerist or other mercenary considerations.

We have to go on improving the ideological education of

Communists and insist upon stricter compliance with Party discipline and unqualified fulfillment of the requirements set by the Rules. In each Party organization the Communists should themselves create an atmosphere of mutual exactingness that would rule out all possibility of anyone disregarding Party norms. In this context, we should support and disseminate the experience of many Party organizations in which Communists report regularly to their comrades, and where character references to Party members are discussed and endorsed at Party meetings. This helps to give all Party members without exception a higher sense of responsibility to their organization.

We suffer quite a lot of damage because some Communists behave unworthily or commit acts that discredit them. Of late a number of senior officials have been discharged from their posts and expelled from the Party for various abuses. Some of them have been indicted. There have been such cases, for example, in the Alma-Ata, Chimkent, and some other regions as well as in some republics, and also in ministries and departments. Phenomena of this kind are, as a rule, generated by violations of Party principles in selecting and educating cadres, and in controlling their work. The Party will resolutely go on getting rid of all who discredit the name of Communist.

At this Congress I should like to say a few more words about *efficiency*. This is a question of principle. Any disparity between what is said and done hurts the main thing—the prestige of Party policy—and cannot be tolerated in any form. The Communist Party is a Party whose words are matched by deeds. This should be remembered by every leader, by every Communist. It is by the unity of words and deeds that the Soviet people will judge our work.

Important resolutions have been adopted and interesting ideas and recommendations have been put forward both in the center and in the localities since the April Plenary Meeting. But if we were to analyze what of this has been introduced into life and been mirrored in work, it will be found that alongside unquestionable changes much has still got stuck on the way to practical utilization. No restructuring, no change can take place unless every Communist, especially a leader, appreciates the immense significance of practical actions, which are the only vehicles that can move life forward and make labor more productive. Organizational work cannot be squandered on bombast and empty rhetoric at countless meetings and conferences.

And another thing. The Party must declare a determined and relentless war on bureaucratic practices. Vladimir Ilyich Lenin held that it was especially important to fight them at moments of change, during a transition from one system of management to another, where there is a need for maximum efficiency, speed, and energy. Bureaucracy is today a serious obstacle to the solution of our principal problem—the acceleration of the country's socioeconomic development and the fundamental restructuring of the mechanism of economic management linked to that development. This is a troubling question and appropriate conclusions are required. Here it is important to bear in mind that bureaucratic distortions manifest themselves all the more strongly where there is no efficiency, publicity, and control from below, where people are held less accountable for what they do.

Comrades, of late many new, energetic people who think in modern terms have been appointed to high positions. The Party will continue the practice of including experienced and young cadres in the leadership. More women are being promoted to leadership positions. There are now more of them in Party and local government bodies. The criteria for all promotions and changes are the same: political qualities, efficiency, ability, and actual achievements of the person concerned and the attitude to people. I feel it is necessary to emphasize this also because some people have dropped the Party tradition of maintaining constant contact with rank-and-file Communists, with working people. This is what undermines the very essence of Party work.

The person needed today to head each Party organization is one who has close ties to the masses and is ideologically committed, thinks in an innovative way, and is energetic. It is hardly necessary to remind you that with the personality of a leader, of a Party leader in the first place, people link all the advantages and shortcomings of the concrete, actual life they live. The secretary of a district committee, a city committee, or a regional committee of the Party is the criterion by which the rank-and-file worker forms an opinion of the Party committee and of the Party as a whole.

Cadres devoted to the Party cause and heading the efforts to implement its political line are our main and most precious asset. Party activists, all Communists should master the great traditions of Bolshevism and be brought up in the spirit of these traditions. In the Party, at each level, a principled stand and Party comradeship should become immutable norms. This is the only attitude that can ensure the Party's moral health, which is the earnest of society's health.

2. To Reinforce Ideology's Link to Life and Enrich People's Intellectual World

Comrades,

"You cannot be an ideological leader without . . . theoretical work, just as you cannot be one without directing this work to meet the needs of the cause, and without spreading the results of this theory . . ." That is what Lenin taught us.

Marxism-Leninism is the greatest revolutionary world view. It substantiated the most humane objective that humankind has ever set itself—the creation of a just social system on earth. It indicates the way to a scientific study of society's development as an integral process that is law-governed in all its huge diversity and contradictoriness, teaches us to see the character and interaction of economic and political forces, to select correct orientations, forms, and methods of struggle, and to feel confident at all sharp turns in history.

In all its work the CPSU proceeds from the premise that fidelity to the Marxist-Leninist doctrine lies in creatively developing it on the basis of the experience that has been accumulated. The intricate range of problems stemming from the present landmark character of the development of our society and of the world as a whole is in the focus of the Party's theoretical thinking. The many-sided tasks of acceleration and its interrelated aspects—political, economic, scientific, technological, social, cultural-intellectual, and psychological—require further in-depth and all-embracing analysis. We feel a pressing need for serious philosophical generalizations, well-founded economic and social forecasts, and profound historical researches.

We cannot escape the fact that our philosophy and economics, as indeed our social sciences as a whole, are, I would say, in a state that is some distance away from the imperatives of life. Besides, our economic planning bodies and other departments do not display the proper interest in carrying rational recommendations of social scientists into practice.

Time sets the question of the social sciences, broadly tackling the concrete requirements of practice and demands that social scientists should be sensitive to the ongoing changes in life, keep new phenomena in sight, and draw conclusions that would correctly orient practice. Viability can only be claimed by those scientific schools that come from practice and return to it enriched with meaningful generalizations and constructive recommendations. Scholasticism, doctrinairism, and dogmatism have always been shackles for a genuine addition to knowledge. They lead to stagnation of thought, put a solid wall around science, keeping it away from life and inhibiting its development. Truth is acquired not by declarations and instructions, it is born in scientific discussion and debate and is verified in action. The Central Committee favors this way of developing our social sciences, a way that makes it possible to obtain significant results in theory and practice.

The atmosphere of creativity, which the Party is asserting in all areas of life, is particularly productive for the social sciences. We hope that it will be used actively by our economists and philosophers, lawyers and sociologists, historians and literary critics for a bold and innovative formulation of new problems and for their creative theoretical elaboration.

But in themselves ideas, however attractive, do not give shape automatically to a coherent and active world view if they are not coupled to the sociopolitical experience of the masses. *Socialist ideology draws its energy and effectiveness from the interaction of advanced ideas with the practice of building the new society.*

The Party defines the basic directions of ideological work in the new edition of the CPSU Program. They have been discussed at Plenary Meetings of the CPSU Central Committee and at the USSR Practical-Scientific Conference held in December 1984. I shall mention only a few of them.

The most essential thing on which the entire weight of Party influence must be focused is that every person should understand the urgency and landmark character of the moment we are living in. Any of our plans would hang in the air if people are left indifferent, if we fail to awaken the labor and social vigor of the masses, their energy and initiative. *The prime condition for accelerating the country's socioeconomic development is to turn society toward new tasks and draw upon the creative potential of the people, of every work collective for carrying them out.*

It is an indisputable fact that intelligent and truthful words exercise a tremendous influence. But their significance is multiplied a hundredfold if they are coupled to political, economic, and social steps. This is the only way to get rid of tiresome edification and to fill calls and slogans with the breath of real life.

Divergence of words from reality dramatically devalues ideological efforts. No matter how many lectures we deliver on tact and how much we censure callousness and bureaucracy, this evaporates if a person encounters rudeness in offices, in the street, in a shop. No matter how many talks we may have on the culture of behavior, they will be useless if they are not reinforced by efforts to achieve a high level of culture in production, association between people, and human relations. No matter how many articles we may write about social justice, order, and discipline, they will remain unproductive if they are not accompanied by vigorous actions on the part of the work collective and by consistent enforcement of the law.

People should constantly see and feel the great truth of our ideology and the principled character of our policy. Work and the distribution of benefits should be so organized and the laws and principles of socialist human relationships so scrupulously observed that every Soviet citizen should have firm faith in our ideals and values. Dwellings, food supplies, the quality of consumer goods, and the level of health care—all this most directly affects the consciousness and sentiment of people. It is exactly from these positions that we should approach the entire spectrum of problems linked to the educational work of party and government bodies, and mass organizations.

Exceedingly favorable social conditions are created for boosting the effectiveness of ideological work in the drive to speed up socioeconomic development. But nobody should count on ideological, political, labor, and moral education being thereby simplified. It must always be borne in mind that however favorable it may be the present situation has its own contradictions and difficulties. No concession in its assessments should be allowed.

It is always a complex process to develop social consciousness, but the distinctive character of the present stage has made many pressing problems particularly sharp. First, the very magnitude of the task of acceleration determines the social atmosphere, its character and specific features. As yet not everybody has proved to be prepared to understand and accept what is taking place. Second, and this must be emphasized, the slackening of socioeconomic development was the outcome of serious blunders not only in economic management but also in ideological work.

It cannot be said that there were few words on this matter or that they were wrong. But in practice purposeful educational work was often replaced by artificial campaigns leading propaganda away from life with an adverse effect on the social climate. The sharpness of the contradictions in life was often ignored and there was no realism in assessing the actual state of affairs in the economy, as well as in the social and other spheres. Vestiges of the past invariably leave an imprint. They make themselves felt, being reflected in people's consciousness, actions, and behavior. The lifestyle cannot be changed in the twinkling of an eye, and it is still harder to overcome inertia in thinking. Energetic efforts must be made here.

Policy yields the expected results when it is founded on an accurate account of the interests of classes, social groups, and individuals. While this is true from the standpoint of administering society, it is even truer where ideology and education are concerned. Society consists of concrete people, who have concrete interests, their joys and sorrows, their notions about life, about its actual and sham values.

In this context I should like to say a few words about *work with individuals as a major form of education*. It cannot be said that it receives no attention, but in the ideological sphere the customary "gross" approach is a serious hindrance. The relevant statistics are indeed impressive: tens and hundreds of thousands of propagandists, agitators, and lecturers on politics, the study circles and seminars, the newspapers and journals with circulations running into millions, and the audiences of millions at lectures. All this is commendable. But does not the living person disappear in this playing around with figures and this "coverage"? Do not ideological statistics blind us, on the one hand, to selfless working people meriting high recognition by society and, on the other, to exponents of antisocialist morality? That is why maximum concreteness in education is so important.

An essential feature of ideological work today is that it is conducted in a situation marked by a sharp confrontation between socialist and bourgeois ideology. Bourgeois ideology is an ideology serving capital and the profits of monopolies, adventurism and social revenge, an ideology of a society that has no future. Its objectives are clear: to use any method to embellish capitalism, camouflage its intrinsic anti-humaneness and injustice, to impose its standards of life and culture; by every means to throw mud at socialism and misrepresent the essence of such values as democracy, freedom, equality, and social progress.

The psychological warfare unleashed by imperialism cannot be qualified otherwise than as a specific form of aggression, of information imperialism which infringes on the sovereignty, history, and culture of peoples. Moreover, it is direct political and psychological preparations for war, which, of course, have nothing in common with a real comparison of views or with a free exchange of ideas, about which they speak hypocritically in the West. There is no other way for evaluating actions, when people are taught to look upon any society uncongenial to imperialism through a gunsight.

Of course, there is no need to overestimate the influence of bourgeois propaganda. Soviet people are quite aware of the real value of the various forecasters and forecasts, they clearly see the actual aims of the subversive activities of the ruling monopoly forces. But we must not forget that psychological warfare is a struggle for the minds of people, for shaping their outlook and their social intellectual bearings in life. We are contending with a skillful class adversary, whose political experience is diverse and centuries-old in terms of time. He has built up a mammoth mass propaganda machine equipped with sophisticated technical means and having a huge well-trained staff of haters of socialism.

The insidiousness and unscrupulousness of bourgeois propagandists must be countered with a high standard of professionalism on the part of our ideological workers, by the morality and culture of socialist society, by the openness of information, and by the incisive and creative character of our propaganda. We must be on the offensive in exposing ideological subversion and in bringing home truthful information about the actual achievements of socialism, about the socialist way of life.

We have built a world free of oppression and exploitation and a society of social unity and confidence. We, patriots of our Homeland, will go on safeguarding it with all our strength, increasing its wealth, and fortifying its economic and moral might. The inner sources of Soviet patriotism are in the social system, in our humanistic ideology. True patriotism lies in an active civic stand. Socialism is a society with a high level of morality. One cannot be ideologically committed without being honest, conscientious, decent, and critical of oneself. Our education will be all the more productive, the more vigorously the ideals, principles and values of the new society are asserted. Struggle for the purity of life is the most effective way of promoting the effectiveness and social yield of ideological education and creating guarantees against the emergence of unhealthy phenomena.

To put it in a nutshell, comrades, whatever area of ideological work we take, life must be the starting point in everything. Stagnation is simply intolerable in such a vital, dynamic, and multifaceted matter as information, propaganda, artistic creativity, and amateur art activity, the work of clubs, theaters, libraries, and museums—in the entire sphere of ideological, political, labor, moral, and atheistic education.

In our day, which is dynamic and full of changes, the *role of the mass media* is growing significantly. The time that has passed since the April Central Committee Plenary Meeting has been a rigorous test for the whole of the Party's work in journalism. Editorial staffs have started vigorously tackling complex problems that are new in many respects. Newspapers, journals, and television programs have begun to pulse with life, with all its achievements and contradictions; there is a more analytical approach, civic motivation, and sharpness in bringing problems to light and in concrete criticism of shortcomings and omissions. Many constructive recommendations have been offered on pressing economic, social, and ideological issues.

It is even more important today to make sure that the mass media are effective. The Central Committee sees them as an instrument of creation and of expression of the Party's general viewpoint, which is incompatible with departmentalism and parochialism. Everything dictated by principled considerations, by the interests of improving our work will continue to be supported by the Party. The work of the mass media becomes all the more productive, the more thoughtfulness and timeliness and the less pursuit after the casual and the sensational there are in it.

Our television and radio networks are developing rapidly, acquiring an up-to-date technical level. They have definitely entered our life as all-embracing media carrying information and propagating and asserting our moral values and culture. Changes for the better have clearly appeared here: television and radio programs have become more diversified and interesting, and there is a visible aspiration to surmount established stereotypes, to take various interests of audiences into account more fully.

But can it be said that our mass media and propaganda are using all their opportunities? For the time being, no. There still is much dullness, inertia has not been overcome, and deafness to the new has not been cured. People are dissatisfied with the inadequate promptness in the reporting of news, with the superficial coverage of the effort to introduce all that is new and advanced into practice. Justified censure is evoked by the low standard of some literary works, television programs, and films that lack not only ideological and aesthetic clarity but also elementary taste. There has to be a radical improvement of film distribution and of book and journal publishing. The leadership of the Ministry of Culture, the State Television and Radio Committee, the State Film Committee, the State Publishing Committee of the USSR, and the news agencies have to draw practical conclusions from the innumerable critical remarks from the public. The shortcomings are common, but the responsibility is specific, and this must be constantly in the minds of ideological cadres.

The Party sees the main objective of its *cultural policy* in giving the widest scope for identifying people's abilities and making their lives intellectually rich and many-sided. In working for radical changes for the better in this area as well, it is important to build up cultural-educational work in such a way as to fully satisfy people's cultural requirements and interests.

Society's moral health and the intellectual climate in which people live are in no small measure determined by the state of *literature and art*. While reflecting the birth of the new world, our literature has been active in helping to build it, molding the citizen of that world—the patriot of his homeland and the internationalist in the true meaning of the word. It thereby correctly chose its place, its role in the efforts of the entire people. But this is also a criterion which the people and the Party use to assess the work of the writer and the artist, and which literature and Soviet art themselves use to approach their own tasks.

When the social need arises to form a conception of the time one lives in, especially a time of change, it always brings forward people for whom this becomes an inner necessity. We are living in such a time today. Neither the Party nor the people need showy verbosity on paper, petty dirty-linen washing, time-serving, and utilitarianism. What society expects from the writer is artistic innovation and the truth of life, which has always been the essence of real art.

But truth is not an abstract concept. It is concrete. It lies in the achievements of the people and in the contradictions of society's development, in heroism and the succession of day-to-day work, in triumphs and failures, in other words, in life itself, with all its versatility, dramatism, and grandeur. Only a literature that is ideologically motivated, artistic, and committed to the people educates people to be honest, strong in spirit, and capable of shouldering the burden of their time.

Criticism and self-criticism are a natural principle of our society's life. Without them there can be no progress. It is time for literary and art criticism to shake off complacency and servility to rank, which erodes healthy morals, and to remember that criticism is a social duty and not a sphere serving an author's vanity and ambitions.

Our unions of creative workers have rich traditions, and they play a considerable role in the life of art and of the whole of society, for that matter. But even here changes are needed. The main result of their work is measured not by resolutions and meetings, but by talented and imaginative books, films, plays, paintings, and music which are needed by society and which can enrich the people's intellectual life. In this context, serious consideration should be given to suggestions by the public that *the standard for judging works nominated for distinguished prizes should be raised.*

Guidance of intellectual and cultural life is not a simple matter. It requires tact, an understanding of creative work, and most certainly a love of literature and art, and respect for talent. Here much depends upon the ability to propagate the Party's cultural policy, to implement it in life, on fairness in evaluations, and a well-wishing attitude to the creative work and quests of the writer, the composer, and the artist.

Ideological work is creative work. It offers no universal means that are suitable to all occasions; it requires constant quest and the ability to keep abreast of life. Today it is particularly important to have a profound understanding of the nature of present-day problems, a sound scientific world view, a principled stand, a high cultural level, and a sense of responsibility for work in any sector. *To raise society's level of maturity and build communism means steadfastly to enhance the maturity of the individual's consciousness and enrich his intellectual world.*

The Party thinks highly of the knowledge, experience, and dedication of its ideological activists. Here, at our Congress, a word of the highest appreciation must be said to the millions of Party members who have fulfilled and continue to fulfill honorably an extremely important Party assignment in one of the main sectors of its work. We must continue to assign to ideological work such comrades who by personal example have proved their commitment, are able to think analytically, and know how to hear out and talk with people, in short, highly trained in political and professional terms, and capable of successfully carrying out the new tasks of our time.

VI. THE RESULTS OF THE DISCUSSION OF THE NEW EDITION OF THE PARTY PROGRAM AND OF THE AMENDMENTS TO THE PARTY RULES

Comrades,

The Political Report of the CPSU Central Committee examines the Party's program goals, its present-day economic and political strategies, the problems of improving inner-Party life, and the style and methods of work, that is, all that constitutes the core of the drafts of the new edition of the Program and of the amendments to the CPSU Rules. Therefore, there is no need to set them forth here in detail. Let me only dwell on some of the points of principle, taking into account the results of the Party-wide and nationwide discussion of the drafts of these documents.

What are these results? First of all, the conclusions and provisions of the CPSU Program and Rules have met with widespread approval. The Communists and all Soviet people support the Party's policy of accelerating the country's socio-economic development and its Program's clear orientation toward the communist perspective and the strengthening of world peace. They point out that the new historical tasks are based on in-depth analysis of the urgent problems of the development of society.

The new edition of the Program has also evoked a wide response abroad. Progressives take note of its profoundly humanist character, its addressing itself to man, its passionate call for mutual understanding among nations and for ensuring a peaceful future to humanity. Our friends abroad are inspired by the Soviet Union's unremitting striving for lasting comradely relations and all-round cooperation with all the countries of the socialist world system and its firm support of the peoples' anti-imperialist struggle for peace, democracy, social progress, and the consolidation of independence. Many of the sober-minded public figures in bourgeois countries take note of the peaceful orientation of our Program, of the CPSU line for disarmament and for normal, sound relations with all the countries.

The preparation and discussion of the pre-Congress documents have invigorated the Party's ideological and political work and furthered the social activity of millions of working people.

The drafts of the new edition of the Program and of the Rules have been thoroughly discussed at meetings of primary Party organizations, at district, city, area, regional and territorial election conferences, and at congresses of the Communist parties of Union Republics. Since the beginning of the discussion, over six million letters were received in connection with the draft Program alone. They came from workers, collective farmers, scientists, teachers, engineers, doctors, Army and Navy servicemen, Communists and non-Party people, veterans and young people. Assessing the new edition of the Program as a document that meets the vital interests of the Soviet people, they made numerous proposals, and suggested additions and more precise wordings. I believe it would be useful to dwell on some of them.

Stressing the novelty of the draft under discussion, the authors of some of the letters suggest adopting it at the Congress as the Fourth Party Program. It will be recalled that the adoption of new Party programs, initially the second and then the third, was necessitated by the fact that the goals set in the preceding Program had been reached. In our case, the situation is different.

The Party's basic tasks of developing and consolidating socialism, of improving it in every way on a planned basis, and of ensuring Soviet society's further advance to Communism, remain in force. The document submitted for your consideration reiterates the theoretical and political guidelines which have stood the test of time.

At the same time, much has changed in our life in the quarter of a century since the adoption of the Third Party Program. New historical experience has been accumulated. Not all of the estimates and conclusions turned out to be correct. The idea of translating the tasks of the full-scale building of communism into direct practical action has proved to be premature. Certain miscalculations were made, too, in fixing deadlines for the solution of a number of concrete problems. New problems related to improving socialism and accelerating its development, as well as certain questions of international politics, have come to the fore and become acute. All this has to be reflected in the Party's Program document.

Thus, the assessment of the submitted document as a new edition of the Third Party Program is justified in reality and is of fundamental importance. It affirms the main goals of the CPSU, the basic laws governing communist construction, and at the same time shows that the accumulated historical experience has been interpreted in a creative manner, and that the strategy and tactics have been elaborated in conformity with specificities of the present turning point.

The public has paid great attention to those provisions of the Program which describe the stage of social development reached by the country and the goals yet to be attained through its implementation. Various opinions were expressed on this score. While some suggest that references to developed socialism should be completely removed from the Program, others, on the contrary, believe that this should be dealt with at greater length.

The draft sets forth a well-balanced and realistic position on this issue. The main conclusions about modern socialist society confirm that our country has entered the stage of developed socialism. We also show understanding for the task of building developed socialism set down in the Program documents of the fraternal parties of other socialist countries.

At the same time, it is proper to recall that the thesis on developed socialism has gained currency in our country as a reaction to the simplistic ideas about the ways and period of time for carrying out the tasks of communist construction. Subsequently, however, the accents in the interpretation of developed socialism were gradually shifted. Things were not infrequently reduced to just registering successes, while many of the urgent problems related to the switching over of the economy to intensification, to raising labor productivity, improving supplies to the population, and overcoming negative things were not given due attention. Willy-nilly, this was a peculiar vindication of sluggishness in solving outstanding problems. Today, when the Party has proclaimed and is pursuing the policy of accelerating socioeconomic development, this approach has become unacceptable.

The prevailing conditions compel us to focus theoretical

and political thought not on recording what has been achieved, but on substantiating the ways and methods of accelerating socioeconomic progress, on which depend qualitative changes in various spheres of life. An incalculably deeper approach is wanted in solving the cardinal issues of social progress. The strategy of the CPSU set out in the new edition of the Program is centered on the need for change, for stepping up the dynamism of society's development. It is through socioeconomic acceleration that our society is to attain new frontiers, whereupon the advantages of the socialist system will assert themselves to the fullest extent and the problems that we have inherited from the preceding stages will be resolved.

Divergent opinions have been expressed, too, concerning details of the Program provisions. Some people hold that the Program should be a still-more-concise document, a kind of brief declaration of the Party's intentions. Others favor a more detailed description of the parameters of economic and social development. Some letters contain proposals for a more precise chronology of the periods that Soviet society will pass through in its advance to communism.

According to Lenin's principles of drafting program documents and the traditions that have shaped up, the Program should present a comprehensive picture of the modern world, the main tendencies and laws governing its development, and a clear, well-argued account of the aims which the Party is setting itself and which it is summoning the masses to achieve. At the same time, however, Lenin stressed that the Program must be strictly scientific, based on absolutely established facts, and that it should be economically precise and should not promise more than can be attained. He called for maximum realism in characterizing the future society and in defining objectives. "We should be as cautious and accurate as possible," Lenin wrote. ". . . But if we advance the slightest claim to something that we cannot give, the power of our Program will be weakened. It will be suspected that our Program is only a fantasy."

It seems to me that the submitted edition of the Program is meeting these demands. As for the chronological limits in which the Program targets are to be attained, they do not seem to be needed. The faults of the past are a lesson for us.

The only thing we can say definitely today is that the fulfillment of the present Program goes beyond the end of the present century.

The tasks that we are to carry out in the next 15 years can be defined more specifically, and have been set out in the new edition of the Program, and in greater detail in the Guidelines for the Economic and Social Development of the USSR Until the Year 2000. And, of course, the 12th Five-Year Plan, a big step in the economy's conversion to intensive development through the acceleration of scientific and technological progress, will occupy an important place in the fulfillment of our Program aims.

Many of the responses and letters received by the CPSU Central Committee Commission which drew up the new edition of the CPSU Program are devoted to social policy. Soviet people approve and support measures aimed at enhancing the people's well-being, asserting social justice everywhere, and clearing our life of everything that is contrary to the principles of socialism. They make proposals that are aimed at ensuring an increasingly full and strict fulfilment of the principle of distributing benefits according to the quantity and quality of labor, and at improving the social consumption funds; at tightening control over the measure of labor and the measure of consumption, at doing away firmly with unearned incomes and attempts at using public property for egoistic ends; at eliminating unjustified distinctions in the material remuneration of equal work in various branches of the economy, at doing away with any leveling of pay, etc. Some of these proposals are reflected in the draft. Others must be carefully examined by Party, government and economic bodies, accounted for in legislative acts and decisions, and in our practical work.

The provisions of the Program concerning the development of the people's socialist self-government have aroused considerable interest during the countrywide discussion. Unanimous support is expressed for the all-round democratization of socialist society and the maximum and effective enlistment of all the working people in running the economic, social and political processes. The concrete steps taken in this field have also been commended, and ideas expressed that the capacity of work collectives as the primary cell of immediate, direct democracy should be shown more clearly when dealing with the problems of improving the administration of the affairs of society and the state. These ideas have been taken into account.

Concern for enhancing the role of cultural and moral values in our society prompted suggestions that the education of Soviet people should proceed more distinctly in the spirit of communist ideals and ethical norms, and struggle against their antipodes. The Program Commission saw fit to accept these proposals, so that the principles of lofty ideological commitment and morality should imbue the content of the provisions of the Party Program still more fully.

About two million people expressed their ideas concerning the CPSU Rules. Having examined the results of the discussion, the Central Committee of the Party has deemed it essential to introduce in the draft Rules a number of substantive additions and clarifications aimed at heightening the vanguard role of the Communists, the capability of primary Party organizations, at extending inner-Party democracy, and at ensuring unflagging control over the activity of every Party organization, every Party worker.

In support of the idea of making more exacting demands on Communists, some comrades suggest carrying out a purge to free the Party of those whose conduct and way of life contradict our norms and ideals. I do not think there is any need for a special campaign to purge the ranks of the CPSU. Our Party is a healthy organism: it is perfecting the style and methods of its work, is eradicating formalism, red tape, and conventionalism, and is discarding everything stagnant and conservative that interferes with our progress; in this way it is freeing itself of persons who have compromised themselves by their poor work and unworthy behavior. The Party organizations will continue to carry out this work consistently, systematically, and unswervingly.

The new edition of the Program and also the proposed changes in the Party Rules register and develop the Bolshevik principles of Party building, the style and methods of Party work and the behavioral ethics of Communists that were elaborated by Lenin and have been tried and tested in practice.

On the whole, comrades, the discussion of the CPSU Program and Rules has been exceptionally fruitful. They have helped to amplify many ideas and propositions, to clarify formulations and to improve wordings. Allow me, on behalf of our Congress, to express profound gratitude to the Communists and all Soviet people for their businesslike and committed participation in discussing the pre-Congress documents.

It is the opinion of the Central Committee of the Party that the submitted drafts, enriched by the Party's and people's experience, correspond to the spirit of the times and to the demands of the period of history through which we are now living. They confirm our Party's fidelity to the great doctrine of Marxism-Leninism, they provide scientifically substantiated answers to fundamental questions of domestic and international affairs, and they give the Communists and all working people a clear perspective.

*   *   *

Comrades, those are the Program aims of our further development which have been submitted for the consideration of the 27th Congress.

What leads us to think that the outlined plans are feasible? Where is the guarantee that the policy of accelerating socioeconomic progress is correct and will be carried out?

First and foremost, the fact that our plans rest on the firm foundation of Marxist-Leninist theory, that they are based on the inexhaustible riches of Lenin's ideas.

The CPSU draws its strength from the enormous potentialities of socialism, from the vigorous creative efforts of the masses. At crucial turning points in history the Leninist Party has on more than one occasion demonstrated its ability to find correct roads of progress, to inspire, rally and organize the many-million masses of working people. That was the case during the revolution, in the years of peaceful construction and in the years of wartime trials, and in the difficult postwar period. We are confident this will be the case in future, too.

We count on the support of the working class because the Party's policy is their policy.

We count on the support of the peasantry because the Party's policy is their policy.

We count on the support of the people's intelligentsia because the Party's policy is their policy.

We count on the support of women, young people, veterans, all social groups and all the nations and nationalities of our Soviet homeland because the Party's policy expresses the hopes, interests, and aspirations of the entire people.

We are convinced that all conscientious, honest-minded Soviet patriots support the Party's strategy of strengthening the might of our country, of making our life better, purer, more just.

Those are the powerful social forces that stand behind the CPSU. They follow it, they have faith in the Communist Party.

The surging tide of history is now speeding toward the shallows that divide the second and third millennia. What lies ahead, beyond the shallows? Let us not prophesy. We do know, however, that the plans we are putting forward today are daring, and that our daily affairs are permeated with the spirit of socialist ethics and justice. In this troubled age the aim of our social and, I would add, vital strategy consists in that people should cherish our planet, the skies above, and outer space, exploring it as the pioneers of a *peaceful* civilization, ridding life of nuclear nightmares and completely releasing all the finest qualities of the human being, that unique inhabitant of the universe, for constructive efforts only.

The Soviet people can be confident that the Party is fully aware of its responsibility for our country's future, for a durable peace on earth, and for the correctness of the charted policy. Its practical implementation requires above all persistent work, unity of the Party and the people, and cohesive actions by all working people.

That is the only way we will be able to carry out the behests of the great Lenin—to move forward energetically and with a singleness of will. History has given us no other destiny. But what a wonderful destiny it is, comrades!

(Mikhail Gorbachev's report was heard with great attention and repeatedly punctuated with prolonged applause.)

VI

SPEECH
At the Close of the 27th Party Congress

March 6, 1986

Dear Comrades,

The 27th Congress is about to close.

It is up to history to give an objective evaluation of its importance. But already today we can say: the Congress has been held in an atmosphere of Party fidelity to principle, in a spirit of unity, exactingness, and Bolshevik truth; it has frankly pointed out shortcomings and deficiencies, and made a profound analysis of the internal and external conditions in which our society develops. It has set a lofty moral and spiritual tone for the Party's activity and for the life of the entire country.

Coming to this rostrum, delegates put all questions frankly, and did not mince words in showing what is impeding our common cause, what is holding us back. Not a few critical statements were made about the work of all links of the Party, of government and economic organizations, both at the center and locally. In fact, not a single sphere of our life has escaped critical analysis. All this, comrades, is in the spirit of the Party's finest traditions, in the Bolshevik spirit.

More than 60 years ago, when summing up the discussion on the Political Report of the RCP(B) Central Committee to the 11th Party Congress, Lenin expressed a thought that is of fundamental importance. He said: "All the revolutionary parties that have perished so far, perished because they became conceited, because they failed to see the source of their strength and were afraid to discuss their weaknesses. We, however, shall not perish, because we are not afraid to discuss our weaknesses and will learn to overcome them."

It is in this way, in Lenin's way, that we have acted here at our Congress. And that is the way we shall continue to act!

The Congress has answered the vital questions that life itself has put before the Party, before society, and has equipped every Communist, every Soviet citizen, with a clear understanding of the coming tasks. It has shown that we were right when we advanced the concept of socioeconomic acceleration at the April 1985 Plenary Meeting. The idea of acceleration imbued all our pre-Congress activity. It was at the center of attention at the Congress. It was embodied in the Political Report of the Central Committee, the new edition of the Party Program, and the amendments to the Party Rules, as well as in the Guidelines for the Economic and Social Development of the USSR for the 12th Five-Year-Plan period and for the Period Ending in the Year 2000. These documents were wholeheartedly endorsed and approved by the delegates to the Congress.

The adopted and approved general line of the Party's domestic and foreign policy—that of the country's accelerated socioeconomic development, and of consolidating world peace—is the main political achievement of the 27th CPSU Congress. From now on it will be the law of life for the Party, for its every organization, and a guide to action for Communists, for all working people.

We are aware of the great responsibility to history that the CPSU is assuming, of the huge load it has taken on by adopting the strategy of acceleration. But we are convinced of the vital necessity of this strategy. We are confident that this strategy is a realistic one. Relying on the inexhaustible potentials and advantages of socialism, on the vigorous creative activity of the people, we shall be able to carry out all the projected objectives.

To secure the country's accelerated socioeconomic development means to provide new powerful stimuli to the growth of the productive forces and to scientific and technological progress through the improvement of socialism's economic system, and to set in motion the tremendous untapped potentials of our national economy.

To secure acceleration means conducting an active and purposeful social policy by closely linking the improvement of the working people's well-being with the efficiency of labor, and by combining all-round concern for people with the consistent implementation of the principles of social justice.

To secure acceleration means to provide scope for the initiative and activity of every working person, every work collective, by deepening democracy, by steadily developing the people's socialist self-government, and by ensuring more openness in the life of the Party and society.

To secure acceleration means to bring ideological and organizational work closer to the people and direct it toward the elimination of difficulties and the practical solution of our tasks by associating this work more closely with the actual problems of life, by getting rid of hollow verbiage and didacticism, and by increasing people's responsibility for their jobs.

Comrades, we can and must accomplish all this!

The CPSU is entering the post-Congress period better organized, more cohesive, more efficient, with a well-considered long-term policy. It is determined to act with purpose, aware of all the complexity, the great scope and novelty of the tasks it faces, undaunted by difficulties and obstacles.

It is up to us to reach every Soviet citizen and bring home the essence and spirit of the Congress decisions. Not only must we explain the basic concepts of the Congress; we must also organize in practice all work in line with present-day demands.

Very many interesting proposals were made and many profound thoughts expressed at our Congress and in the pre-Congress period. They must be carefully examined, and everything valuable and useful should be put into effect.

The most important thing now is to convert the energy of our plans into the energy of concrete action. This idea was very well expressed by a delegate to our Congress, Vasily Gorin, chairman of a Belgorod collective farm.

"All over the country," he said, "in every work collective, a difficult but, we are sure, irreversible process of renovation and reconstruction is now under way. It passes through the hearts and minds of Soviet people and calls for complete dedication on the part of each and everyone. Above all in their work."

Yes, comrades, acceleration and radical changes in all spheres of our life are not just a slogan but a course that the Party will follow firmly and undeviatingly.

Many delegates noted that departmentalism, localism, paper work, and other bureaucratic practices are a big obstacle to what is new and progressive. I wish to assure you, comrades, that the Central Committee will resolutely eliminate all the obstacles standing in the way of accelerating socio-economic progress, strengthen discipline and order, and create the organizational, moral and material prerequisites for the maximum development of creative activity, bold search, and socialist enterprise. I am confident that this will meet with broad and active support on the part of the entire Party and of all working people.

The Party committees, from top to bottom, are the organizers of the work of implementing the instructions of the Congress. What we now need are a concrete, businesslike and consistent style of work, unity of words and deeds, use of the most effective ways and means, a thorough consideration of people's opinions, and efficient coordination of the actions of all social forces.

Sluggishness, formalism, indifference, the habit of letting good ideas get bogged down in empty and endless round-about discussions and attempts to "adjust to readjustment" must be completely overcome.

One of the main conclusions of the Congress is that all Party committees should act as genuine bodies of political leadership. In the final analysis, the success of all our efforts to implement the general line of the 27th Party Congress will be determined by the conscious participation of the broadest masses of the people in building communism. Everything depends on us, comrades! The time has come for vigorous and united actions. The Party calls on every Communist, every Soviet citizen, to join actively in the large-scale work of putting our plans into practice, of perfecting Soviet society, of renovating our socialist home.

Comrades, the Congress has strongly reaffirmed that socialism and peace, and peace and constructive endeavor, are indivisible. Socialism would fail to carry out its historic mission if it did not lead the struggle to deliver humanity from the burden of military threats and violence. The main goal of Soviet policy is security and a just peace for all nations. We regard the struggle against war and military preparations, against the propagation of hatred and violence as an inseparable part of the democratization of all international relations, of the genuine normalization of the political climate in the world.

In one respect the nuclear danger has put all states on an equal footing: in a big war nobody will be able to stand aside or to profit from the misfortunes of others. Equal security is the imperative of the times. Ensuring this security is becoming increasingly a political issue, one that can be resolved only by political means. It is high time to replace weapons by a more stable foundation for the relations among states. We see no alternative to this, nor are we trying to find one.

Unfortunately, however, in the international community there are still some who lay claims to a special security, one that is suited only to themselves. This is illustrated by the thinking in Washington. Calls for strength are still in fashion there, and strength continues to be regarded as the most convincing argument in world politics. It looks as though some people are simply afraid of the possibility that has appeared for a serious and long-term thaw in Soviet-American relations and in international relations as a whole.

This is not the first time we have come up against this kind of situation. Now, too, the militaristic, aggressive forces would of course prefer to preserve and perpetuate the confrontation. But what should we do, comrades? Slam the door? It is possible that this is just what we are being pushed into doing. But we very clearly realize our responsibility for the destinies of our country and for the destinies of the world. We do not intend, therefore, to play into the hands of those who would like to force humankind to get used to the nuclear threat and to the arms race.

Soviet foreign policy is oriented toward a search for mutual understanding, toward dialogue, and the establishment of peaceful coexistence as the universal norm in relations among states. We have both a clear idea of how to achieve this and a concrete program of work for maintaining and consolidating peace.

The Soviet Union is acting and will continue to act in the world arena in an open and responsible way, energetically and in good faith. We intend to work persistently and constructively to eliminate nuclear weapons, radically to limit the arms race, and to build reliable international security that is equal for all countries. A mandate to preserve peace and to curb the arms race resounded forcefully in speeches by delegates to our Congress. The Party will unswervingly carry out this mandate.

We call on the leaders of countries that have a different social system to take a responsible approach to the key issue of world politics today: the issue of war and peace.

The leadership of the CPSU and the Soviet state will do its utmost to secure for our people the opportunity to work under the conditions of freedom and a lasting peace. As reaffirmed by the Congress, our Party and the Soviet Union have many allies, supporters and partners abroad in the struggle for peace, freedom, and the progress of mankind.

We are sincerely happy to see here the leaders of the socialist countries. Allow me, on behalf of the Congress, wholeheartedly to thank the Communist Parties and peoples of these countries for their solidarity with the CPSU and the Soviet Union!

For a number of the fraternal parties in socialist countries this is also a congress year. The problems and tasks that the very course of history has set before the ruling Communist Parties are similar in many respects. And by responding to them, each party contributes to the treasure chest of world socialism's combined experience. We wish you every success, dear friends!

The CPSU is grateful for the warm greetings addressed to it by the representatives of communist, revolutionary-democratic, socialist and social-democratic parties, of democratic, liberation, and antiwar forces and movements. We highly appreciate their understanding and support of the idea advanced by the Congress of establishing a comprehensive system of international security and the plan for eliminating nuclear arms before the end of the century. The CPSU is convinced that they are consonant with the true interests of all nations, all countries, and all humanity.

Comrades, our Congress has shown that at the present stage, which is a turning point in our country's social development, the Leninist Party is equal to its historic tasks. On behalf of the delegates representing our entire Party, I should like to say from this rostrum that we Communists set great store by the confidence placed in us by the workers, the farmers, the intelligentsia, by all Soviet people. We put above all else the interests of the people, of our Motherland, of socialism and peace. We will spare neither effort nor energy to translate into life the decisions of the 27th Congress of the Communist Party of the Soviet Union.

(Mikhail Gorbachev's speech was heard with great attention and repeatedly punctuated with prolonged applause.)

VII

TELEVISED SPEECH
On the Resumption of U.S. Nuclear Testing

Moscow, March 29, 1986

Good evening, dear comrades!

At our meeting tonight I would like to share my views with you on the situation that has emerged around the Soviet Union's moratorium on nuclear tests.

Several days ago the United States carried out yet another nuclear explosion. It is clear to us all that the timing was not chosen at random. The blast was staged just before the end of the Soviet Union's unilaterally declared moratorium. Yesterday it was learned that in the coming days, in the near future, the United States intends to set off yet another nuclear device.

Soviet people, like people of good will in all countries, are incensed by these actions of the United States. They write about this in their letters to the Party's Central Committee and request that an assessment be made of the resulting situation. They ask how this should all be understood, what conclusions should be drawn, why the United States has taken such a step, and how our country's leadership intends to act in these conditions.

We consider it our duty to respond to these questions, and this, in effect, is the reason for our meeting tonight.

I must tell you frankly that we regard the present actions of the American administration, which is continuing nuclear tests despite the pressing demands of the peoples, as a pointed challenge to the Soviet Union, and not only to the Soviet Union but to the whole world, to all peoples, including the American people.

The question of ending nuclear tests has acquired tremendous importance now that whole mountains of inflammable nuclear material have been stockpiled in the world. This much is clear.

Firstly, the ending of nuclear tests is the most realistic way of achieving an end to the arms race. Without such tests it is impossible to either perfect or develop new types of nuclear

213

arms. In short, if together with the United States and other nuclear powers we were to reach an accord on ending nuclear explosions, it would be possible to get the entire process of nuclear disarmament out of the deadlock.

Further, continued testing inflicts a tremendous and perhaps not yet fully understood harm on the environment, on the natural surroundings in which we all live. Do we not feel obliged to show concern for our own home? And not only for ourselves, but for our children and grandchildren as well.

And finally, in this difficult endeavor we need not start from scratch, so to speak. A definite road has already been traversed and joint experience acquired: that is, tests in the atmosphere, in water and on land have not been conducted for many years now; nor have there been explosions in outer space.

It was with due account precisely for these circumstances that, after thoroughly weighing all the pros and cons, eight months ago, on the day of the 40th anniversary of the tragedy of Hiroshima and Nagasaki, the Soviet Union put forward an initiative of extraordinary importance—to stop all nuclear explosions both for military and peaceful purposes. And it called on the United States of America and other nuclear states to follow its example—to start an advance along the road of nuclear disarmament.

I have already had an opportunity to say that in conditions of unabating tension in the international situation this was not an easy decision for us to make. If you like, this step required both an awareness of the responsibility resting on the governments of nuclear powers, and the necessary political will. In acting as it did the Soviet leadership had the mandate of its people, which knows the price of peace and sincerely strives for its preservation and consolidation, for cooperation with all peoples.

Acting in this way, we proceeded from the deep conviction that the world in its development has entered a stage which calls for new approaches to international security matters. Today, in the nuclear and space era, one cannot think in the categories of the past. All must ultimately come to realize that everything has radically changed. The question now is not only of the preservation of peace but of the survival of humanity as well.

These are the motives behind our decision to announce the unilateral moratorium on nuclear tests.

The good initiative of the Soviet Union—and I am immensely pleased to say this—has been regarded with understanding and general approval in the world. Our action has been highly appreciated by the working people of all countries: Communists and Social Democrats, liberals and conservatives, Christians and Moslems, a multitude of public organizations, prominent political figures, scientists and cultural figures, and millions of ordinary people.

How did the other side conduct itself? That is, the U.S. Administration.

In words, it stands for the elimination of nuclear weapons. It has made a good number of statements on that score. But in actuality, a gap between words and practical policy has again manifested itself. The U.S. government has continued to conduct nuclear tests despite the Soviet Union's call and example, despite persistent demands on the part of the American people and the peoples of the whole world.

We set certain hopes on the Geneva meeting with the President of the United States of America and expected to reach an agreement with him on this matter as well. As you remember, encouraging statements were made there by both sides as well as jointly, statements to the effect that nuclear war is inadmissible, that such a war cannot be won, that neither side would seek nuclear superiority.

The results of the Geneva meeting prompted us to take yet another step of good will: to extend the moratorium until March 31 of this year. We thereby confirmed in deed our responsible attitude toward the dialogue between the leaders of the two powers, and we hoped, of course, for reciprocal steps on the part of the U.S. Administration.

I think you will agree that our Statement of January 15 of this year, which set forth a concrete and realistic program for the elimination of nuclear arms, is yet another illustration of our true intentions—to put an end to nuclear confrontation. In taking this step, we thought least of all of how to gain extra "propaganda points," as journalists say in such cases, of how to outsmart or outdo the other side. We consider such an approach to the burning problems of present-day politics inadmissible. Our actions were motivated by our responsibility both to the Soviet people and to other peoples, the responsibility for the removal of the nuclear threat, for the preservation and strengthening of peace.

In February the leaders of six nonaligned states, expressing the prevailing sentiments in world public opinion, urged the leaders of the Soviet Union and the United States to refrain from nuclear explosions until a new Soviet-American meeting. We consented to this.

It would have seemed natural for the U.S. Administration to support the Soviet Union's initiative with practical actions and to respond to the expectations of the peoples. And, at any rate, to confirm precisely through deeds its own statements made in Geneva. But that did not happen.

Everything indicates that the ruling circles of the United States have placed the narrow selfish interests of the military-industrial complex above the interests of the whole of humanity and the American people itself. The manner in which this is done is also quite significant: it is demonstrative, arrogant, disregarding the opinion of the world community. There is neither a sense of realism nor of responsibility.

It is becoming increasingly obvious that the U.S. ruling circles continue to lay emphasis on the pursuance of a militaristic line, to bank on force so as to dictate their will to other countries and peoples. Statements are openly made that it is precisely in this way that they will also influence the policy of the Soviet Union.

What can be said about that? These are ill-fated attempts. Nobody has ever succeeded in using the methods of power-politics against our state, while now they are simply preposterous. The peoples of other countries are also ever more vigorously rejecting the outdated policy of diktat in international relations.

The Soviet political leadership is now faced with the difficult question of how to react to this behavior of the United States.

Our position is clear. We believe that the world has now entered a period when responsible decisions must be taken. Yes, precisely a period when they are absolutely necessary. We will not deviate from the policy of preserving and strengthening peace, which was most definitely confirmed by the 27th Congress of the CPSU. Fulfilling the wish of its people, the

USSR will further step up its efforts to ensure universal security, and will do so in cooperation with all countries and their peoples.

As for our unilateral moratorium, I can say that it continues to remain in effect till March 31, 1986. But even after that date, as was announced, we will not conduct nuclear explosions if the United States acts likewise. We are again giving the U.S. Administration a chance to take a responsible decision—to end nuclear explosions.

Otherwise, the Soviet Union will resume testing. This must be made absolutely clear. We regret it, but our own security and that of our allies will force us to do so. I am saying all this in order that there be nothing left unsaid on that issue.

At the same time I cannot stress enough that our main intention is to stop the nuclear arms race. The simplest, most explicit and effective step in that direction would be to put an end to nuclear explosions.

We have proposed that talks be started immediately on a total ban on nuclear weapons testing, covering issues of verification. All variants are acceptable to the Soviet Union— bilateral Soviet-American talks, tripartite talks with the participation of Great Britain, or multilateral ones within the framework of the Geneva Disarmament Conference.

We have come to the conclusion that the situation requires immediate action. It is not yet too late to halt the nuclear arms race. The first major stride in that direction is needed. Putting an end to nuclear testing by everyone concerned— first of all by the Soviet Union and the United States, as well as by the other nuclear powers—could become such a step. We attach tremendous significance to the solution of this task which concerns the fate of all nations.

I am ready to meet with President Reagan as soon as possible in London, Rome, or in any other European capital that will agree to receive us, in order to reach agreement on this question. And I do not feel that there are political, technical, or any other insurmountable obstacles to this. What is needed is the necessary political will and understanding of our mutual responsibility. We propose to meet, exchange views on this crucial problem and issue instructions to draft an appropriate agreement.

We hope that this proposal of the Soviet Union will be duly

appraised and correctly understood by the President of the United States of America, and by the governments of the countries of Europe, Asia, Africa, and Latin America, of the whole world.

Time is running out. On behalf of the Soviet people we call on the American people and its government, on the peoples and governments of all countries to work vigorously, by practical actions, for the ban on nuclear explosions to become a fact, an immutable norm of interstate relations.

Mankind is standing on a line that requires the utmost responsibility. The consequences of the nuclear arms race can become dangerously unpredictable. We must act together. This matter is of concern to everyone.

This is what I wanted to tell you, dear comrades, at our meeting tonight. Goodbye.

VIII

EXCERPT FROM A SPEECH
SPEECH
To the Auto Workers at Togliatti,
USSR

April 8, 1986

And now, comrades, a few words about international affairs. The other day I had a meeting with American Congressmen and promised them that I would tell you precisely what I told them. We do not have two policies. We have one policy which expresses the interests of the Soviet people and takes account of the interests of all other peoples.

The 27th CPSU Congress produced a comprehensive analysis of all the controversies and interrelationships in today's world. What is needed to resolve its problems is an entirely new way of thinking, an innovative approach, and an awareness of the fact that the arms race and the development of military technology have reached a critical point. This is what we proceed from. In so doing, we understand that we exist side by side in world politics with an opposing system in terms of class and that from the point of view of safeguarding peace we are confronted by such a serious reality as the United States. At the same time, the leadership of that country still cannot drop past habits and, to all appearances, does not want to reckon with the reality of the Soviet Union.

This fact, however, does not stop us from seeking a way out of confrontation. For we have no alternative. The other alternative is a race toward nuclear catastrophe. Our conduct and our policy are prompted not only by our principles and morality, but also by the fact that we understand that any other approach is unrealistic. This is why I went to Paris and to Geneva. This is why the Soviet Union has put forward a large number of major initiatives. This is why we set out immediately after Geneva to translate the accords achieved there and the Joint Statement into practical actions:

We extended our unilateral moratorium on nuclear explosions two times and offered immediately to begin talks on ending nuclear tests altogether;

—at the Vienna and Stockholm conferences we put forward compromise proposals, meeting the West halfway;

—another major initiative was our Statement of January 15, which contains a concrete and clear plan for the elimination of weapons of mass destruction and for reductions in other weapons to limits that are adequate for defensive purposes;

—we took into account the anxiety of Europeans about medium-range missiles and tactical nuclear weapons and came up with a compromise option for the European zone;

—we suggested the mutual withdrawal of the Soviet and U.S. navies from the Mediterranean; the 27th CPSU Congress not only approved all these measures, but also formulated basic principles for establishing a comprehensive international security system.

But what about those in the West, on whom putting an end to the arms race and improving the international climate also depend directly? What has their attitude been since Geneva? What is their policy? To begin with, we have not received a satisfactory reply to the Statement of January 15, and what they have sent us avoids the heart of the matter and attempts to make do with half-measures and to mislead the world public with vague promises.

As for a reply on the substance of the Statement, it is being provided by the actions of the United States and by the real policy of NATO. In Geneva both sides agreed that just as in the nuclear arms race, there could be no winners in a nuclear war. But when we put forward a simple and clear, stage-by-stage plan for the reduction and elimination of nuclear arsenals, we were told: "No!"

Or another example: over the years they have kept harping that the Russians cannot be trusted because they do not permit on-site inspections. We have agreed to such inspections. In response, President Reagan offers us to "verify" not a ban on nuclear explosions but a procedure for improving nuclear weapons. As an American newspaper aptly remarked the other day, this is the same as asking a man advocating the abolition of capital punishment to witness an execution.

We, naturally, have not accepted and will not accept such an offer. We put the matter differently: let us discuss both our proposal on ending explosions and the American proposal on verification. The only thing that the U.S. Administration seems to have retained from Geneva is talk about a new meeting between the U.S. President and the General Secretary of the CPSU Central Committee. To make the matter absolutely clear I shall say once again: I'm for holding such a meeting. We set no preconditions for it. But we want it to take place in accordance with what the President and I agreed upon, namely, that it should mark a *step forward*, that is, produce *practical* results toward ending the arms race.

One more thing. Our meeting can take place if the atmosphere of Geneva is preserved, or it would be more correct today to say *revived*. Just look at what is taking place. Soon after Geneva, an anti-Soviet campaign, full of every type of fabrication and insults to our country, was relaunched with a vengeance in the United States.

Subsequently, more serious matters have arisen, namely, the demand that the Soviet Union reduce the number of its diplomats in New York by 40 percent. An American naval squadron appeared off the shores of the Crimea—and they did not conceal the fact that the action was sanctioned by the top authorities. An attack was launched against Libya to show America's might and to demonstrate that it was at liberty to do whatever it wished. A high-yield nuclear explosion was carried out in Nevada with an obviously provocative purpose just before our moratorium expired. And when I proposed a meeting without delay concerning just one but truly urgent question, that of nuclear explosions, it took less than a day to answer: "No!"

Do the people in Washington think that they are dealing with chickenhearts? Do they believe that today it is possible to behave like reckless gamblers? Is this how they in the U.S.A. understand the spirit of Geneva? Do they think that we do not see how the Soviet-American dialogue that has just been started is being misused to cover up the fulfillment of military programs? All this makes us wonder what content and what meaning Washington is imparting to a new Soviet-American meeting.

And what about Western Europe? In reply to our proposals, which also meet the wishes of the European public and many governments, they are now saying: the American missiles cannot be removed from Europe because the Soviet Union has a greater supply of conventional weapons. But our January Statement unambiguously offers reductions in conventional weapons and armed forces.

They also say another thing: the U.S.A. will have to remove the missiles across the ocean, while Moscow will merely ship them to Siberia, from which they can easily and promptly be brought back. In saying this, they pretend not to know that the USSR offers to *eliminate* these missiles, rather than ship them anywhere. In sum, they stand for peace in words, but for missiles in deeds. No, neither Britain nor France has demonstrated a serious approach in this respect.

Consider the attitude to the Strategic Defense Initiative. The West European governments and big businesses are using all sorts of pretexts for getting increasingly more involved in that disastrous plan, and they are thus becoming participants in a new, even more dangerous round of the arms race.

A final, and perhaps, the most essential point. The U.S.A. is putting its Star Wars program into full gear. The President claims that this is a defensive and nonnuclear program. But the general, who heads that project, describes in public how the space weapon will be able to hit the enemy on earth, while the U.S. Secretary of Defense says that it includes nuclear components.

Let me state frankly: If, contrary to common sense, the U.S.A. persists in pursuing this policy, we shall find a convincing response, and not necessarily in outer space. We well know the potentials of contemporary science, our own potentials. There is nothing that the U.S.A. can do and we cannot. Yet we are against such an option, we are against the absurd American logic on armament. To us, a ban on space-strike weapons *does not pose the problem of fearing to lag behind, but that of responsibility.*

I wish to say the following in this connection: it is high time to give up trying to build relations with the USSR on the basis of erroneous concepts, on illusions. One of the most dangerous illusions is to consider the Soviet Union's peaceful intentions and proposals as a sign of weakness. And so: the arms race will not wear us out, we cannot be taken from outer space, and shall not be outdone in technology. Nothing good will come of these attempts.

As can be seen from the numerous letters pouring into the

Central Committee, not a few Soviet people are concerned whether it might happen that under cover of peace talks and fruitless negotiations the West will make a spurt in the arms race to which we shall not have enough time to react. I can assure you, comrades, that this is not going to happen. We can see very well the difference between words and deeds. The Soviet Union builds its policy with due regard for the whole totality of real factors. We shall not be taken by surprise. The Soviet state has proved repeatedly that it is able to meet any challenge. If need be, it will give a fitting answer this time, too. We do not lay claims to a greater security, as the 27th Congress stressed, but we shall not agree to a lesser security either.

Certainly, nobody expected that the implementation of our program to advance toward peace without wars and weapons would proceed smoothly, like a Zhiguli car driving down a good asphalt road. We are in for a long and tough struggle. Not only detente, but even a warming-up in Soviet-American relations does not suit certain circles. They are trying to find any pretext to frustrate an improvement of the international situation, which began to manifest itself after Geneva. And the whole world knows the identity of these circles. They are the circles associated with the business of manufacturing arms, those who work for the military-industrial complex which sends its representatives to the upper echelons of power and takes them back after they have loyally served its aims there. They are those who earn billions on the arms race and confrontation.

At our Congress we outlined the main directions in the struggle against nuclear war. And we shall act consistently and perseveringly. Our potential is considerable.

Our true friends—the socialist countries—support us in this great effort. We have a special responsibility toward them, that is, our common responsibility for the destiny of socialism. It is very important that we pursue the policy of peace jointly, coordinating our strategy for the future and each important step toward peace.

A majority of the world community supports preserving peace, including the governments and peoples of the non-aligned countries, of the Third World, and the working people of the capitalist countries.

We want to preserve the achievements of Paris and Geneva. We shall not let ourselves be provoked, nor shall we pour fuel on the bonfire of the cold war which is currently being kindled. One should not play politics in this nuclear age.

We shall count on the common sense of the working people of all countries, the common sense of ordinary people, the growing sense of self-preservation, the awareness of new realities by political figures and parties, including those in the NATO countries.

As for us, we must always remember: carrying out the tasks of perfecting socialist society is the main front on which the success of the struggle for peace is ensured. The state of our national economy, the development of science and engineering, a qualitative restructuring of the economy, and the building up of the spiritual, intellectual, and moral potential of the Soviet state are of decisive significance. In the final count, it all depends on the work put in by every one of us. In a word, a strong, healthy economy ensures success to the policy of peace. That is where foreign policy and domestic policy link up.

IX

TELEVISED SPEECH
On the Reactor Accident at Chernobyl

Moscow, May 14, 1986

Good evening, comrades,

As you all know, a misfortune has befallen us—the accident at the Chernobyl nuclear power plant. It has painfully affected Soviet people and has caused anxiety in the international public. For the first time ever, we have had to deal in practice with a force as sinister as nuclear energy, which has escaped control.

Considering the extraordinary and dangerous nature of what has happened at Chernobyl, the Politburo has taken into its hands the entire organization of work aimed at ensuring the speediest cleanup of the accident and minimizing its consequences.

A government commission was formed and immediately left for the scene of the accident, while at the Politburo a group was formed under Nikolai Ivanovich Ryzhkov to solve urgent problems.

All work is actually proceeding on a round-the-clock basis. The scientific, technical, and economic potentials of the entire country have been put to use. Operating in the area of the accident are organizations of many Union ministries and agencies that are under the guidance of ministers, as well as prominent scientists and specialists, units of the Soviet Army and the Ministry of Internal Affairs.

A huge share of the work and responsibility has been taken on by the Party, government, and economic bodies of the Ukraine and Byelorussia. The operating staff of the Chernobyl nuclear power plant are working selflessly and courageously.

So, what happened?

According to specialists, the reactor's capacity suddenly increased during a scheduled shutdown of the fourth unit. The considerable emission of steam and the subsequent reaction led to the formation of hydrogen, an explosion, damage to the reactor, and the resulting radioactive discharge.

It is still too early to pass final judgment on the causes of
the accident. All aspects of the problem—design, construction, technical, and operational—are under the close
scrutiny of the government commission. It goes without saying that once the investigation of the causes of the accident is
completed, all necessary conclusions will be drawn and measures will be taken to rule out a repetition of anything of the
sort.

As I have said already, this is the first time that we have
encountered such an emergency, when it was necessary
quickly to curb the dangerous force of the atom, which had
escaped from control, and to keep the scale of the accident to
a minimum.

The seriousness of the situation was obvious. It was necessary to evaluate it quickly and competently. And as soon as we
received reliable initial information, it was made available to
Soviet people and sent through diplomatic channels to the
governments of other countries.

On the basis of this information practical work was begun
to clean up the accident and minimize its grave consequences.

In the resulting situation we considered it our top priority
duty, a duty of special importance, to ensure the safety of the
population and to provide effective assistance to those who
had been affected by the accident. The inhabitants of the
settlement near the station were evacuated within a matter of
hours and then, when it became clear that there was a potential threat to the health of people in the adjoining zone, they
too were moved to safe areas. All of this complex work required the utmost speed, organization, and precision.

Nevertheless, the measures that were taken failed to protect many people. Two of them died at the moment of the
accident—Vladimir Nikolayevich Shashenok, an adjuster of
automatic systems, and Valery Ivanovich Khodemchuk, an
operator in the nuclear power station. As of today, 299 people
have been hospitalized, diagnosed as having radiation sick-
ness of a varying degree of gravity. Seven of them have died.
Every possible form of treatment is being given to the others.
The best scientific and medical specialists of the country,
specialized clinics in Moscow and other cities are taking part.

They have the most modern means of medicine at their disposal.

On behalf of the CPSU Central Committee and the Soviet Government, I express our profound condolences to the families and relatives of the deceased, to the work collectives, to all who have suffered from this misfortune, who have been struck by personal loss. The Soviet government will take care of the families of those who died and other victims of the accident.

The inhabitants of the areas that heartily welcomed the evacuees deserve the highest praise. They responded to the misfortune of their neighbors as if it were their own and, in the best traditions of our people, showed consideration, responsiveness, and attention.

The CPSU Central Committee and the Soviet Government are receiving thousands upon thousands of letters and telegrams from Soviet people and also from foreign citizens expressing sympathy and support for the victims. Many Soviet families are prepared to take children into their homes for the summer and are offering material help. There are numerous requests from people asking to be sent to work in the area of the accident.

These demonstrations of humaneness, genuine humanism, and high moral standards cannot but move every one of us.

I repeat, assistance to people remains our top priority task.

At the same time intensive work is under way at the station itself and in the adjacent territory to minimize the scale of the accident. Under the most difficult conditions the fire was extinguished and prevented from speading to the other power units. The staff of the station shut down the three other reactors and brought them under control. They are under constant observation.

A stern test has been passed and continues to be passed by all—firemen, transport and building workers, medics, special chemical protection units, helicopter crews, and other detachments of the Ministry of Defense and the Ministry of Internal Affairs.

In these difficult conditions much depended on a correct, scientific evaluation of what was happening, because without such an evaluation it would have been impossible to work out and apply effective measures for coping with the accident and its consequences. Our prominent specialists from the Academy of Sciences, leading specialists from union ministries and agencies as well as in the Ukraine and Byelorussia are successfully dealing with this task.

I must say that people have acted and are continuing to act heroically, selflessly. I believe we shall have an opportunity to name these courageous people and to assess the value of their exploit.

I have every reason to say that despite the full gravity of what has happened, the damage turned out to be limited. To a decisive degree this is due to the courage and skill of our people, their loyalty to duty, the concerted manner in which everybody taking part in eliminating the consequences of the accident is acting.

This task, comrades, is being solved not only in the area of the nuclear power station itself, but also in research institutes, and at many of the enterprises in our country that are supplying everything necessary to those who are directly engaged in the difficult and dangerous struggle to cope with the accident.

Thanks to the effective measures taken, today it is possible to say that the worst is over. The most serious consequences have been averted. Of course, the event is not over yet. We cannot rest content. Extensive and long work still lies ahead. The level of radiation in the station's zone and in the territory in the immediate vicinity still remains dangerous to human health.

As of today, therefore, the top priority task is to eliminate the consequences of the accident. A large-scale program for the decontamination of the territory of the electric power station and the settlement, of buildings and structures, has been drawn up and is being implemented. The necessary manpower, material and technical resources have been concentrated for that purpose. In order to prevent the radioactive contamination of the water basin, measures are being taken at the site of the station and in the adjacent territory.

Organizations of the meteorological service are constantly monitoring the radiation levels on the ground, in the water and atmosphere. They have the necessary technical facilities at their disposal and are using specially equipped planes, helicopters, and monitoring stations.

It is absolutely clear—all these operations will take much time and will require no small efforts. They should be carried out meticulously, in a planned and organized manner. The area must be restored to a condition that is absolutely safe for the health and normal life of people.

I cannot fail to mention one more aspect of the affair. I am referring to the reaction abroad to what happened at Chernobyl. In the world as a whole, and this should be emphasized, the misfortune that befell us and our actions in that complicated situation were treated with understanding.

We are profoundly grateful to our friends in socialist countries who have shown solidarity with the Soviet people at a difficult moment. We are grateful to the political and public figures in other states for their sincere sympathy and support.

We express our kind feelings to those foreign scientists and specialists who showed their readiness to assist us in overcoming the consequences of the accident. I would like to note the participation of the American doctors Robert Gale and Paul Tarasaki in treating affected persons and to express gratitude to the business circles of those countries that promptly reacted to our request for the purchase of certain types of equipment, materials, and medicines.

We are grateful for the objective attitude to the events at the Chernobyl nuclear power plant that was shown by the International Atomic Energy Agency (IAEA) and its Director-General Hans Blix.

In other words, we highly appreciate the sympathy of all those who responded to our misfortune and our problems with an open heart.

But it is impossible to ignore and not to assess politically the way the event at Chernobyl was treated by the governments, political figures, and the mass media in certain NATO countries, especially the U.S.A.

An unrestrained anti-Soviet campaign was launched. It is difficult to imagine what was said and written these days— "thousands of casualties," "mass graves of the dead," "Kiev desolate," and "the entire land of the Ukraine poisoned," and so on and so forth.

Generally speaking, we faced a veritable mountain of lies—most brazen and malicious lies. It is unpleasant to recall all this, but it must be done. The international public should know what we had to face. It must be done to find the answer to the question: what, in fact, was behind this highly immoral campaign? Its organizers, to be sure, were not interested in either true information about the accident or the fate of the people at Chernobyl, in the Ukraine, in Byelorussia, in any other place or country. They were looking for a pretext to exploit in order to try to defame the Soviet Union and its foreign policy, to lessen the impact of Soviet proposals on the termination of nuclear tests and on the elimination of nuclear weapons, and, at the same time, to dampen the growing criticism of the U. S. conduct on the international scene and of its militaristic course.

Bluntly speaking, certain Western politicians were after quite definite aims—to wreck the possibilities for balancing international relations, to sow new seeds of mistrust and suspicion toward the socialist countries.

All this was made completely clear during the meeting of the leaders of "the Seven" held in Tokyo not so long ago. What did they tell the world, what dangers did they warn humanity of? Of Libya, groundlessly accused of terrorism, and of the Soviet Union, which, it turns out, failed to provide them with "full" information about the accident of Chernobyl. But not a word about the most important issue—how to stop the arms race, how to rid the world of the nuclear threat. Not a word in reply to the Soviet initiatives, to our specific proposals on the termination of nuclear tests, on ridding mankind of nuclear and chemical weapons, on reducing conventional arms.

How should all this be interpreted? One involuntarily gets the impression that the leaders of the capitalist powers gathered in Tokyo wanted to use Chernobyl as a pretext for distracting the attention of the world public from all those problems that make them uncomfortable, but are so real and important for the whole world.

The accident at the Chernobyl station and the reaction to it have become a kind of test of political morality. Once again two different approaches, two different lines of conduct were revealed for everyone to see.

The ruling circles of the U. S. A. and their most zealous allies—in particular the FRG—regarded the mishap only as another chance to put up additional obstacles impeding the development and deepening of the current East-West dialogue, progressing slowly as it is, and to justify the nuclear arms race. What is more, an attempt has been made to prove to the world that talks, and, particularly, more agreements with the USSR are impossible, and thereby to give the green light to further military preparations.

Our attitude to this tragedy is absolutely different. We realize that it is another sound of the tocsin, another grim warning that the nuclear era necessitates a new political thinking and a new policy.

This has strengthened our conviction still more that the foreign policy course worked out by the 27th CPSU Congress is correct and that our proposals for the complete elimination of nuclear weapons, the ending of nucler explosions, the creation of an all-embracing system of international security meet those inexorably stringent demands that the nuclear age makes on the political leadership of all countries.

As to the "lack" of information, around which a special campaign with a political content and nature has been launched, in the given case this matter is an invented one. The following facts confirm that this is so. It is well known that it took the U.S. authorities 10 days to inform their own Congress and months to inform the world community about the tragedy that took place at the Three Mile Island atomic power station in 1979.

I have already said how we acted.

All this makes it possible to judge those persons and the way they choose to inform their own people and foreign countries.

But the essence of the matter is different. We hold that the accident at Chernobyl, just as the accidents at U. S., British and other atomic power stations, poses to all states very serious problems which require a responsible attitude.

Over 370 atomic reactors now function in different countries. This is reality. The future of the world economy is virtually unimaginable without the development of atomic power. Altogether 40 reactors with an aggregate capacity of over 28 million kilowatts now operate in our country. As is known, humankind derives a considerable benefit from atoms for peace.

But it stands to reason that we are all obliged to act with even greater caution, and to concentrate the efforts of science and technology to ensure the safe harnessing of the great and formidable powers contained in the atomic nucleus.

To us, the indisputable lesson of Chernobyl is that in the course of the further development of the scientific and technical revolution the question of equipment reliability and safety, the question of discipline, order and organization, assume priority importance. Everywhere and in everything the most stringent demands are needed.

Further, we deem it necessary to support a serious deepening of cooperation in the framework of the International Atomic Energy Agency (IAEA). What steps could be considered in this connection?

First, creating an international system for the safe development of nuclear power based on the close cooperation of all nations dealing with nuclear power engineering. A system of prompt warning and supply of information in the event of accidents or faults at nuclear power stations, specifically when this is accompanied by radioactive emissions, should be established in the structure of this regime. Likewise it is necessary to organize an international mechanism, both on a bilateral and multilateral basis, for the speediest rendering of mutual assistance when dangerous situations emerge.

Second, for the discussion of the entire range of matters it would be justifiable to convene a highly authoritative specialized international conference in Vienna under the IAEA auspices.

Third, in view of the fact that the IAEA was founded back in 1957 and that its resources and staff are not in keeping with the level of the development of present-day nuclear power engineering, it would be expedient to enhance the role and capabilities of that unique international organization. The Soviet Union is ready for this.

Fourth, we believe that the United Nations Organization and its specialized institutions, such as the World Health Organization (WHO) and the United Nations Environment Program (UNEP), should be more actively involved in the effort to ensure safe development of peaceful nuclear activity.

For all this, it should not be forgotten that in our world, where everything is interrelated, alongside the problems of atoms for peace, there also exist the problems of atoms for war. This is the major issue of today. The accident at Chernobyl showed again what an abyss will open if nuclear war befalls mankind. For inherent in the stockpiled nuclear arsenals are thousands upon thousands of disasters far more horrible than the Chernobyl one.

At a time of increased attention to nuclear matters, and after having considered all circumstances connected with the security of its people and all humanity, the Soviet Government has decided to extend its unilateral moratorium on nuclear tests till August 6 of this year, the date on which more than 40 years ago the first atomic bomb was dropped on the Japanese city of Hiroshima, resulting in the death of hundreds of thousands of people.

We again urge the United States to consider most responsibly the measure of danger looming over humanity, and to heed the opinion of the world community. Let the leaders of the United States show their concern for the life and health of people by deeds.

I reiterate my proposal to President Reagan to meet without delay in the capital of any European state that is prepared to accept us or, say, in Hiroshima, in order to reach agreement on a ban on nuclear testing.

The nuclear age forcefully demands a new approach to international relations, the pooling of efforts of states with different social systems for the sake of putting an end to the disastrous arms race and of a radical improvement of the world political climate. Broad horizons will then be cleared for the fruitful cooperation of all countries and peoples. This will benefit all people on earth!

X

MEETING
With Armand Hammer and Robert Gale

Moscow, May 15, 1986

On May 15 Mikhail Gorbachev received in the Kremlin the prominent American industrialist and public figure Armand Hammer, and Robert Gale, a physician.

The Soviet leader expressed deep gratitude for the compassion and understanding displayed by them and for their prompt concrete assistance in connection with the misfortune that has befallen the Soviet people—the accident at the Chernobyl nuclear power plant. Their noble deed reflected the sentiments of many rank-and-file Americans and public figures who are now sending sincere, moving letters and telegrams to Moscow, some of which Mikhail Gorbachev showed to Armand Hammer and Robert Gale.

The Soviet people view what Armand Hammer and Robert Gale have done as an example of how relations between the two great peoples should be built, given the political wisdom and will to do so by the leadership of both countries.

Deeply disappointing, however, is the way Washington has been acting during these difficult days. It has made shameful speculations on the accident and gross attempts to use it to discredit the entire policy of the Soviet Union and to sow mistrust toward its peace initiatives. The people will make their own assessments of the position taken by everyone in the face of this tragedy and, we hope, will draw the right conclusions: primarily that it is necessary to redouble, to increase tenfold the efforts to put an end to nuclear tests, eliminate nuclear weapons, and ensure reliable international cooperation in the peaceful uses of atomic energy.

Mikhail Gorbachev informed Mr. Hammer and Dr. Gale that the situation in the disaster area had been brought under control and that people there were working selflessly and heroically. The entire potential of Soviet science, he said, was brought into play effectively to eliminate the aftermath of the accident and to learn everything that should be learned.

Stressing that human life was the most valuable thing, Mikhail Gorbachev said that now the top priority was to help the people who were affected by the accident, and that the main concern of the Soviet state was to do its best to protect and rehabilitate their health and make up for the damage they suffered.

Responding to a question from Mikhail Gorbachev about the treatment of the accident victims, Dr. Gale related what had already been done and what could still be done and spoke highly of the work of his colleagues—Soviet physicians. He emphasized that everyone in the world should now realize that if a nuclear war breaks out, medicine will not be able to help, and it will simply be of no use to anyone.

During the conversation, Armand Hammer raised the question of a Soviet-U.S. summit meeting. Mikhail Gorbachev confirmed his consent in principle to a new meeting and repeated that two simple things are needed for it: a readiness to produce a tangible practical result, if only in one or two matters of concern to the whole world, and an appropriate political atmosphere.

As concerns the first thing, the Soviet leader stressed that the meeting cannot be held to an American script, adding that this apparently is what the Soviet Union is expected to agree to. Nor will the meeting be held to a Soviet script, Mikhail Gorbachev continued, stressing that a common platform must be sought that is oriented toward concrete results. Referring to the political atmosphere, he noted that it had grown even worse as a result of the vicious anti-Soviet campaign that Washington launched in connection with the Chernobyl accident.

At the conclusion of the warm and frank conversation, Mikhail Gorbachev thanked Armand Hammer and Dr. Gale once again.

Anatoly Dobrynin, Secretary of the CPSU Central Committee, also took part in the conversation.

XI

MEETING
With British Members of
Parliament

Moscow, May 26, 1986

On May 26 Mikhail Gorbachev, General Secretary of the CPSU Central Committee, received a British parliamentary delegation made up of representatives of all the parliamentary parties, including the Labour "shadow" foreign secretary Denis Healey, and led by Lord Whitelaw.

A personal message from Prime Minister Margaret Thatcher was passed on to Mikhail Gorbachev by Lord Whitelaw.

In the course of a frank and friendly conversation, the two sides explained their positions on a broad range of outstanding international issues and on Soviet-British relations.

Both sides agreed that it was necessary to stop the arms race and to look for mutually acceptable solutions to other questions of general concern to humankind in today's complex, diverse, controversial but interrelated world. Mikhail Gorbachev noted that this calls for a new way of thinking, one that respects the realities of the nuclear and space age. International security, he continued, cannot be built by proceeding from your own interests while ignoring the security interests of others, and no serious talks are possible with such an approach.

The Soviet leader pointed out the great opportunities for expanding fruitful political dialogue and economic and cultural relations, for parliamentary exchanges and for human contacts between the two countries, and noted that the hopes that arose in these fields 18 months ago are still to be fulfilled.

Various aspects of the problem of ending nuclear tests, to the solution of which Britain could make a substantial contribution, were discussed at the meeting. It was suggested that the sides consider a joint Soviet-British initiative on resuming the tripartite talks that were broken off in 1980, especially since at that time the USSR, the U.S.A. and Britain had agreed that nuclear weapons tests should be banned. There was also an exchange of opinions on a chemical weapon ban. Well-founded argumented replies were given on all issues of disarmament and verification that were consonant with the Soviet position. As for reducing conventional armaments, Mikhail Gorbachev said that the Warsaw Treaty countries would propose a detailed draft agenda for such talks in the near future.

The situation around Afghanistan and in the Middle East, and humanitarian issues were also touched upon.

While discussing nuclear missiles in Europe, Mikhail Gorbachev made a new proposal. If Britain takes an official decision to eliminate its nuclear weapons, the Soviet Union will be prepared to reduce its nuclear potential accordingly. If Britain also removes foreign nuclear weapons from its territory, the Soviet Union will guarantee that its nuclear weapons will not be targeted at British territory and will never be used against Britain. The entire package of issues arising in this context, he said, could become a subject for discussion and working out of agreed-upon decisions by the two countries.

Mikhail Gorbachev, when asked about a new meeting with the U.S. President, outlined the Soviet approach. The Soviet Union, he said, is for such a meeting and does not put forward any preconditions. This meeting should tackle the major issues of concern to the whole world and take decisions that will strengthen international security, build trust and help curb the arms race. He went on to say that the meeting should take place in an atmosphere consonant with the character of the Geneva accords rather than in one that contradicts them. He emphasized that dialogue cannot go on endlessly with nothing being decided, that the meeting cannot be used as a cover for a buildup in armaments. The Soviet Union does not agree to this. Its approach is related to what it has been prompted to by practice and to what is expected of it by the peoples.

When the West presents Soviet disarmament initiatives and the Soviet Union's persevering efforts toward detente as

"Moscow's intrigues," as being propagandist, utopian, or a manifestation of weakness, the Soviet leader continued, it is viewed in the Soviet Union as a sign of narrow-mindedness and inability to understand the real state of affairs in the contemporary world. The crux of the matter is that the Soviet Union is aware of its high responsibility for the fate of civilization.

Mikhail Gorbachev thanked the parliamentarians for their sympathy and assistance in connection with the Chernobyl accident and asked that this be conveyed to the British people along with his best wishes.

Lord Whitelaw spoke highly of the character and content of the conversation, thanked the host for his hospitality and noted that such discussions and other contacts lead to greater mutual respect and broader cooperation.

THE FIVE-YEAR PLAN: 1986–1990

The Economic and Social
Development of the USSR and
the Tasks of Party Organizations
in Carrying It Out

Moscow, June 16, 1986

Comrades,

Today we will discuss the progress made in carrying out the general policy line determined by the Congress, sum up the preliminary results, draw the lessons from our post-Congress work and define the immediate tasks of the Party.

Little time has passed since the Congress. However, the responsibility of the moment and the scale of the tasks facing society today are so great that we must constantly feel the pulse of changes and check our intentions and plans against the way things are actually going. In other words, we will discuss the most important problems at the moment, how the energy of our plans is being translated into the energy of our actions, what problems and difficulties have arisen and how we should act further.

The 27th Congress of the CPSU set all spheres of Soviet society—political, economic and spiritual—in motion. Social development was given a strong dynamic impetus which stimulated political awareness of the masses. The atmosphere of exactingness and truthfulness which prevailed at the Congress is exerting a mobilizing influence on all practical work. Soviet people meet with enthusiasm and support innovative projects and demand that reorganization should be universal and be carried out in a businesslike manner. All this shows that the ideas of the Congress are becoming firmly implanted in people's minds and are an objective guarantee that the ongoing changes are irreversible.

Today we are even more convinced than before that the decisions we adopted at the Congress are correct and in keeping with the fact that we are living at the critical time. They have a special part to play in the destiny of this country and of socialism in general, and this will have far-reaching consequences for the development of the whole world. We realize better and to a fuller extent the scale and depth of the changes initiated by the Party and all sorts of difficulties we must overcome. We also understand better what our possibilities are today and what possibilities we will have in future.

The interest of other countries in the Congress does not abate. It is especially keen in the socialist countries. The Congress's decisions gave a powerful impetus to the struggle for peace and social progress. Approval and support from our friends convince us that we are going the right way. They also remind us that we have great responsibility for following this course consistently and purposefully.

Sober-minded people in the nonsocialist part of the world could see once again that our extensive plans for social and economic development are inseparably linked with a foreign policy which is aimed at promoting peace and all-round international economic cooperation.

Our plans evoked a different reaction from the militarist and aggressive forces led by U.S. reactionary circles. Their animosity is particularly strong now that they are waging a struggle against the Soviet proposals on ways of improving the international situation and shaping international relations that would be adequate to the realities of the nuclear and space age.

In short, comrades, we will be discussing key problems of the five-year plan, taking into account both domestic needs and external conditions. The plan is the basis for our work in the immediate years ahead and over a longer period.

At this stage of work since the Congress we must show an ability to reorganize and build, seek new forms and methods, and not allow success to go to our heads even for a moment. Fast economic growth rates, high efficiency and major positive changes in the social field are now becoming the main yardstick for assessing performance. We will be judged not by our intentions alone, but primarily by real changes in society, by practical results.

I. THE FIRST RESULTS OF REORGANIZATION

Comrades, it is from the point of view of practical work and results that we must assess the activities of all Party committees, government and economic agencies, public organizations and work collectives.

This approach will enable us not only to find our bearings in the current situation but to proceed further. We must do this also because, as experience shows, we are dealing not only with positive trends, which, of course, are predominant in society, but also with factors which hinder the reorganization process. Some of these factors are objective, but most of them are due to sluggishness, bad habits and outdated psychology.

People who are exerting themselves today are those who strongly supported the stand of the 27th Congress and became actively involved in the common effort, who do not spare either time or energy and are contributing to the process of reorganization. However, there are quite a few people who, while realizing the political need to work in a new way, simply do not know how to do this in practice. We must help them in every way possible. We must also realize that there are still people who have not grasped the essence of the changes that are under way, who take a wait-and-see position or simply do not believe that the economic and political breakthrough charted by the Party can be successfully carried out.

The Congress's directive on encouraging the creative activity of the masses as the basis of accelerated growth is having a profound influence on our society. It is closely related to the drive for social justice, greater democracy and complete openness, and for ridding society of all manifestations of petty-bourgeois psychology. Soviet people are showing a growing interest in politics and economics, culture and morality, in public life in general. And this is having an important effect on labor and political activity, discipline and order in the country.

Soviet people have also demonstrated extraordinary organizational abilities and patriotism in emergencies, as was the case with the Chernobyl accident. The breakdown at the atomic power station was a severe trial. At that difficult time workers, firemen, engineers, physicians, scientists, and soldiers displayed great fortitude, courage, and selflessness.

The country has risen as one to combat the consequences of the accident. The CPSU Central Committee and local Party and government organizations are flooded with letters from people who want to be sent to Chernobyl. An extensive fund-raising campaign has been launched to help the families affected by the accident. Many work collectives have pledged to work several shifts free of charge in order to help them.

Allow me on behalf of our Plenary Meeting to convey deep condolences to the bereaved families, and cordially thank all those who, risking their lives, did everything they could to contain the accident and who are working selflessly today to eliminate its consequences.

Comrades, we are faced with complex tasks in all sectors of social and economic advancement. Of course, it would be naive to think that it would take us only a few months to overcome the lag and shortcomings that have accumulated over years. However, a trend toward higher rates of economic growth is now apparent. We attribute this mostly to the hard work of the people and the positive processes taking place in society.

In the first five months of this year industrial production rose by 5.7 percent compared to the same period last year. There are also positive changes in sectors which have been lagging behind for many years, i.e., in the mining, iron-and-steel industries, and in railway transport. The timber, wood-working, cellulose, and paper industries are performing better. Workers of the oil industry have not yet overcome their difficulties. However, encouraging trends are evident there too. A number of branches of mechanical engineering are developing rapidly. Intense work is also under way in the agricultural sector.

In many regions and areas of the Russian Federation, the Ukraine, Byelorussia, the Baltic Republics and elsewhere the active work carried out by Party, government and economic organizations and work collectives shows what we can achieve if we encourage initiative and foster creative and businesslike attitudes at workplaces.

The main thing now is to consolidate the rates of growth already achieved and then to increase them. This is feasible, but it would require major efforts since we are at the very start of restructuring, when not everything that needs to be done organizationally has been done, and when the economic levers and incentives crucial for further economic change for the better have not yet swung into full action.

An analysis of economic changes would be far from complete if, along with obvious successes, we fail to note the weak points, the things which impede our advance. I must say that reorganization is still taking place too slowly. Many enterprises still rely on rush work and abide by the old slogan of "fulfilling plans no matter what." The turn to quality, efficiency and new management methods is a difficult and painful process. However, it should be absolutely clear that the Central Committee will firmly support all that is sound and is in keeping with the decisions of the Congress, all that promotes reorganization and the movement forward. We will be just as firm in combating all that stands in the way of this process.

That which is new that was initiated by the April Plenary Meeting and further elaborated in the decisions of the 27th Congress, calls for a profound restructuring not only of the economic sphere, but of society as a whole. This is no simple process. It requires efforts and serious changes in the mentality of our cadres, of all working people. We have succeeded in overcoming passive attitudes to some extent, increasing responsibility, improving organization and giving more room to initiative. At the same time, the restructuring process is not yet smooth enough at enterprises, in the field of management, in research institutions, artistic collectives, and in the work of Party and government bodies. Old ways of doing things and inertia are slowing down progress.

Sometimes words are substituted for deeds, no practical action is taken following criticisms, and self-criticism resembles self-flagellation. Some managers are lavish in issuing appeals for openness and publicity, they quite correctly speak about the important role of the work collective, and about promoting democratic principles. Regrettably, it all stops at that. Restructuring becomes a mere illusion: everything is all right in words, but there is no real change—and the restructuring process marks time.

The post-Congress period has shown that the complicated structure and inefficient performance of our management bodies considerably hamper our progress and the introduction of new management methods. The redistribution of rights and responsibilities between the central economic bodies and ministries, on the one hand, and enterprises, production associations and work collectives, on the other, has proved to be a painful process.

Even though the functions of management bodies have

changed, some officials try to hold on to their leadership position at all cost. Still, no ministry, no central office, however efficient, can successfully solve every problem, given today's large-scale economy, and replace the creative search of work collectives. That simple truth has to be brought home to everybody.

A blind faith in the omnipotence of management bodies is reflected in the fact that the central bodies still receive requests to set up more and more management bodies and appoint more and more staff members. Some republics try, quite unjustifiably, to copy the central management structures and have asked the USSR Council of Ministers for permission to set up new ministries and other central departments, though they have already 50 or more ministries, central departments and other management bodies.

The past few months have clearly shown that it is impossible to carry out social restructuring without changing the style and methods of Party work at every level. Those matters should be discussed in detail, and I shall return to them later.

Now, I should like to stress the tremendously important role of the leaders of Party bodies in asserting the new style. The consistent and vigorous reorganization of Party work depends on the position they take, on their behavior and work.

In this connection I have to call special attention to the part played by the first secretaries of the Central Committees of the Communist Parties of the Union Republics, of territorial and regional Party committees, and, last but not least, of city and district Party committees. They must set the tone at work, show political insight and a profound understanding of the tasks at hand, have organizational abilities and a sense of responsibility, and be able to assess their own and others' work critically—in a word, they must display the Party spirit in the loftiest sense. Only then can a district, city, region or republic hope to achieve good results in their work and create an atmosphere of constructive search and endeavor.

Comrades, what are the main conclusions to be drawn from our work in the first months after the Congress?

The main thing is that the Party and the people actively support the Congress's political line. The Party reorganizes itself as it organizes and rallies the working people. The past few months have once again demonstrated that restructuring is everybody's concern, from a rank-and-file Communist to a Central Committee secretary, from a shop-floor worker to a minister, from an engineer to an academician. We can accomplish this task only if it truly becomes a national concern. We have to overcome every obstacle in its way.

Another important conclusion. There is no replacing people's creative initiative with instructions, even the best of them. Restructuring presupposes the all-round encouragement of independence and initiative by work collectives and by every worker. Today it is inadmissible—and practically impossible—to solve all questions at the center. Everybody has to realize that. Work collectives at enterprises and associations have to shoulder most of the responsibility for day-to-day decision-making. As to creating the necessary economic, legal and social conditions for fruitful work, for progress in science and technology, that is strictly the obligation of central management bodies.

And lastly, the time that has elapsed after the Congress, and the latest developments, have clearly confirmed the vital importance of the lesson of truth of which the Congress participants spoke. In all situations, we should remember Lenin's warning: "Illusions and self-deceptions are terrible, the fear of truth is pernicious." The Party and the people need the whole truth, in big things and small. Only the truth instills in people an acute sense of civic duty. Lies and half-truths produce warped mentality, deform the personality and prevent one from making realistic conclusions and evaluations without which an active Party policy is inconceivable.

II. DECISIVE STAGE IN THE IMPLEMENTATION OF THE PARTY'S ECONOMIC STRATEGY

Comrades, we will now discuss the new five-year plan and the tasks which the Party and all working people must carry out in order to fulfill that plan.

The 12th Five-Year Plan has a special role to play. The rates of socioeconomic development and the level of people's well-being will depend on the foundation which we will lay over the coming years for the implementation of radical reforms in the national economy, and on the acceleration of scientific and technological progress.

As you know, the drafting of the new five-year plan has not been easy. As calculations show, the old methods of management and dead-stop planning were only leading our economy into a dead end. For a whole year we had persistently sought new approaches which would create the conditions for deepening the process of production intensification and ensure more rapid introduction of the latest achievements of science and technology in production. The Guidelines for the Economic and Social Development of the USSR, meeting the requirements of the present-day economic and social policy of the Party, were submitted to the 27th CPSU Congress for consideration and approval.

In drafting the new five-year plan we were able to reach the highest level, in terms of most of the quantitative and, more importantly, qualitative indicators, as regards the targets outlined in the Guidelines for the country's economic and social development. The draft plan has been thoroughly discussed in the Politburo of the CPSU Central Committee, has been approved by it and is being now submitted for discussion by this Plenary Meeting.

Which particular aspects of the plan should be given special attention?

First of all, I would like to say that on the whole the plan corresponds to the directives of the 27th Party Congress. It provides for the concentration of efforts and resources in the key areas of economic development and for changes in the structural and investment policies in the interests of the intensification of social production. The plan is aimed at raising the efficiency of the economy, saving resources, increasing the effect of economic levers and incentives and using stable work standards and new methods of economic management.

One can get a clear picture of the changes in the economy by looking at the absolute increment figures envisaged in the plan. The principal ones among them are 50 percent higher than in the previous five-year period. For example, the national income will grow by 124,000 million rubles compared to 79,000 million in the 11th Five-Year-Plan period. Industrial output growth will add up to 200,000 million rubles compared to 133,000 million and the average annual increment in the gross agricultural output to 29,000 million rubles compared to 10,000 million in the preceding five-year period. It should be noted here that the planned growth rates are to be achieved from the very start of the new five-year-plan period.

The high targets envisaged in the plan call for a new approach to defining the sources of economic growth. The decisive factor here is a radical improvement of the production efficiency indicators through more rapid scientific and technological progress. This is the basis, comrades, on which the whole plan is built.

In the new five-year-plan period the share of the accumulation fund in the national income is to be increased to 27.6 percent. This will create real conditions for boosting the absolute growth figures in capital investments. In the terms of the national economy as a whole, the rates of their growth will rise from 15.4 percent in 1981-1985 to 23.6 percent. The plan envisages an extensive program of technical modernization and retooling of many enterprises now in operation. The appropriations for these purposes will go up by 70 percent, while their share in the overall capital investments will exceed 50 percent by the end of the current five-year-plan period.

The new five-year period will see large-scale mechanization and automation of production and the introduction of new technologies. All this will lay the groundwork for improving working conditions and relieving more than five million people of manual jobs by 1990, or more than twice as many as over the previous five years. Large-scale measures have been taken to save material and energy resources.

On the whole, comrades, the series of measures aimed at introducing new achievements of science and technology in production and at improving economic management methods, envisaged by the plan, will make it possible to increase the average annual rates of national income growth to 4.1 percent, or nearly by a third compared to the previous five-year period.

There are also plans for carrying out a broad social program on the basis of accelerated development of the economy. The real incomes of the population will grow; the supply of foodstuffs and consumer goods will be improved; services industry will be extended and new measures will be taken to upgrade the health service and public education.

Special attention is being given to the housing construction program. The housing stock will be increased by 595 million square meters; the new houses will be of better quality and have more amenities. The rates of housing construction will be particularly high in the countryside. All these are important measures, but they should not make us complacent. The search for new ways of improving the Soviet people's living conditions must be continued with the use of all available means and possibilities. Cooperative and individual house-building should be actively promoted.

About four-fifths of the national income are to be spent on improving the people's well-being. The defense capability of the country will be maintained at a proper level, too.

In a word, the 12th Five-Year Plan is an important step in carrying out the economic and social policy worked out by the 27th Congress of the CPSU. Essentially, it is a program of action for each branch, each republic, the entire national-economic complex and the society as a whole. The Politburo believes that there is every ground for the Plenary Meeting of the Central Committee to endorse this plan and instruct the Council of Ministers to submit it for consideration by a session of the Supreme Soviet of the USSR. Nikolai Ryzhkov will report to the deputies on this plan.

A. Past Mistakes Must Not Be Repeated

Objectively assessing the plan submitted, it must be openly stated that strenuous work will be required for its fulfilment. It is essential that we attain the goals set, carry through the reconstruction of the economy so as to create conditions for the further growth of its efficiency. Comrades, all this must be accomplished in the next five years.

Performance has improved somewhat in the recent period. However, this has been achieved primarily by drawing on the reserves that are readily available in order to ensure long-term and stable success. It is necessary to look for more cardinal measures. Our experience in building socialism has taught us that at turning points in the society's development we must boldly make drastic changes and not be afraid of decisive reforms.

We all know what the Russian economy was like before the Great October Revolution. Its industrial production was only 12.5 percent that of the United States. For Lenin and the Bolshevik Party it was absolutely clear that socialism would be able to win only by embarking on a basic reconstruction of the economy and by achieving the highest possible labor productivity. From the first years of Soviet government the Party worked for a major renovation of the national economy, using all available resources to this end.

With Lenin's plan for the building of socialism our people soon created a material-technical base for industry, with factories equipped with machinery advanced for that time serving as the core. Industries guaranteeing rapid technical progress were set up, and the reequipping of large-scale production proceeded apace. The economy focused primarily on advancement in science, the promotion of education, and the training of qualified research and engineering personnel.

It was precisely in this way that the rapid pace of economic and social development was achieved. In a historically short time, the formerly backward peasant country became one of the world's leading industrial states. By the fifties, despite enormous losses in the war, the volume of our industrial production had reached 30 percent, and by 1970, 75 percent of the U. S. level; the USSR's national income was two-thirds that of the United States.

But in the seventies and the eighties we lost to a certain extent our previous dynamism. The economy did not succeed in switching over from extensive to intensive development in time. By inertia the previously achieved level guided economic planning. Departmental interests hindered the transfusion of capital investments and resources into more promising industries. The volume approach to assessments of the economy distorted the real state of affairs and gave false indications of its condition.

The structure of our production remained unchanged and did not meet the requirements of scientific and technological progress. The Soviet Union produces considerably more iron ore and steel than the U. S. A. though it manufactures significantly fewer engineering products; it produces as much timber, but fewer timber products. Under these circumstances, each unit of increment in the national income or in industrial and agricultural output requires of us more resources.

In order to rectify the situation, it is necessary to see clearly the causes of the lag. They boil down primarily to serious errors in the policy of capital investments. The reductions in investment increases from one five-year period to the next were entirely unjustified. As a result, such basic industries of machine-building as machine-tool construction, instrument-making, computer technology and the manufacture of modern structural materials were not properly developed. Furthermore, capital construction was conducted ineffectively, and the building time of projects increased, and the stores of uninstalled equipment grew.

We perceive the rapid growth and accumulation of fixed production assets in the country as a great achievement and, by and large, this is correct. But at the same time, comrades, we cannot fail to see that negative trends in the reproduction of these assets accumulated in the course of a number of years. Unjustified enthusiasm over the construction of new enterprises and neglect of the requirements of existing ones became typical of the planning agencies and many ministries. The bulk of machinery and equipment went to the new facilities, whereas a timely replacement of the obsolete equipment in existing factories and plants was not effected. The process of asset renewal was too slow and their age structure deteriorated.

Among the negative effects of the extensive reproduction of fixed assets is excessive swelling in the repairs sphere. In industry alone equipment repairs cost 10,000 million rubles, and of this sum over 3,000 million goes to the repair of equipment which is being operated beyond the standard maintenance time limits.

It should also be mentioned that such an approach slows the turnover of the country's metal stock. Rather than sending the obsolete machinery for remelting at the appropriate time, the metal is tied up, so to speak, in low-efficiency equipment repeatedly subjected to expensive repairs. In order to produce new machinery, the production of pig iron, steel and rolled metal, as well as the output of iron ore, coal and other mineral resources must be increased.

And finally, the extensive forms of the buildup of fixed production assets have led to an artificial shortage of labor. Some people still cling to this life-buoy when explaining the causes of low growth rates, or failure to make contract deliveries or fulfil the plan. Naturally, we are aware of the demographic situation in the country. But we may ask: if there is a labor shortage, then why continue to build ever new enterprises, and on the basis of obsolete equipment at that, and not infrequently turn out outdated products?

This is precisely the way things stand. At present, in industry alone there are about 700,000 job vacancies. And this is when equipment operates practically for only one work shift. If the shift ratio is raised to 1.7, the number of job vacancies in industry will exceed 4 million. Thousands of millions of rubles have been spent on creating these vacancies. So it works out that old machines function in the existing enterprises, and the new ones have no workers to operate them. The money has been spent, but there are no proper returns.

Comrades, today at the Plenary Meeting I consider it necessary to draw special attention to the fact that the shortcomings in investment policy have had the most adverse effect on the development and the technical level of the engineering industries.

The share of machine-building capital in the total volume of investments was unjustifiably down-rated. Both the planning bodies and the ministries had a hand in this. The prestige of creativity in engineering was undermined, and the once world-famous national schools of technology designers withered away. A pernicious philosophy of imitation and mediocrity has taken shape. As a result, some products are not up to the present-day level of science and technology.

So what is the trouble, comrades? What is the fundamental cause of the situation with the technological standards of our machines? It lies first of all in the fact that until now we have not made a systems analysis of the latest world achievements. Attainment of top quality and reliability was, in effect, not envisaged in the designing of new technology. True, we have recently begun to evaluate technology on the basis of analogues. However, it is not the latest foreign models that are used as standards. This is a sad example of the outmoded thinking and eyewash on the part of those who are responsible for the creation of essential technology. Whom are they deceiving? As it turns out, they are deceiving their own people.

The existing orientation on an average or even low technological level of products was to a certain extent permitted by the standards which were in effect. The system of standards did not encourage designers to search for new ideas, nor did it raise a barrier in the way of producing outdated machines and equipment. Apparently, a kind of inferiority complex that emerged at some research institutes and design offices has also played its part. They tried to justify the poor results of their work by claiming that it was impossible to work better. Nor was there complete success in stimulating effective work among scientists, designers, and engineers.

For many years proper attention was not given to the development of scientific research and experiment, and necessary investments and resources were not channeled in this direction. Naturally all this could not but tell on the technological level of machine-building and on the rates of scientific and technological progress.

Such was the situation prior to the April Plenary Meeting. It was comprehensively analyzed by the Central Committee. Measures worked out were unanimously approved by the Plenary Meeting and the Party Congress. I want to repeat to those who are trying to pull us backwards: we cannot and will not put up with this attitude and must stem all attempts to perpetuate the former approaches and errors, first and foremost in the sphere of scientific and technological progress.

I am sure that the Plenary Meeting of the Central Committee will adopt a principled line in this fundamental question of our home policy and will support all the necessary measures of the Politburo and the government designed to revolutionize the development of our economy and lead it to the vanguard positions of scientific and technological progress. I have already spoken about the responsibility in this connection which lies on the members of the Central Committee elected by the 27th Congress of the CPSU. Comrades, we must not shun this historic responsibility.

What should be done first of all in order to optimally fulfill the rigorous 12th Five-Year Plan and create the necessary prerequisites for the further acceleration of scientific and technological progress?

B. To Accelerate Modernization and Energetically Develop Machine-Building

In our efforts to realize the Party's economic strategy we will rely heavily on the reorientation of the investment and structural policy: we will increase the share of capital investments in the modernization and retooling of industrial enterprises now in operation, accelerate the development of machine-building, and shorten the investment cycle.

We have recently taken some far-reaching measures with respect to the cardinal issues of economic growth. I am referring to the resolutions calling for a fundamental reorganization of metal production, broader and more effective application of chemicals, modernization of engineering, faster advance in computerization, installation of flexible production systems, rotor lines, automated design systems, industrialization of capital construction, and improvement of design-and-estimate work. Guidelines have been laid for resource saving. Work of tremendous importance is under way to upgrade the quality of output in every sector of the national economy. Finally, solid groundwork has been laid for a transfer to new methods of economic management and administration.

The decisions taken are oriented toward intensive economic growth through more timely application of advances in science and technology. The whole of this work must be carried out, comrades, with all determination in every respect. Naturally, we must act now within the framework of the five-year plan. Within this framework, we have vast opportunities for the further intensification of the national economy and enhancement of its efficiency.

Speaking of reserves, I would like to begin with the problem of better utilization of fixed production assets and optimization of their renewal. For this, comrades, is the key component of the wealth of a socialist society, the material base of our economic potential. We must set things right as

far as the use of fixed production assets is concerned, and
ensure a genuinely proprietary, rational attitude toward them
and their effective renewal.

We can bring about a substantial qualitative improvement
in our economic performance, above all, higher productivity
and increased returns on capital, if we accelerate the renewal
of fixed production assets, discard their outdated part as soon
as possible, and use technically modern machinery and
equipment more intensively in various ways, including by
raising the equipment shift ratio. By cardinally renewing
fixed production assets and reducing the scale of new construction, we can make substantial capital investments available for speedier social development, above all, the development of housing construction.

These, comrades, are potentialities of vast proportions
which fall in the mainstream of the Party's present economic
policy. They are not a figment of imagination divorced from
life but an actual reality confirmed, notably, by the initiative
of the Leningrad Party organization.

While working out means for continued intensification of
industrial production, the Leningrad regional Party committee has analyzed the draft economic development plans of
industrial enterprises for the 12th Five-Year Plan period. It
turned out that the overwhelming majority of the ministries
are still committed to extensive development in the enterprises under their jurisdiction in this region. Close to 40
percent of the capital investments are earmarked for new
construction and for the expansion of operating capacities. At
the same time, the scope of the technological updating of
production is clearly insufficient.

Following a thorough investigation of the state of affairs,
the regional Party committee has arrived at the correct conclusion: new and advanced components of the fixed production assets must be used in two or three shifts, and the assignments of the 12th Five-Year Plan must be carried out on that
basis. In the meantime outdated equipment must be phased
out and the space thus released used for the installation of
modern productive capacities. This means, as our Leningrad
comrades have calculated, about three million square meters
of space. The proportion of advanced types of machinery in

the total machine-tool inventories of the city and the region will double by the end of the five-year-plan period as machinery and equipment are renewed. There will be a rise in quality standards in industry.

Decisive cuts in new building will allow the Leningraders to decrease capital investments for the purpose. Some of the resources thus saved will be directed toward the technical modernization of the enterprises concerned, but the bulk of it will be used to expand housing construction and provide more amenities in towns and villages. In this way, major technological, economic and social problems are being tackled integrally.

As you know, the Politburo of the Central Committee has considered and approved the proposals of the Leningrad regional Party committee and found that they open up quite a promising area of accelerated development of social production. The initiative thus taken is one of national importance. This is an effective means which should be followed by the industries of other regions.

We see the changeover to a two-shift work regime as an important initiative today. This type of work schedule has long been standing practice in many countries. There enterprises crucial to scientific and technological progress work in two or even three shifts. This reflects a determination to make the best possible use of advanced equipment and replace it with even more effective equipment as soon as possible. Workers on afternoon and night shifts are encouraged by additional incentives. Our central offices must address themselves to this matter without delay and advance proposals for improved moral and material incentives for workers on afternoon and night shifts. We expect the All-Union Central Council of Trade Unions to make an active and constructive contribution to this matter of great national importance.

Even in the early stages, as the initiative of the Leningraders was being discussed, someone suggested that it would not be so simple to get engineering factories to operate in two or three shifts. This, indeed, is not a simple thing. But we have the right to say: why is it that people can work three shifts at continuous production plants, such as metallurgy or chemistry, as well as in the food or textile industries, where, incidentally, female labor predominates? Why then is there only one-shift work, as a rule, in the engineering and metal-working industries where working conditions are certainly no worse?

The Politburo believes that all ministries and departments in conjunction with local Party, government, trade union, and Komsomol bodies must immediately get down to the actual job of intensifying production, taking into account the Leningraders' initiative. In this context, it is important to remodel the operation of transport services, institutions of learning, day-care centers and all the social services in order to create proper conditions for effective work.

In switching over to a multishift work schedule, it is obviously worthwhile to allow the regions, territories and republics to retain the overall capital investments they are entitled to under the five-year plan, leaving them free to use the resources they save by reducing the amount of new industrial construction for updating their productive capacities and advancing their social and cultural development. And they, in their turn, must guarantee the achievement of their five-year-plan targets. Such proposals have, incidentally, already come from some Party and local government officials. I think they must be supported.

One of the most urgent issues of the new five-year plan is to speed up the technological updating of operating production capacities. The plan envisages a substantial increase in capital investments for these purposes. But there are many additional opportunities and possibilities here as well.

The Central Committee of the CPSU set great store by the initiative of the Volzhsky motor works and the Sumy research and production association, which resolved to reach new frontiers of technological progress, improve the quality of products and ensure fast economic growth rates through the use of internal reserves and the upgrading of the organization and methods of managing production. Many other enterprises are emulating their practices. More than 200 other large industrial enterprises are to adopt the principles of self-financing and self-sufficiency next year.

The work collectives of the ZIL motor works, the Leningrad metal works, the Voronezh synthetic rubber factory, the Rosa

Luxemburg knitwear factory in Kiev, the Ekranas plant in Panevezys, Lithuania, and hundreds of other enterprises are successfully utilizing internal reserves to enhance efficiency at each workplace.

Many enterprises in the machine-tool manufacturing industry are being reorganized for the production of advanced machine-tools and equipment capable of increasing productivity many times over and ensuring high quality of products. These include the machine-tool-making associations and plants of Leningrad, Ivanovo, Gomel, Odessa and Ulyanovsk.

The instrument-making and electronics industries are doing their best to speed up the development of computers and microprocessors. They have now created realistic opportunities for quickly solving the problem of organizing the production of high-performance computers and ensuring large-scale production of technological means for electronizing engineering and other sectors of the economy. The 12th Five-Year Plan envisages a 140 percent increase in the production of computers, as compared with the previous five-year-plan period, and manufacture of 1.1 million personal computers.

The practices of Byelorussian railway workers are gaining ever wider recognition. Ten railways have already adopted new methods of organizing and stimulating work. The implementation of this project of national importance will ensure the more efficient functioning of transport and, at the same time, make it possible to increase labor productivity and release nearly 100,000 workers. Such creative attitudes toward work deserve high praise and active support. Generally speaking, a creative search is taking place in all sectors of the economy and in all regions of the country.

Comrades, retooling and modernization of production call for new attitudes. You are aware of how many plants were retooled in the past. Thousands of millions of rubles were spent on replacing obsolete equipment. Nevertheless, the efforts often failed to produce the desired result. One of the chief reasons for this was poor quality of detail design, often based on low-efficiency technology and antiquated methods of labor organization. New equipment often differed from the old only by the date of manufacture.

How are ministries dealing with the problem of modernization now, in this time of change? What projects are to be tackled in the new five-year-plan period?

A sample analysis of plant modernization projects of some industrial ministries has been made at the request of the Central Committee. What are its results? By no means could all projects be accepted as matching modern standards. Many of them require thorough revision. Moreover, some of them had become outdated, and it was thus recommended that they no longer be implemented.

Here are a few examples. The plan for the reconstruction of the Voznesensk hydraulic press plant was drawn up by the Kharkov Ukrgipromash Institute of the Ministry of Machine Building. Note the figures programmed into this plan: the number of workers is to be increased more than five-fold, while labor productivity is to be raised by a mere 70 percent. Moreover, only one-third of this growth is to be achieved through technical solutions, and the remaining two-thirds through a rise in prices on the products.

The situation in other places is much the same. The state institute for the design of textile industry enterprises drafted a plan for the reconstruction of the Moscow printed-calico factory of the Ministry of Light Industry of the USSR: half of its machine fleet is to be made up of equipment that has been manufactured without modernization for more than 15 years. It is impossible to produce high-quality fabric of the required assortment, or to achieve high productivity of labor with this machinery.

The question is where are they sending the country, those wretched planners and ministerial officials who endorsed these plans? It is clear that such plans can discredit the idea of accelerating scientific and technological progress, and burden the economy with enormous expenditures.

So, comrades, we must learn important lessons from all this. We must review promptly, and in the shortest possible time, all plans for technical retooling and reconstruction which are slated for implementation in the 12th Five-Year-Plan period. Those which do not correspond to the tasks of speeding up scientific and technological progress should be discarded without hesitation, their implementation prohibited, while the funds thus saved should be channeled into the development of high-technology production.

Responsibility for the level of the plans for technical retooling and reconstruction should lie, above all, with the ministries which are called upon to be true technical headquarters of industries. Above all it is they who should be held accountable. The attention of ministers was drawn to these questions at a conference held in June of last year. They were directly instructed to review the plans for technical retooling and reconstruction.

The approach to business has to be changed dramatically, comrades. We cannot allow thousands of millions to be invested in obsolete projects which are based on technically unsound solutions. In so acting, we will not rise to the modern world standards of production. And we cannot, I would even say we must not, accept this.

Everyone is aware of the urgency of the problem of supplying the people with products of light industry. Some specialists propose building new enterprises for this purpose. Nobody rules out this path of development, particularly as it concerns the output of modern materials and goods. But basically the task of expanding the production of goods can only be solved through the technical retooling and reconstruction of light-industry enterprises. The main thing is to find the correct solutions to this problem.

Calculations reveal the following information. If the most advanced equipment and technologies are used in the reconstruction of enterprises, we will be able to increase their effectiveness by 30 to 40 percent.

Evidently, we must proceed in the following manner: where such equipment exists reconstruction should be conducted vigorously, and where it is absent reconstruction should be put off for two or three years until the production of efficient equipment starts to run smoothly, and then it will be possible to make up for the delay on a new production basis. Generally speaking, ministries and central offices must approach these matters with utmost responsibility, and stop clinging to the old. Otherwise, they will let down their own people.

Comrades, you well realize that plans for updating the national economy on the basis of the latest scientific and technological achievements depend, in the final analysis, on machine-building. It is here that all of today's burning economic questions are focused. We will not be able to cope with the tasks the Congress sets before us unless we quickly modernize machine-building and reorient it to produce new machine systems and sophisticated equipment for all branches of the national economy.

This matter was recently discussed at the conference of machine-building branch leaders at the CPSU Central Committee. We had a serious talk with the ministers. The discussion showed that we cannot afford to limit ourselves to the measures charted by the well-known resolution on developing machine-building. Additional and equally extensive efforts are needed in order to thoroughly update the machine-building complex. Proposals have been elaborated on instruction from the Central Committee for additional measures to accelerate progress in machine-building.

First of all, guidelines have been established for an overall improvement in the technological standards of machines, instruments and other equipment, for an increase in the production of items equipped with automatic control devices, for a dramatic rise in the output of special-purpose technology to be used at the very enterprise which produces it, and for a substantial expansion of the capacities of stock preparation shops. Measures have been worked out to further step up science and production integration, and consolidate the experimental bases of scientific research institutes and design bureaus.

When implemented, these measures will ensure that 80 to 95 percent of the total output of basic nomenclature goods will correspond to world standards by the year 1990, with the figure for newly developed products reaching practically 100 percent. It is planned to switch production entirely to top-quality articles between 1991 and 1993.

The share of microprocessor equipment will grow sharply, as will the automation of research and development work. The demands of the instrument-making industry for the latest electronic equipment will be met in full.

Machine-building enterprises will be reequipped much quicker, with 38 to 40 percent of Soviet-manufactured technology to be assigned for this purpose. In 1990, the production of special technologies for use at enterprises producing them will reach 4,000-4,200 million rubles, as compared with the initially planned 2,500 million.

Capital investments in developing the machine-building complex are fully ensured by contract allocations and equally distributed for each year of the five-year-plan period. In order to concentrate investments on the crucial lines of scientific and technological progress, and observe the specified time limits in construction, it is planned to freeze more than a hundred outdated-design machine-building projects now under construction.

Major steps are envisaged to improve the economic mechanism in machine-building. Beginning next year, the number of confirmed assignments will be drastically cut by means of increasing the role of such general indices as profit, labor-efficiency growth and decrease of relative consumption of basic materials and resources.

The planning of machinery and equipment production in tons is ruled out. Solutions to most of the questions determining the interaction of industries within the machine-building complex have been found, and other reserves for the further enhancement of the technical level of production revealed. The machine-building ministries have been asked to complete in 1986 the formulation of plans for technically reequipping each enterprise and the industries as a whole on the basis of the broad use of scientific and technological achievements. The solution of the problem of providing the machine builders with high-quality progressive materials will require additional development of component suppliers' capacities. This will also have to be accomplished.

The Politburo has examined and expressed its support for all these proposals. Now it is submitting them to the Plenary Meeting of the Central Committee for approval.

As you see, comrades, the realization of such a very crucial and complex program will call for tremendous effort, strenuous and competent work. It must be carried out—we have no other path. Any other road means relinquishing positions, falling behind. This the CPSU Central Committee cannot accept.

We hope that the heads of the machine-building ministries and the work collectives will treat the fulfillment of this important national task with full understanding and due responsibility. Recalling the lessons of the past, we must warn in advance all those who are responsible for fulfilling the program of modernizing the engineering industry: there must be no retreats from what has been outlined, and no excuses citing objective or subjective reasons will be accepted.

Comrades, speaking of our work for a major technical re-equipping and reconstruction of the economy, we cannot bypass the problems of capital construction. Its volume in the new five-year-plan period is enormous. Almost 1,000,000 million rubles is being allocated for this purpose. More than 500,000 million rubles worth of building and assembly work alone will be carried out. This is 20 percent more than in the 11th Five-Year-Plan period.

Yet, the situation in construction remains unsatisfactory and the process of reconstruction has become protracted. Nearly half the construction trusts chronically fail to fulfill their plans and bring capacities and facilities into operation on schedule. Serious defects mark the organizational structure of the management of construction work. The establishment of design and building associations and firms for the mass industrialized "turn-key" construction of multiple-recurring projects still has not gone beyond good intentions.

Generally speaking, comrades, a thorough streamlining of the entire construction industry will have to be undertaken and progressive experience will have to be more widely utilized.

Everyone is aware of the successes of the Byelorussian builders, for example. In the course of the 11th Five-Year-Plan period, they reduced the number of projects under construction at one time by 21 percent and their average building time by 28.6 percent. Considerable savings in labor and materials were achieved, and at the same time the commissioning of all completed projects and facilities was ensured. The overall volume of capital construction rose by 19 percent, and the commissioning of fixed assets increased by 23 percent. And this was accomplished throughout the entire republic. But this very successful experience has not yet been implemented anywhere outside Byelorussia.

There are good examples in other areas of the country as well. In 1979 a building team led by Nikolai Ilyich Travkin was organized in the Moscow region. Cost-accounting principles and elements of self-management revealed great potentials and ensured the achievement of good results. In 1983, on the basis of this collective, a new prime contractor organization, the PMK-96, was established. And later the entire trust Mosoblselstroi No. 18, led by N. I. Travkin, went over to cost accounting. Here are the results. In the past year the trust delivered 1.5 times more commercial building products than in the previous year. Productivity rose by 25 percent, and production costs were reduced by 12 percent. Having earlier operated at a loss, the trust now received almost 1.5 million rubles in profit. The average pay increased by 11 percent.

It is also important to stress that the successes of the Byelorussian and Moscow builders have been achieved on practically the same material base. Therefore, claims that the shortcomings in capital construction are due to a shortage of labor or transport facilities are often groundless. Experience has shown that capital construction can be successfully conducted with existing potentials. It is essential only to ably utilize everything the builders have right now, and show creativity and economic initiative in work.

We obviously face the need for a cardinal restructuring of capital construction. The time has come to demand prompt action from all those who are responsible for utilizing progressive experience in this industry. It is necessary to change the planning and organization of construction and, of course, to update its material base.

C. Thrifty Management and Skillful Administration

Comrades, there are many other reserves within the framework of the five-year plan which can provide additional momentum to our advance. When we speak of the need for a fundamental restructuring of the economy, we view a substantial improvement in the quality of products as one of its most important results. The Party Congress presented the problem of quality as a nationwide task. The CPSU Central Committee addressed a special letter to all working people.

We can now definitely say that the majority of Soviet people realize the need for an urgent solution to this most important problem.

Many work collectives have taken a much more serious approach to their work. Without particular expenditures, but rather, largely due to a conscientious attitude toward work, stronger labor and technological discipline, the adoption of a series of urgent organizational and technical measures, such enterprises as the Alma-Ata machine-tool manufacturing plant, the Tallinn machine-building works, the Fergana-based Azot amalgamation, the Elektroizolit amalgamation in the Moscow region, the Bakelektrobytpribor production amalgamation and a number of others have sharply reduced the number of unsatisfactory equipment reports and ensured the output of products in strict compliance with the standard requirements. I would like particularly to emphasize the fact that they have achieved a breakthrough in raising the quality of output using practically only the existing equipment.

Thus, decisive steps to improve the quality of machines, equipment and consumer goods can and should be taken today, without waiting for the appearance of new technology. As you know, the Politburo of the CPSU Central Committee and the Council of Ministers of the USSR passed a special resolution. Measures of a technical and economic nature, standardization and certification of products, price-setting, a system of moral and material encouragement are directed at improving the quality of output. A system of state-controlled independent approval of products is being introduced at enterprises.

It is important that the Party committees actively support the work of production collectives and state control and approval bodies in order to right the situation in the near future. The fact that this is realistically possible is evidenced by the experience of those enterprises where the system of independent approval was introduced as an experiment last year.

Radical changes are to be achieved in the utilization of material resources as well. Not long ago the CPSU Central Committee and the Council of Ministers of the USSR passed a resolution that presents challenging tasks as regards the saving of energy and resources. The saving of resources is a decisive means of meeting the growing requirements for materials, fuel and electric power. We hope to receive over one-quarter of the increment of the national income in the current five-year-plan period as a result of this factor.

This is an important task, though not all managers fully realize it and remain locked into the narrow sphere of their outmoded conceptions. The Ministry of the Automobile Industry, the Ministry of Heavy Machine-Building, the Ministry of the Coal Industry, the Ministry of Electric Power Development and Electrification, and the Ministry of Light Industry systematically fail to fulfill the tasks relating to a number of types of resource saving. No small number of enterprises continue to permit direct losses of the most valuable raw materials and products. Thirteen thousand million cubic meters of casing head gas is burnt needlessly in flares every year. Millions of tons of coal are lost in transport by rail. The loss of agricultural produce is high, reaching nearly 20 percent on the whole. And how much electric power, heat and water is still being wasted needlessly? The utilization of secondary resources is still poorly organized.

Let us be frank—we have reached a point beyond which such mismanagement is intolerable, and what's more, we simply cannot afford it. Our scientific and technological policy, planning, and economic and administrative levers should be used to eliminate these ills that have struck root.

We must launch an all-out war on wasteful practices and exercise the strictest economy. Steps should be taken to make the fulfilment of tasks as regards the saving of resources and the level of their utilization one of the main criteria for assessing the performance of every enterprise and collective.

The saving of feedstock and materials should be further encouraged. Can we consider such a practice as normal whereby the payment for the saving of resources amounts to mere kopecks? This simply won't do. Thriftiness should also become a habit; every worker should learn to be thrifty. Thriftiness should be constantly fostered in the rising generation, both in the family and at school.

Comrades, special attention in the five-year plan is devoted to the development of the agroindustrial complex. The planned targets are in line with the policy formulated by the May 1982 Plenary Meeting of the CPSU Central Committee. On the whole, the volume of capital investment, the output of farm produce and the amount of material and technical facilities for the agroindustrial complex have been planned in keeping with the targets of the Food Program. Enterprises that process and store farm produce, and plants making agricultural machinery will be developing at priority rates.

In general, favorable conditions are being created for a buildup of the potential of the farming sector. This is undoubtedly justified. At the same time we must realize that the immense resources being channeled into that sector are not yielding sufficient returns. On the whole, the 11th Five-Year-Plan period was completed with low indicators. This affected the supply of foodstuffs to the population and the rates of the country's economic development.

For the sake of objectivity it should be said that positive changes have been carried out in the farming sector of late.

However, they are not taking place in all branches of the agroindustrial complex, and not in all regions, territories, and republics. We are now faced with the urgent task of ensuring stable output of crops, primarily grain and fodder crops. This is the main problem on whose successful solution the stable development of livestock farming, the incomes of collective and state farms and the economic performance of the processing enterprises largely depend.

Work in the farming sector must be intensified in order to change the situation decisively for the better. We have vast reserves, comrades, for that. They are found above all in the huge potential that has already been created. We now have experience in running an efficient agriculture in practically all zones. Thanks to the measures taken to improve administration and the system of management, the economic and organizational prerequisites have been created for heightening the labor activity of agricultural workers.

Without going into details, I would like to emphasize the main thing once again—to achieve higher productivity in crop farming and livestock breeding intensive technologies should be used on a wide scale. This is both the most realistic and the most efficient way of achieving better results in crop growing and in livestock production.

We should continue our policy of concentrating efforts and means on the decisive branches of the agroindustrial complex. This is a reliable way of getting tangible returns on investments in the countryside. The experience of our country and of other states shows that one should concentrate resources on those farms and in those regions where they promise the best results in terms of the volume of production and of economic efficiency. In this connection, there is every reason to consider once again the question of redistributing resources and allocating them for the specific volumes of production.

Also worth considering is the question of setting up research-and-production amalgamations on a regional scale, and in some cases perhaps also on a district scale, so that they would become catalysts for the accelerated development of the collective and state farms in their zone and help them in applying advanced technologies and advanced methods of husbandry. This approach guarantees a rational use of the economic potential and the achievement of good end results.

Moldavia, the Ukraine and other republics already have experience in this. Amalgamations have been formed there on the basis of zonal institutes, research and experimental farms. Similar work has been carried out in a number of fraternal socialist countries. I believe it would be expedient to study it thoroughly and make active use of it in practice.

If we are to make great achievements in our agroindustrial complex, we must not merely follow traditional paths. It is only by concentrating resources, providing for the priority development of key sectors, and skillfully using the advantages inherent in the new economic mechanism and structure of management that we will be able to work efficiently, increase output quickly and successfully carry out the tasks set by the Food Program of the USSR.

Finally, comrades, our success in the 12th Five-Year-Plan period will depend on how we will further conduct the work to perfect management and the entire economic mechanism. The principles of this work have been defined. On the one hand, we must continue to improve centralized management of the national economy, enhance the role of the State Planning Committee and other economic agencies and specify the functions of ministries, and on the other hand, increase in every way the rights and economic independence of enterprises and amalgamations and also their responsibility for the results of their activity.

I believe everybody agrees with this now. But the practical work to implement democratic centralism in management is not proceeding in a way that is required in the present situation. We have carried out experiments and obtained promising results, but we often shrink back when it comes to disseminating them on a large scale. Much in the system of the economic mechanism has already been tested and it is necessary to introduce what is new more boldly in practice. To operate, so to say, along the entire front. To this end the central economic bodies should, on the basis of the Guidelines laid down by the 27th Congress, draft and adopt more quickly documents necessary for the transition to the new principles of management.

The numerous instructions, regulations and methodological guidelines that we have been accumulating for decades should be reviewed in accordance with the decisions of the Congress and the resolutions adopted after the Congress, and those which contradict the transformation should be resolutely discarded. We will not be able to advance without this, comrades. Genuine centralism in management has nothing to do with a bureaucratic regulation of the multifaceted life of production, research, and design collectives. The system that has formed over many years in which these collectives have been burdened with far-fetched instructions and methods deprives managers and development engineers of the possibility to promptly solve the economic and technical problems that arise.

This results in the loss of profits amounting to many billions of rubles on a nationwide scale. We encounter such phenomena at every step. The Director General of the Kriogenmash research-and-production amalgamation, V. P. Belyakov; the Director General of the Electrosila amalgamation, B. I. Fomin; the Chief Designer of the Zavod Imeni Vladimira Ilyicha amalgamation, V. I. Radin; and many other experienced managers, scientists, and development engineers have written about them.

Order must be installed here and concern shown for a real expansion of the rights of work collectives. This requires that the draft law on the socialist enterprise (production amalgamation) be completed as quickly as possible. This document should be based on the concept of the new conditions of economic management, sum up the recent experience, and consolidate all the best trends in implementing the course toward greater economic independence, in increasing the role and responsibility of enterprises and production amalgamations.

Thereby we will lay the foundation for the optimal distribution of rights and duties among ministries and enterprises, and for legislatively protecting work collectives from petty tutelage and arbitrary administration, from unjustified interference in their day-to-day economic activity. This, comrades, will mean a serious step forward in democratizing the management of our economy and developing the initiative of working people.

As you know, the 27th Congress set the task of really mastering economic methods of managing the national economy. In this connection we will have to ensure first of all the formulation of advanced standards and quotas. The State Planning Committee should head this crucial work and draw ministries and agencies, scientists, specialists of amalgamations and enterprises into it on a broad scale. Moreover, this work should not be dragged out. Without creating substantiated economic standards we will not rid ourselves of the yoke of all sorts of instructions fettering the performance of enterprises, and it will be difficult to move from administrative methods of management to economic ones. This will slow down the application of the principles of self-financing and work without state subsidies, which we intend to use ever more widely.

Finally, mention should be made of the key importance of price-forming in developing economic methods of management. Many unanswered questions have accumulated here. Prices of machinery and equipment, and estimates of construction costs are raised under the pretext of modernization. Changes in the range of products and pursuit of "gross" indicators often bring about an unjustified increase in prices of consumer goods as well.

Regrettably, state and economic bodies often look the other way, so to speak, and quite often themselves turn out to be interested in increasing volumes of production by "playing" with prices. Following last year's audits alone more than 100 million rubles received by enterprises in unlawful profits through violations of price-setting regulations were confiscated and directed into the budget.

I would like to warn you, comrades, that this is an extremely dangerous trend. Artificial price-raising does not cure economic ailments but only corrupts officials and puts a brake on technical progress. Exaggerated prices based on the input approach conceal shortcomings in technology and the organization of production, and generate a disdainful attitude to the search for economic methods of management.

Price increases are justified only if they are due to substantial improvement in the consumer quality of commodities and higher effectiveness of products. We must introduce order in price-forming. The State Committee for Prices must take a more clear-cut and principled stand here. Questions of perfecting crediting and banking in general are also rife. As we switch to new methods of management we must enhance the role of the bank as a key organ of economic management.

I would particularly like to single out a problem, which, if not solved, will make the task of introducing resource-saving technologies and overcoming the input-oriented nature of the economy impossible to successfully attain. I am referring to the notorious "gross" indicators. Various forms of assignments in terms of such indicators play a major role in assessing the performance of industries, regions and enterprises. Since this is so, costly materials are often used for the sake of increasing this "gross," the weight of machines is built up, ton-kilometers are chalked up, intraenterprise turnover is inflated, etc. We are struggling for efficiency, but look at the really ridiculous situation in which economic managers find themselves: they manufacture a cheap product and get a dressing down for failing to meet the target of production in terms of rubles; they introduce a novelty, save resources, and again it turns out that they have put their enterprises and sometimes even the whole industry at a disadvantage.

I will give you the following example. An economic experiment at motor transport enterprises of a number of ministries was started two and a half years ago. The participants in the experiment began planning their work in such a way as to interest people not in ton-kilometers but in the timely delivery of all ordered freight with the least outlay. The causes prompting managers to pad their accounts with nonexistent tons and kilometers were removed.

And here are the results: the fulfillment of orders, that key indicator of work, rose to 100 percent. At the same time demand for motor vehicles and drivers declined and fuel expenditure dropped by 18 percent. The introduction of such conditions of work nationwide would free thousands of motor vehicles and drivers and save more than five million tons of motor fuel.

It would seem that planning bodies should embrace this new method of work. But far from it. Certain high-ranking officials of the State Planning Committees of the USSR and the Russian Federation began to defend the outmoded planning systems with might and main, as the saying goes. The fact is that the earlier planned "gross output" and the volumes of transportation turned out to be exaggerated. Planners did not want to admit that these estimates were no good. This is a fine example of nonacceptance of the new, of reluctance to deal with the restructuring of the economic mechanism and to renounce outdated methods of work.

Gross output indicators still dominate in many sectors. Moreover, efforts are being made again to revive "gross output" as the main evaluating indicator in, for example, construction, and not without approval from the USSR State Planning Committee and the Ministry of Finance of the USSR. This is happening despite the fact that the experience of the leading building organizations testifies otherwise; namely, that their work should be evaluated and encouraged on the basis of finished products, the commissioning of projects, and not on the basis of the volume of construction and assembly work. I believe, comrades, that the time has come to unravel this "gross output tangle," otherwise we will not be able to move ahead and successfully tackle the input mechanism.

Considering questions of management, it is impossible not to mention the responsibility of the USSR State Planning Committee for the solution of national economic problems advanced by life itself. Conceived at its founding as the think tank for managing the economy, the State Planning Committee continues to perform traffic controller's functions in many respects. Not infrequently, it has to deal with matters which top industry executives, and perhaps even directors of enterprises, could sort out. At the same time it does not perform the main function of the strategic planning body of the country.

Routine business hinders planners seeking ways of resolving the main socioeconomic tasks, choosing proportions and priorities in the development of the national economy, defining structural policy, locating productive forces and balancing the economy. This is why we have overlooked many things. Generally speaking, a serious restructuring is required in planning work.

Comrades, discussing questions relating to the long-term development of the country and drawing up measures for the future, we must not lose sight of the tasks of the current moment. The successful fulfillment of the plans for this year, and hence for the entire five-year period, depends on whether these tasks are tackled correctly. Workers in the countryside have some special responsibilities today. The results of the current year in the farming sector are of exceptional importance for us. As you know, fairly good results have been achieved in livestock production in the past five months. It is important that they be consolidated.

However, the main task is to grow and gather in without loss grain, fruits and vegetables, fodder and industrial crops. This is a task of nationwide importance, and should be approached as such in everyday work. And what is especially important in those many regions where present conditions are not easy is to take in and preserve everything that will have been grown, to prevent losses.

A crucial period is beginning in the operation of industry, capital construction and transport. There must be no slackening in the results of work: efforts should be made to try and increase the pace of production growth and to fulfil all the plans without fail. It is important to get ready in time for work in winter. We must learn lessons from the past. With this in mind the CPSU Central Committee and the Council of Ministers of the USSR passed a resolution a few days ago charting specific measures to prepare the national economy for the forthcoming autumn and winter seasons.

The attention of the Party, state, and economic bodies should be directed toward fulfilling it even now. The entire life-sustaining sphere of cities and villages should be put in proper order—the reliable operation of electric power and heat supply systems, the repairs to energy-generating units and the planned commissioning of new capacities, the timely buildup of stocks of fuel at enterprises and in the utilities should be ensured. In short, matters should be dealt with in such a fashion as to ensure that the population does not experience any discomfort in everyday life under any circumstances, that the work collectives operate in the normal production regime, and the economy develops at a stable pace, gaining momentum.

These, comrades, are considerations on the principled and current questions relating to the economic policy—questions the solution of which will determine to a decisive extent the fulfilment of the wide-scale program for transforming the national economy in the 12th Five-Year-Plan period. The fulfillment of the assignments of the five-year plan will provide new evidence of the dynamism and vitality of the socialist system, and will become a major step forward in the realization of the policy course charted by the 27th Congress of the CPSU.

III. ACTIVE EFFORTS TO RESTRUCTURE PARTY WORK

Comrades, when the country's destiny was at stake, or when it was a matter of solving questions of vital importance for its present and future, Lenin emphasized: "The Party is responsible."

Ours is the ruling Party. It has in its hands powerful levers for influencing social processes. The theory and the policy, the ideas and the strength of organization, millions of Communists in production and management, in science, technology and culture are the mighty potential of the Party.

The activity of the millions of working people, and the scope and depth of the people's creative endeavor, which is the decisive factor of acceleration, in many respects depend on how Party organizations operate. Only by placing the human being at the center of Party work will we be able to carry out the tasks set by the Congress. The essence of the radical restructuring of Party work lies precisely in turning to people, to real work.

What has been shown by the months that have passed since the Congress? The ideas of restructuring have been appreciated by the majority of Party cadres and are beginning to manifest themselves in practical activities. New relationships between local and central Party, government and economic bodies have developed. Many practical matters are dealt with faster and with a greater understanding. We have mounted another step where frankness and urgency in the way problems are put and in the level of criticism and self-criticism are concerned.

The Moscow, Leningrad, Kiev, Minsk, Donetsk, Chelyabinsk, Sumy, and Tatar Party organizations are profoundly engaged in the large-scale intensification of production. Questions of developing the economy and the social sphere are being tackled energetically and purposefully by the Communists of Brest, Volgograd, Ulyanovsk, Kharkov, Irkutsk, Lipetsk, Rostov, and of many other regions, territories and republics.

Important steps are being made by all Party organizations. The quest for new forms and methods of work that will accord with the present time is itself proceeding with difficulties. One encounters the idea that the guidelines laid down at the Congress apply to the sphere of big-time politics and that practical work should proceed along its own course, keeping to the beaten track. It can be said that such sentiments still exist within Party circles.

Take, for example, the Kursk regional Party organization. The spirit of imaginative attitude to work, of criticism and self-criticism has by no means penetrated all of the districts there. A domineering style of work has proved exceptionally tenacious. For example, Comrade V. A. Anpilogov, first secretary of the Oktyabrsky Party district committee, and some other Party workers, used to hold a negative view of criticism, cover up for "yes-men" and try to conceal failures. In order to color the real state of affairs, they quite often induced economic managers to resort to report-padding. They showed little concern for the development of the initiative of the Party organization, or for the labor and social activity of people.

Comrade M. S. Shevelev, secretary of the Party organization of the Krasnoye Znamya collective farm, wrote about all this to a central newspaper.

The fallacious methods of work could not have been unknown to the regional Party committee. But, obviously, the bureau and the first secretary of the regional committee, Comrade A. F. Gudkov, failed to rise to the occasion. The regional committee was lavish in giving Comrade Anpilogov the most flattering character references, virtually holding him up as an example to others. When the Central Committee instructed its staff to look into the state of affairs there, it turned out that what Comrade Shevelev had written was the truth pure and simple, and the opinion of the leaders of the Party's regional committee proved to be untenable.

Eventually, the story was brought to an end by the members of the district committee, who gave Comrade Anpilogov a vote of no-confidence and decided to relieve him of the secretaryship. Why did the regional committee fail to notice in time and duly assess the unbecoming style of the work of the secretary of the district committee, and the situation which had developed in the district Party organization? Apparently, the secretaries of the Party's regional committee themselves and the committee's bureau are in no hurry to reorganize their work, and still cling to the obsolete style under which the initiative of working people does not get due support.

Since the Congress, Soviet people have shown a growing interest in the Party's affairs and in the processes taking place in society. They want to find their place in the countrywide work to realize the ideas advanced at the Congress and make their contribution to the restructuring effort. This is borne out by the numerous letters that have been received by the Central Committee and the editorial offices of newspapers. Some of these letters you are holding in your hands. It would seem that the task of the Party committees is utterly clear: it is essential to support the social and labor activity of people in every way. But in many places everything remains as it used to be: initiative runs into a wall of indifference and, at times, overt resistance.

At the Irbit chemical and pharmaceutical plant of the

Sverdlovsk region, the Party bureau and the management, with the backing of the city's Party committee, took to task a shop superintendent who advocated the introduction of advanced forms of organization and remuneration of labor. The initiative of a Communist, a resourceful person, ran into out-and-out red tape. We deemed it necessary to discuss this fact, in view of its exceptional importance, at the CPSU Central Committee. You know what decision the Secretariat of the Central Committee took on this matter. I think there are lessons to be learned from this and not just for the people in Sverdlovsk.

The Congress oriented the Party committees to mastering political methods of leadership. However, the striving of Party bodies to assume managerial functions continues unabated. Just listen to what some Party leaders say. They readily and with expertise speak of the current economic campaign, of milk yields and weight gains, tons, etc. But when the conversation turns to a political analysis of social phenomena, socioeconomic tasks, scientific and engineering problems, and of the resources inherent in the human factor, they are quite often at a loss.

Frankly speaking, we should reorganize and get rid of the elements of arbitrary administration at all levels—from primary organizations to the Central Committee. Only all-round political, organizational and ideological activities at all levels of Party leadership will ensure the accomplishment of the tasks set by the Congress.

An increase in the capacity for action of primary Party organizations is acquiring a particular importance in this context. We have more than once become convinced of their inexhaustible resources. I would say that we should begin restructuring work precisely with developing the independence and vigor of primary organizations, the initiative and activity of Communists. This is the main element, and it should be tackled in real earnest.

This must be done by the Party's district and city committees, which are the closest to work collectives and know the potentials and resources of primary Party organizations. We have quite a number of Party committees at district and city level that in the new situation are giving greater scope to the initiative of the cadres and shift the center of gravity to control of their work by the grass roots, by the public and the press.

At the same time, there is still gravitation to traditional methods of leadership, or rather management. All this, comrades, was practiced at one time out of necessity, as if in compensation for flaws in the economic machinery. At present, such practice is not only unnecessary but harmful, too. One should more boldly renounce a controller's functions. The work collectives and people are the main sphere of the activities of a secretary and of members of a Party district committee.

Recently I have had many meetings and conversations with directors of enterprises, workers, engineers and secretaries of Party committees, and they all agree that opportunities for resourceful work are broadening slowly. Red tape, that twin brother of arbitrary administration and arch opponent of the broad participation of the masses in managerial affairs, makes itself felt.

Take managerial bodies, for example. When one gets directly acquainted with their activities, one can see that some ministers and heads of departments and enterprises have altogether lost the habit of speaking to one another and of establishing direct business contacts, and that everything is done by correspondence. Does this mean that comrades are unable to speak to one another over the telephone, to get together and settle problems or is this an attempt to shield oneself from responsibility by means of documents?

This applies, to a certain extent, to Party bodies. For example, the Tashkent city Party committee and the city's district committees within four months have sent 50–100 percent more of their resolutions to primary Party organizations than in the corresponding period last year. One can come across such excessive reliance on correspondence in other places as well.

Unnecessary paper work, far from being a technical question, is a political one. Just see what any inspection boils down to: a study of information, tables, minutes and plans of activities, and to finding out whether the matter was discussed and whether an appropriate decision was taken. In short, there is a habit of working with paper, and not with people, and of looking at people through paper work. As for how people work, live, what they think, what their problems are and their attitude of mind—all that is remote. Yet Party work is all about precisely these things.

There will be no restructuring if an atmosphere of intolerance to drawbacks, to stagnancy in work, to ostentation and idle talk is not established within the Party and its organizations. This is why, in the spirit of the Congress, we must enhance criticism. What we need is principled criticism, which is directed to an exact address, and which reveals the causes of shortcomings and omissions, and ways of removing them, the criticism that upholds the spirit of concern, and of healthy dissatisfaction with what has been achieved.

Comrades, the concept of acceleration is inseparable from a vigorous personnel policy. The plans for the five-year period envision fundamental measures in personnel training and development of a system of continuous education. All of them are directed at providing professionally competent workers for every area of material production and cultural and intellectual life.

This task is being tackled not only in educational establishments where we have initiated serious reforms. Our time demands that everyone continuously update their knowledge, improve their skills and broaden their ideological, political, scientific, technological and economic horizons. Otherwise one cannot efficiently use the latest technology or be a knowledgeable manager and a skillful administrator.

Special importance is attached today to work with senior managers and officials, called upon to organize the restructuring effort in the areas entrusted to them. By the April 1985 Plenary Meeting, as you know, we have quite a few unresolved personnel issues.

That situation drew criticism from both Communists and non-Party people. The Central Committee made the proper conclusions. Many well-trained and mature Communists, who have proved themselves in practical grass-roots work and who understood the current situation well, were advanced in the course of the review-and-election campaign. There should be continued improvement in the placement of cadres.

While speaking in Togliatti, I noted that now that work is getting under way to accelerate scientific and technological progress, people with an innovative spirit should be particularly valued. All the more so since we are urging everyone to act rather than to sit back and wait. One cannot help seeing that a man with initiative often comes into conflict with outdated regulations that do not meet the new tasks. Everything possible should be done to ensure that questing, creative people do not find themselves in a tight spot and suffer defeat. This is not an abstract discourse.

I would like to illustrate what I have just said with one outrageous example. In Cherkassy there is a plant under the Ministry of the Electrical Engineering Industry and a research institute working in the same field. The institute, which was headed by Comrade A. I. Chabanov, has developed machine tools of a new type and control systems for them. The machine tools won recognition at international exhibitions and orders began to come in for them from our plants and from abroad.

Meanwhile, the plant, which should have been the first to utilize those achievements, stubbornly ignored the new technology. And when last July Comrade Chabanov was appointed acting manager of the plant on a temporary basis, he decided to go ahead with production without waiting for approval of specifications for new products. So, the advanced technology was brought to life and the plant's finances were improved. But then some people began to complain that the new manager had departed from the regulations and padded his reports. And what was the response of the ministry and the regional Party committee?

One cannot say they acted in the spirit of innovation. The manager was relieved of his duties and the case was turned over to the investigating bodies. The CPSU Central Committee and the Procurator General had to interfere to sort things out. No violations, let alone crimes, were found. The matter seemed to be clear. But even after the truth was restored, the Party bureau expelled Comrade Chabanov from the Party. Moreover, a letter sent to the Congress by Communists who had taken his side, was intercepted at the post office by the local authorities and never reached Moscow.

These, comrades, are the sort of facts that one comes across. We turned the case over to the Party Control Committee, and justice has now triumphed, it seems. But the question is: where was the regional Party committee? Could it not have promptly grasped the essence of that case and prevented a breach of Soviet laws and the victimization of a Communist?

At our Plenary Meeting we should state in the most principled manner that the Party committees are called upon to protect the honor of the Party, and not the honor of rank. Everything is important in Party work, not least the way a person is met at the Party committee, the way he is talked to, the way the questions that trouble him are settled and, finally, the role the Party committee plays in his fate.

What continues to happen is this. A Communist shares his doubts or expresses his personal opinion in a city or district Party committee. But instead of giving him a substantive answer, they tell him: "Don't forget the place you are in." And what is that place? It is his home. Where else should he take his problems and concerns if not to his Party committee? And because Party comradeship means a Bolshevik standard of relationships among Communists regardless of rank or title, he has every right to expect to be treated with sensitivity and attention rather than receiving a high-handed reception.

The spirit of comradeship should pervade our entire Party life. Making stricter demands on the performance of one's duties, it is necessary to always draw a clear distinction between Party principle and a dressing-down that denigrates human dignity. Deviations from this rule—and we know of such cases—crush the human soul, sow uncertainty in the work collective and depress public interest and activity. We cannot reconcile ourselves to such things.

We should continue to work perseveringly to ensure that a healthy atmosphere in our society gains ground and becomes firmly established. I would say that, in this context, the war on drunkenness and alcoholism remains among the most urgent tasks. We should be guided in this war by the opinion of our people rather than those who are addicted to alcohol. We have assumed a commitment to our entire people to wage a resolute battle on drunkenness, and it is our Party duty to fulfill this mandate.

We should also fulfill the mandate to step up the war on unearned incomes. The recent major resolutions on this matter were welcomed by society with satisfaction. They should be put into practice in such a way that, while rooting out this phenomenon, which is alien to socialism, they contribute to improving the living conditions of the working people.

To sum it all up, comrades, we should strictly respect our main socialist principle: supporting and encouraging honest and conscientious work in every way and waging an uncompromising struggle against all parasitic elements, against those who would like to live at the expense of others, at the expense of society.

We should proceed from the fact that as the tasks in the social, economic, cultural and intellectual fields grow more complex, the demands on ideological work will also grow. I would like to note today the great contribution that is being made by the press, television, radio and the other mass media to the process of restructuring. They are doing a great deal to broaden publicity, to translate the democratism of our society into practice, and to raise serious, socially meaningful problems. Today it is especially important for our press to sensitively detect the emergence of everything new and advanced that is generated by the restructuring in all areas of life, and to help put it within the reach of the entire society. The objectivity, high exactingness and responsibility of the mass media are inviolable principles of the Party press, that guarantee them their authority.

The newspaper is the face of the Party committee. It reflects the style and methods of its work, its standards of leadership and its attitude to every outstanding problem. If the Party committee restructures itself, the press follows suit. I would like to draw your attention to the fact that the degree of publicity and effectiveness in many local newspapers is still far below that of the centrally published press. As an analysis of this matter shows, this is directly dependent on the position of the Party committees. Hence the need, both in the Party committees and in the editorial offices, to draw the correct conclusions in a self-critical manner. I am certain that they will be made.

In short, we count on stepping up efforts in the ideological sphere and on the rallying power of truthful ideas which bring together millions for a common cause.

IV. ON THE RESULTS OF THE BUDAPEST MEETING OF THE POLITICAL CONSULTATIVE COMMITTEE

Comrades, I shall now move on to the second item on the Plenary Meeting's agenda.

The documents of the recent regular meeting of the Political Consultative Committee (PCC) of the Warsaw Treaty member countries have been published. What could one say about the importance of the PCC meeting? First of all, it should be pointed out that the meeting took place immediately after several fraternal parties had held their congresses. So, it is only natural that the foreign-policy principles endorsed at the highest Party forums should be in the focus of collective discussion. Because of that, the meeting acquired a greater dimension, and the emphasis in the discussion was on matters of a strategic, global nature.

It was particularly stressed that the course of accelerated socioeconomic development adopted by our Party and by other fraternal parties had evoked a broad international response and, as it was implemented, would have an increasing effect on the entire course of world social development. It was pointed out that this was exactly what worried our class adversary most of all.

There was an exchange of views on the course of events in Europe and in the international arena over the period of time that had elapsed since the Sofia PCC meeting and the Soviet-U.S. summit meeting in Geneva. All participants in the meeting agreed that the situation remained complex and that there were no grounds so far for speaking of a relaxation of tension.

You know about the steps we have taken to make sure that the positive trend that originated in Geneva will not fade away or be lost to view in the whirlpool of international life. They include a concrete plan for the elimination of nuclear weapons by the end of this century, a moratorium on nuclear explosions, and proposals on the destruction of chemical weapons. Our initiatives have helped to improve and will continue to help improve the international climate.

But it is precisely the prospect for a relaxation of tension that is being regarded in the West and, first of all, by the reactionary ruling upper crust in the United States, as a threat to their interests. Recent months and weeks have seen a series of rejections of Soviet proposals on cardinal questions of present-day development: the refusal to end nuclear tests; the renunciation of existing agreements on strategic arms; and the refusal to keep outer space weapon-free. In addition, there is an unwillingness to conduct negotiations in good faith in Geneva and Vienna.

Washington's actions in Berne showed a haughty disregard for the interests of all countries of Europe, and not only of Europe, and as a result no important accords on human rights were achieved. A total nonacceptance of present-day realities alone can explain why the U.S. leaders are counting on brute force, on the nuclear fist, on terroristic piratical acts closely combined with ideological intolerance and hatred. They continue to assess the present world situation in terms of Star Wars and nuclear warheads, the arms race and militarist blackmail, thus more and more undermining the security of the entire world and of their own country.

It is becoming increasingly clear that the real threat to U.S. security does not come from outside. The threat, and a substantial one at that, is being posed by that country's military-political elite, its adventuristic behavior in the world arena.

The 27th CPSU Congress proposed sensible ways of resolving the problems facing humanity. Our objectives are absolutely clear. They are: acceleration of the country's social and economic development, broad international cooperation that benefits all, disarmament and the elimination of nuclear weapons, and peace for humanity. Hence our political course both inside the country and in the international arena. As more and more people on earth come to know the truth about the Soviet Union's policy, there will be more and more supporters of this course.

This in fact is what is worrying the ruling circles of imperialism. They regard the Soviet initiatives as a formidable obstacle in the way of the implementation of their imperial designs aimed at world domination and social revenge. Unable to offer the peoples a peaceful historical alternative, one that would meet the interests of all, they are whipping up militarist psychosis which they think can put a brake on historical progress and help them preserve economic and political power. Moreover, they are pinning their hopes on the possibility, however illusory, to hinder the implementation of our plans, impede the development of the socialist countries, push us off from the course of the 27th CPSU Congress and keep us in the fetters of the arms race.

It stands to reason, comrades, that the main aim of our foreign policy should be the frustration of these dangerous plans. The Soviet Union will continue persistently to try and bring about the implementation of its initiatives which accord with the cherished hopes of our people, of all peoples in the world. But we will never allow the United States to achieve superiority in nuclear missiles. And here our Leninist foreign-policy course and the might of our defense rest on the reliable basis of the strategy of accelerating socioeconomic development worked out by the Party and clearly reflected in the draft 12th Five-Year Plan which we are discussing.

The destiny of peace must not be put into the hands of imperialism; imperialist reaction must not be allowed to succeed in imposing a deepening of the military-political confrontation on humanity. This would mean only one thing—sliding toward nuclear war. This was the conclusion expressed in the speeches of all the participants in the Political Consultative Committee conference.

We have discussed with our friends the existing situation in our talks with the United States at Geneva. The following question has now arisen: should we continue marking time at the Geneva talks squabbling with the Americans, something that fully suits them, or search for new approaches that will make it possible to clear the road to a reduction of nuclear arms? Having decided to firmly adhere to the course of searching in practice for a mutually acceptable agreement at Geneva we offered the Americans the following interim variant:

a) that agreement be reached on nonwithdrawal from the ABM Treaty for at least 15 years and that work in the field of SDI be limited to the level of laboratory research, i.e., the threshold the United States has already actually approached;

b) that the strategic offensive arms (ICBMs, SLBMs, and heavy bombers) be limited by equal ceilings. In this case the question of medium-range weapons, including long-range land-based cruise missiles, capable of reaching the territory of the other side, should be solved separately.

This variant once again demonstrates the Soviet Union's desire for a mutually acceptable accord. Although, of course, we would prefer to agree at once on a drastic 50 percent reduction in strategic offensive arms capable of reaching each other's territory.

We have also submitted a draft agreement on medium-range missiles in Europe. We agreed that in the event of a zero ratio between the Soviet Union and the United States in this type of arms, there should remain as many British and French nuclear missiles in the European zone as there are now. We have also stated that we will not increase the number of medium-range missiles in Asia.

In other words, the Soviet Union has made new steps facilitating the search for mutually acceptable accords at the Geneva talks. Time will show the attitude of the United States to this. In any case, it should be clear: if the American side ignores our initiatives this time once again, it will become obvious that the present U.S. Administration is engaged in an unseemly game in a most serious matter on which the future of humanity depends.

The problem of ending nuclear tests has now acquired a special acuteness. To a certain extent this is also a result of the accident at the Chernobyl nuclear power plant. This accident showed that even a small emission of radioactive substances brings misfortune and alarm to thousands of people.

As they expressed their sincere sympathy and offered disinterested help to us, all honest people saw in this accident a far more serious danger. They ask themselves and others: what will happen if the military uses of atomic energy get out of control, accidentally or through evil design? The explosion of even one nuclear bomb would become a far more terrible tragedy for the peoples of many countries. This is what the earth's people have been increasingly pondering.

The United States of America is assuming the gravest responsibility before humanity in refusing to end nuclear testing and join the Soviet moratorium. The world is alarmed by the American behavior. But the seriousness of the situation also calls for doubling and trebling the efforts for ending all nuclear tests and eliminating nuclear weapons.

The misfortune of Chernobyl is our misfortune. We will be able to overcome it. We sincerely and profoundly thank everyone for the sympathy and assistance expressed in connection with the accident. But let Chernobyl, as well as other cases in which atomic energy stopped obeying man, serve as a stern warning to those who have yet to fully realize the nuclear menace that is looming over the world, and who still regard nuclear weapons as a political instrument.

I would like to comment particularly on the new Soviet-American summit meeting. We are in favor of dialogue with Washington. We are not slamming the doors shut: a new meeting with the U.S. President is possible, but, clearly, it requires an atmosphere that would open up prospects for reaching real agreements. We have said this to President Reagan and to the entire world. This position has met with understanding among friends.

But how is the U.S. Administration acting? It is sabotaging the disarmament talks and has declared its intention not to comply with the SALT-II Treaty, saying it was "dead"! Actions that further aggravate the international situation are being taken throughout the world.

A legitimate question arises: Does Washington really want a new meeting, or is all the talk around it merely an attempt to delude world public opinion?

The significance of the Political Consultative Committee meetings is known to be largely determined by the new initiatives they advance. Central to the Budapest meeting was the jointly elaborated, detailed proposal for reducing conventional armaments and armed forces throughout Europe, from the Atlantic to the Urals. Its content is known to you. We are talking about a 25 percent reduction in the armed forces of both sides in the upcoming years. Thus the speculations that nuclear disarmament in Europe, in the event of the preservation of conventional armed forces at their current level, would be to the disadvantage of the West European states are refuted. The fact that the West has not found it possible to simply dismiss this proposal is quite revealing.

Several other important initiatives were agreed upon in Budapest. The idea of pooling the efforts of all countries in peaceful uses of outer space and of creating a special international organization for this purpose was approved. This idea, which was put forward shortly before the meeting, in the speech in Čsepel, has already found expression in the proposal sent to the UN Secretary-General. Questions pertaining to the continued advancement of the concept of establishing a comprehensive system of international security were discussed.

Special mention should be made of the lively, constructive atmosphere of the Budapest meeting.

All comrades—and this is a telltale sign of the times— viewed concrete issues in the light of the common foreign-policy strategy of the allied socialist states. In short, Budapest revealed the unity, the creative cooperation which enriches socialism's international policy and lends even greater weight to its actions in the world arena.

All participants in the conference noted with satisfaction that the work of the supreme body of the Warsaw Treaty Organization has shown greater dynamism and efficiency of late. The decisions adopted at Budapest are a major contribution of the socialist countries to the struggle for improving the international situation.

To sum it up, comrades, we have always made maximum efforts to preserve and consolidate peace, and we will continue to do so. In this noble undertaking, we feel active support for our position from our friends, from all peace-loving forces on earth.

Comrades! Such are the main lessons and conclusions of our post-Congress development, which we must study and use in full measure to advance with success. Such are the domestic and international conditions in which we have started implementing the decisions of the 27th CPSU Congress.

The political task of the five-year plan is to restructure our economy, create a modern material and technical base to ensure faster development of Soviet society, solve major social tasks and maintain a reliable defense of the country. There is not a moment to lose. Everything that we have planned must be done in time, for at issue are the might and prosperity of our country, the positions of socialism in the international arena and the consolidation of peace throughout the world.

A memorable date is approaching—the 70th anniversary of

the Great October Socialist Revolution. Our common patriotic and internationalist duty is to meet that remarkable holiday with rapid economic and sociopolitical advances, with achievements and successes worthy of the land of the October Revolution.

I think that it is necessary, on behalf of the Plenary Meeting, to call on all working people to develop nationwide socialist emulation in order to successfully attain the targets set by the 12th Five-Year Plan, and to appeal to them to transform bold plans into the energy of practical actions. The Central Committee is calling on every Soviet worker to take part in the emulation campaign, to rank among the best during the five-year-plan period, and to make a tangible personal contribution to the common cause at his or her workplace.

The attention of the Party committees and of all Party organizations should be focused on how to tackle the tasks set by the Congress and how to conduct political, economic, organizational and educational work to attain and exceed the targets of the five-year plan. Herein is the highlight of the moment. Therefore, there must be more analysis, more action, greater efficiency, less vague talk and fewer references to objective circumstances.

From every leader and from every Communist the Party expects concrete deeds to lead us forward along the projected road, not vows and assurances. The Central Committee will support the initiative and innovative quest of Party organizations, work collectives, ministries and departments, aimed at achieving the best results. To act persistently and energetically, with initiative, and with a high sense of responsibility is what life today requires of each and every one of us. I am confident that the appeal of the Plenary Meeting will find understanding and response in the working class, among farm workers and the intelligentsia, and will be embodied in the heroism of the everyday, routine work of millions of people. On this, comrades, everything depends!

XIII

A DINNER SPEECH
In Honor of François Mitterrand,
President of the French Republic

Moscow, July 7, 1986

Esteemed Mr. President and Madame Mitterrand, Ladies and Gentlemen,

Comrades,

We are glad to receive in Moscow the President of the French Republic and his wife, members of the French Government, and distinguished representatives of friendly France. The warm welcome the residents of the French capital accorded us in Paris, and the businesslike and candid conversations with the President, statesmen and politicians still remain fresh in our memory.

I would like your present visit to Moscow to be a memorable and interesting one for you. I would like you to feel what is uppermost in the minds of the Soviet people, what their hopes and plans are at this crucial juncture in the development of our society. The basic aims of the strategy of the 27th CPSU Congress are to tap the entire social, economic and democratic potential of socialism, to provide the needed impetus to the country's development and to raise the people's standard of living. Our plans are bold and the work vast; we will abandon all that is outdated or has not proved its value. We are trying out new methods and searching for solutions that are appropriate for attaining the present-day objectives.

The entire country has come into motion. The Soviet people are ready to give their talent, abilities, knowledge, experience and energy to the common cause; this reminds one of the most stirring moments in the history of our nation.

Our plans can be feasibly achieved if peace is to reign. And thus this is our basic policy in international affairs: everything possible must be done to consolidate peace and end the arms race.

The Soviet Union is demonstrating with concrete measures, proposals and unilateral actions, its will to alter the dangerous course of events and to ensure that distrust and hostility at long last be replaced with sensible cooperation based on awareness of our common responsibility for the fate of the world.

I have already said more than once that our goal is not to convert anyone to our belief. And we are not aiming to be winners on some diplomatic "chessboard." Present-day diplomacy must put forth detente as its goal, for a sound and mature policy of detente will benefit all.

This applies to Europe in particular, for Europe is threatened not only by the mortal danger of nuclear war. There are more than 150 atomic reactors and hundreds of chemical plants on European territory. Only a few conventional artillery shells can destroy a reactor and thus take a great toll of human lives. Whether the armed conflict be conventional or nonconventional, it would trigger a catastrophe with global consequences.

Everyone realizes that the Europeans are fed up with the nerve-racking confrontation and tension. They need the fresh air of detente. Here in Europe one has greater perception of the graveness of the international situation and the increased threat of war. For it is in Europe that powerful military groups oppose each other, that mountains of arms have been accumulated and ever-new nuclear missiles are being deployed. But then again Europe is also the continent where states with different social systems—members of military alliances as well as neutral states—have gained the valuable experience of peaceful coexistence.

The economic and political potential of Europe is so great that it should and could speak out more definitely and confidently on its own behalf and press for progress at all the ongoing talks.

Political thought must be completely rid of the tendency to view Europe as a "theater of operations." Europe must set an example of coexistence by sovereign, different, and yet peaceful states—states that are aware of their interdependence and that are building relations on trust.

To achieve this goal the most vital task to be accomplished is the releasing of Europe—from the Atlantic to the Urals—

from the explosive burden of armaments. The USSR, together with its allies, recently advanced major proposals for the reduction of armed forces and conventional armaments in Europe. This move can eradicate all fears, both hypocritical and actual, that the elimination of nuclear arms in Europe would shift the balance in favor of socialist countries, which, allegedly, have an edge in conventional armaments.

Let us approach this entire issue from a new direction: if the West would make corresponding reductions in those types of arms of which it possesses more, we will be quick to eliminate any "surplus" in those types of arms of which we have more. In other words, let us seek a balance at a lower level. This task is a realistic and urgent one, and we have the right to expect a positive and definite response from the West.

Although Europe is referred to as "the Old World," it nevertheless possesses a sense of the new, and a sensitivity for historic changes. This became clear with the emergence of a unique phenomenon described as the European process, "the spirit of Helsinki." It has withstood the first trials and continues serving stability and peace in Europe.

This process must be conducted in all spheres—political, economic, humanitarian and cultural. All three "Helsinki baskets" must be filled with fresh fruit that is good for us all. Our approach is similar to the coming forum which is so important for Europe—the meeting in Vienna of representatives from states participating in the European Conference. We believe that this meeting might signify a turn for the better, which we are ready to promote. We would like to count, in this, on cooperation with France and other countries.

But the first stage of the Stockholm Conference must be completed before the Vienna meeting begins. The situation there gives rise to concern; there is little time left. All participants should have long ago shown a responsible and flexible approach. Only through major mutual concessions on a basis of equality and equal security can success be ensured. The Soviet Union and France, who initiated the Stockholm forum, could already at this stage come to an agreement as to how to promote this.

The human rights issue becomes ever more acute as we approach the 21st century. People are refusing to tolerate arbitrary rule and lawlessness either within their own coun-

tries or in international relations. And this is only natural, for
it is a reflection of the level civilization has reached. We
approach this matter with the highest criteria, maintaining
that this issue embodies the advanced ideals of social justice
and at the same time is one of the components of the all-
embracing system of international security. A statement to
this effect was made at the 27th Party Congress.

The very emergence of Soviet society was made possible by
a great revolution which emancipated the people and gave
rights to tens of millions of working people.

A nation without rights, as to this day some people portray
the Soviet Union, could never have been able to astound the
world by transforming a backward country into a major
power. And this major power is confidently making further
progress. Naturally, we are staunch adherents of a socialist
way of life and take pride in our achievements. But we are not
going to mark time and be content with what we have already
accomplished.

We are also prepared to cooperate in the international
arena on humanitarian issues. These are not mere words. We
are searching for practical solutions in this field as well.

But what happened at the Berne conference on human
contacts, for instance? Progress toward agreement on positions had nearly been achieved, but the United States
quashed this opportunity.

And yet the Soviet Union has unilaterally set about working
on the proposals which we put on the table at Berne. Moreover, the USSR is prepared to adhere to the Berne draft—even
though it was not passed—in its bilateral relations with those
states which would like to reach an appropriate agreement
with us.

Our meeting with you, Mr. President, is taking place almost
twenty years to the day after the historic visit of Charles de
Gaulle to the Soviet Union. That visit not only ushered in a
new stage in Soviet-French relations; it was also a precursor
to positive changes on the European scene as a whole.

Over these past twenty years it has been shown clearly that
when two sides, especially if they are great powers, display at
the national level will and perseverance for the furthering of
political, economic, cultural, and other contacts, everyone
stands to gain. We would like the Soviet Union and France to

continue to set such a good example, which is much needed by Europe and the world as a whole.

We attach great importance to economic, scientific and technological cooperation with France, including such vital areas as the peaceful exploration of space and the development of a reliable safety regime for nuclear power engineering and controlled thermonuclear fusion. Achievements of great interest have already been made in this field, and the basis has been established for long-term and stable cooperation to the end of this millennium and beyond.

The Soviet Union has the firm intention to broaden areas of concord and cooperation between the USSR and France and to do everything possible to make Soviet-French dialogue once again a powerful source of sensible tendencies in world politics.

We wish health and happiness to the President of France and Mme. Mitterrand, and prosperity to the French people.

XIV

MEETING

With Representatives of the
International Forum of Scientists
for a Nuclear Test Ban

Moscow, July 14, 1986

Professor G. B. Marini Bettolo presented Mikhail Gorbachev a declaration to the leaders of all nuclear powers, and especially the Soviet Union and the United States. The declaration was approved unanimously at the forum.

Handing over the document, the professor said:

Dear Mr. General Secretary, it is a great honor and pleasure for me to convey to you, on behalf of all the participants in the International Forum of Scientists for a Nuclear Test Ban, the text of a declaration which we have been drafting for three days. This document is the result of open, constructive and mutually beneficial discussions. Our declaration was approved unanimously.

This was made possible due to the atmosphere created by the Soviet Union's unilateral moratorium on nuclear testing and to the cooperation between scientists in the use of seismic monitoring to verify that nuclear tests are not being conducted.

Mr. General Secretary, allow me to express our hope that all the heads of state will appreciate and accept our actions and efforts in the interests of all mankind.

Mikhail Gorbachev: You are guests and I am here at your request, therefore if anyone would like to say something, please go ahead.

Professor Frank von Hippel: I have been asked to say a few words in addition to what my colleague has said. The Soviet Union's unilateral moratorium on nuclear explosions is of exceptional importance. It has exerted a tremendous influence on world public opinion and has demonstrated the Soviet Union's growing confidence in a new way of thinking. It demonstrates once again the realization in the Soviet Union that the introduction of new nuclear weapons cannot change the fact that both the Soviet Union and the United States have the ability to destroy each other many times.

This new way of thinking is also gaining ground in the United States. The majority of physicists at leading U.S. universities have signed an open letter, in which they state that they consider the SDI program dangerous and express their refusal to work for this project.

The Soviet moratorium on nuclear explosions has also strengthened the position of this new outlook in U.S. public opinion. According to the public opinion polls, the majority of Americans want the United States to join the Soviet moratorium. The latest studies show that 56 percent of all Americans support this idea.

Such matters are the prerogative of the President, and therefore the U.S. Congress usually does not interfere in deciding such questions. Nevertheless, a considerable minority of Congressmen believe that the allocations for nuclear testing must be cut back.

The first such proposal submitted to Congress will most likely be defeated, but if it is supported by a considerable number of Congressmen and if it is defeated by a narrow margin, the positions of opponents of nuclear testing will grow much stronger. In that case, we could expect some positive developments this year. However, this will happen only if the Soviet Union's unilateral moratorium continues.

The forces for peace in the United States have been reinforced considerably due to cooperation between the Academy of Sciences of the USSR and the U.S. Natural Resources Defense Council. The American public fears that the Soviet Union is concealing secrets and this fear is being exploited by the advocates of new nuclear weapons. Your consent to the installation of American seismic equipment in the area of Semipalatinsk, near the Soviet nuclear test range, shows that the Soviet Union has indeed taken a new attitude. This fact is revealed clearly by your willingness to allow others to observe your activities.

To judge by an article in *The New York Times*, the American public is showing interest in our joint venture and this interest can be expected to grow as our joint activity expands. Apart from the fact that seismologists are anxious to dispel fears of Soviet secrecy, they are likewise actually confirming that with specialized instruments it is possible to prevent even the smallest nuclear explosion from being concealed.

I have a seismographic chart which clearly shows how several years ago an earthquake in Kamchatka was monitored in Norway. It also shows a monitored small nuclear explosion—500 tons—which occurred at the same time roughly 2,000 kilometers away from the monitoring device. Thus this kind of equipment can monitor even the most insignificant nuclear explosions.

Yevgeni Velikhov: I would like to mention very briefly the fact that scientists from thirty-two nations have attended our forum and that over seventy people have taken the floor. Among these people are seismologists and physicists who at one time worked on nuclear weapon development. The consequences of using nuclear weaponry were also discussed.

This has been a broad forum, and the major conclusions are the following. It has been convincingly demonstrated that today the problem of control practically does not exist as a technical problem and that the methods of verification worked out by geophysicists are absolutely reliable. Of course, there are various possibilities of concealing nuclear explosions. But it is clear that the improvements made in seismic technology have practically eliminated such possibilities. This is the objective of the joint research activities by the Academy of Sciences of the USSR and the U.S. Natural Resources Defense Council. The question of the importance of a total nuclear test ban was also discussed at the forum. In particular the speakers noted that underground nuclear tests have been and will continue to be used to develop new means of nuclear warfare and thus destabilize the world situation. Therefore, a total ban on tests is essential to close all channels for the qualitative development of nuclear weapons.

[Another speaker at the forum was Professor Cochran. Working with Soviet scientists, he has already installed seismic equipment near Semipalatinsk and obtained his first oscillogram.]

O. Nathan: The speech made by Dr. Theodore Taylor, one of the creators of atomic weapons in the U.S.A., made a great impression on us. He explained that the development of new nuclear weapons by testing requires a lot of time. He claimed, therefore, that the Soviet Union need not be concerned that the United States still has not reached a rational decision concerning nuclear tests. Furthermore, Dr. Taylor contends that the Soviet Union should continue its moratorium without fearing that the Americans might develop new weapons within a short period of time.

Mikhail Gorbachev: Is this the Teller who advocates escalation of the arms race?

Voices: No, they simply have similar names.

Mikhail Gorbachev: Otherwise I would have expressed doubts in the advisability of heeding the views you have just related because Teller's opinion is well known to us.

Joseph Rotblat: I would like to say a few words about the public opinion polls on the Soviet initiative which were taken in Great Britain. The following question was asked: "Should Great Britain reciprocate the Soviet Union's unilateral nuclear moratorium?" Eighty-four percent of the answers were "Yes." What was most interesting, was that this question was answered in the affirmative by 60 percent of the Conservatives, that is, Margaret Thatcher's supporters.

Mikhail Gorbachev: This is interesting in itself and also interesting from a political viewpoint: presidents and prime ministers secure their posts by receiving a majority of votes in elections . . .

Joseph Rotblat: . . . A few remarks about the role of scientists who participated in this forum.

Although we are scientists, we are discussing an issue which is mostly political. But scientists have played a very important and sometimes negative role in this issue. At times we have been forced into this role. I'm speaking as one of those who began the work of developing the atomic bomb in Great Britain at the beginning of the Second World War. Later, however, many scientists voluntarily and even enthusiastically participated in the nuclear arms race. This race is continually fueled by new scientific discoveries, which not only provide an impulse to the nuclear race but at times determine its rate.

Almost any scientific achievement can be used for destructive purposes very quickly. But this is absolutely wrong, for the situation must be the reverse: science must serve the welfare of mankind.

The opportunities for international cooperation among scientists are vast. The Chernobyl disaster can serve as an example. A program which would benefit entire generations could be developed in connection with this disaster.

In the course of the discussion on the problems of banning nuclear tests, we, as scientists, gave our recommendations to you, a political leader. These recommendations can help you in your continuing work to stop the nuclear arms race.

And we hope that the efforts we have undertaken here will help restore the tarnished image of science as a creative force working for the good and welfare of mankind.

Thomas Cochran: I am proud of having been granted the honor of meeting you.

As you know, only one month ago our U.S. Natural Resources Defense Council signed an agreement with the USSR Academy of Sciences. As was noted by previous speakers, the principal goal of our cooperation is to refute the opinion popular among American politicians and the American people that it is impossible to guarantee the infallible detection of all nuclear explosions in the Soviet Union. We are thereby trying to prove that the United States must also stop its tests immediately and work for an agreement banning all nuclear tests.

We have selected our best seismologists from the Universities of California and Colorado for this cooperation effort. We arrived in your country only six days ago. Owing to the assistance of Soviet experts from the Institute of Earth Physics, we have already installed our equipment at one of the three chosen sites. The first seismograms have already been obtained from Karkaralinsk, which lies about 200 kilometers west of the testing ground.

Mikhail Gorbachev: The White House does not believe that the Soviet Union will agree to any, even the most radical, forms of control, both national and international, including on-site inspection and installation of monitoring equipment.

And actually such work has already been accomplished and without any red tape, and moreover without the political leadership; well, not entirely without it, for the political leadership cannot be excluded altogether. Your only concern should be to verify whether tests are being conducted or not, rather than to exercise control over continued testing and improvement of nuclear weapons.

Thomas Cochran: I believe we have fully disproved the arguments advanced by the White House that a comprehensive treaty on banning nuclear tests is impossible and does not lend itself to complete verification.

Mikhail Gorbachev: We are of the same opinion. I believe no one, neither the Soviet Union nor the United States, can count on deceiving the other. The search for new ways to damage the security of the other side must cease. Such an approach is inadmissible. I believe that this is also a sign that a new way of thinking has recently developed. Security must be equal. Otherwise, suspicion and uncertainty appear, and stability is upset as a result of the suspicion and mistrust. Hence the arms race accelerates as each side seeks to increase its own security, just in case. This is the psychological result of such a situation. And this is why a new way of thinking is essential.

Thomas Cochran: The cooperation between Soviet and American scientists can be described as quite exceptional. The assistance offered by Academician Velikhov and the other members of our joint experiment is worthy of all praise. We will find it very difficult to reciprocate when Soviet scientists come to the United States.

The joint Soviet-American research program, which is the topic of discussion, has already met with favorable reaction in the United States. Our research program must be enlarged if the new method, the new approach is to be consolidated. The program proves that scientists not only can make important political statements but can also conduct very valuable scientific tests on a joint basis.

Angel Balevski: I would like to say a few words in connection with the statement made by my colleague from Denmark. I do not know who will outstrip whom; that is unknown. But I do know that the continuation of American nuclear experiments evokes constant fear among mankind. This psychological aspect is very important and I spoke about it at the forum. It is terrifying. All the more so when people fail to perceive the deterioration of the human spirit. It is terrible to live in constant fear, and I think we must allow people to rest from this fear and live a human life. No one has the right to hold humanity in the grips of continuous tension. No matter what the intention may be, this is a crime.

Sune Bergström: I was chairman of the International Committee of Experts in Medical Sciences and Public Health to consider the effects of nuclear war, a committee established by the World Health Organization. Two years ago we submitted a report on the results of our work. The unique cooperation between Soviet and American scientists made a great positive impact on world public opinion.

Mikhail Gorbachev: I welcome the substantial contribution made by medical scientists. I am referring, first of all, to Academician Chazov and Professor Lown. It was of great importance that the whole world heard the competent statement of the outstanding representatives of medical science on the possible consequences of a nuclear conflict and also on the ability of medical science to perform its functions if some madman unleashed a nuclear war.

Sune Bergström: As many have stressed at the forum, the cooperation in verifying nuclear explosions has already improved the international climate. We now consider it important to extend our activites beyond the bounds of this sphere and include other major problems, especially those concerning the developing countries.

If your scientists and your academicians came forward with such an initiative, it could play a tremendous role and make possible the formulation of a long-term program for improving international relations in general.

O. F. Lenci: First of all, I would like to say that the unilateral Soviet moratorium on nuclear explosions has helped in many ways to create a new atmosphere. This fact is recorded in the declaration passed by our forum. The moratorium is, in effect, the first real step toward a comprehensive treaty on the prohibition of nuclear weapon tests, which, in turn, can lead one day to the complete elimination of nuclear weapons.

I also believe that the preservation and extension of the Soviet moratorium on nuclear explosions will be influential in other countries, and especially in my country, Italy. It does not possess nuclear weapons but holds membership in certain organizations. I think that countries such as Italy can play a role in the solution of this problem, different from the one which they are playing today. For instance, such countries could be induced to take more vigorous actions for the conclusion of an agreement on the complete ban on nuclear weapons.

Pyotr Fedoseyev: A distinctive feature of the forum was that there was not just a feeling of concern for the current international situation, but also a desire to act continuously and to show initiative for a ban on tests and against nuclear weapons in general.

The agenda for the round-table discussion concluding the conference included a program of follow-up action as one of its items.

It was proposed both at the forum and in the lobby that the action group continue its activities; the group should not only continue to circulate the adopted documents world-wide and to popularize the results of the forum, but should also serve as a liaison and source of information for the scientific community. The group has pledged to continue its work.

Anatoli Alexandrov: I have attended many international forums, but I would like to point out that this is the first time I have seen such a community of views. We, all of us, representatives of various countries, may have had differing opinions on certain questions, but we were unanimous in our belief that a nuclear war must be prevented, that such a war would be tantamount to the destruction or degradation of mankind.

Mikhail Gorbachev: It would be degradation at the very least, but the most likely result would be destruction.

Anatoli Alexandrov: All agreed that the Soviet Union's unilateral moratorium on nuclear tests was an extremely important move which received response throughout the world. Each called it in his own way—the first step, or the most important step—but these were basically different shades of the same meaning.

All were also unanimous in the belief that all other nuclear countries, beginning with the United States, and nonnuclear states, too, must join the Soviet Union in this endeavor. This would be of paramount importance now, and would serve to relax the colossal tension present today in international relations.

Koji Fushimi: I highly appreciate the bold decision of the Soviet leader to stop underground nuclear testing. This is not only my opinion but, I believe, that of a great many Japanese citizens. I have with me several things which testify to this sentiment among the Japanese people. Here is one of them, a message from the religious leaders of Hiroshima. [He presents the message to Mikhail Gorbachev.]

Derek Paul: Five years ago my colleagues and I founded the organization called Science for Peace. Since then I have attended many different conferences on disarmament, the campaign for peace, etc., in the Soviet Union, and I would say that this forum which I have just attended has made a greater impression on me, for reasons already mentioned. All of us—in any case, the forum participants from the West—will return home more optimistic and resolved in our hope to accomplish something, however small, in the name of peace.

Mikhail Gorbachev: First of all, I would like, through you, to greet all the participants of the Moscow forum of scientists. This forum has discussed the most burning problem of today—the problem of preserving human civilization.

The initiative which was realized at this forum of scientists from more than 30 countries is extremely important, as is everything which is being done today in the effort to stop the arms race and begin a real disarmament process.

I have already had occasion to say, and I will take advantage of this meeting to repeat, that we still hear people ask why we are in such a hurry, and whether it might not be better to draw out the drive against the arms race for many years and even decades. This type of thinking is erroneous. We have reached a stage in the scientific and technological revolution when new discoveries can spur on the arms race and create a situation in which it will be far more difficult to even start talks.

Let us presume that the arms race spreads to outer space. Who can say for certain what will happen then? There are just a few dozen satellites and spaceships in space right now, but emergencies of all kinds happen to them time and again. So what if echelons of military systems are moved there? They would be controlled by computers, which would issue data, but would not analyze the reasons for whatever was happening up there. As a result, the "decisions" upon which the fate and lives of millions of people depend would be made at the technical rather than political level. The whole of civilization would become technology's hostage.

Or take conventional arms. In this sphere, too, scientific discoveries serve as the basis for the appearance of weapons which, in terms of destructive capacity, are not at all inferior to nuclear weapons. In addition, there are chemical and biological weapons. The consequences of their use would be no less disastrous.

Thus we have all reached the point beyond which unpredictable processes can begin. Everyone must act today—politicians, scientists, and people everywhere.

This morning I received the Russian-language text of your forum's declaration. I want to state my attitude toward this document straight away: it is a responsible document and one which meets the interests of all countries regardless of their political systems, and of all people regardless of what political organizations they identify themselves with. This document has special significance because it was drawn up and approved by people competent in their field, and approved unanimously at that, which gives it even more weight.

The results of your forum show that the preconditions now exist in the world for the formation of new approaches to, and a new way of thinking about, the solution of the main questions of the day—halting the nuclear arms race and beginning disarmament. And this process should start, as you have correctly pointed out, with an end to nuclear tests.

You have informed the entire world public in your declaration that we are all now faced with the simple and harsh reality that human civilization will not survive a nuclear war. This warning is timely and convincing, and it demands a great sense of responsibility.

You raise the question of reducing the risk of nuclear war and of the need for energetic measures. The Soviet leadership will support this call, and it agrees with your view that the ending of nuclear tests should be the first step in this direction.

Convincing arguments have been voiced both in the declaration and at our meeting here to the effect that it is possible to verify that nuclear tests have been terminated. This is of immense importance, as it reflects the opinion of people who know what they are talking about.

We are assisting and will continue to assist Soviet and American scientists in carrying out their initiative designed

to use special equipment to make sure that no nuclear explosions are taking place. I have no objection to a single line in
your document.

You have asked the Soviet Government to reexamine the
possibility of extending the moratorium. Well, in the first
place, it is still in effect. And that is the most important thing,
so there is still time and it must not be wasted. Naturally,
your request will be considered most carefully. The Soviet
Government will make a decision, which will then be conveyed to you. But, frankly speaking, this decision will depend
largely on whether or not the United States of America is
going to begin disarmament after all.

Following the meeting with the U.S. President in Geneva,
where we agreed to move in the direction of making the
contents of our accord meaningful and concrete, we began
acting in precisely such a manner. We extended the moratorium—extended it twice. We put forward a program for
the complete elimination of nuclear weapons within 15 years.
We came up with new, far reaching proposals on the abolition
of chemical weapons, including measures to verify that the
industries producing them are being dismantled. We put forward an enormous program for the reduction of conventional
arms so as to allay the fears of the peoples of the Western
countries. Finally, we recently put on the table compromise
proposals at the Geneva talks. I spelled them out in a letter to
President Reagan—they concern both medium-range missiles
and reductions in strategic nuclear weapons.

Naturally, we expect adequate response from the American
side and from the West in general. So far we are not satisfied
with the position of either the American Administration or
the other Western governments. That Administration has
taken a negative stand regarding an end to nuclear tests. At
one time the issue of verification was used as an argument.
Now that this problem, as we see, is being conclusively resolved by virtue of the well-known position of the Soviet
Union and of your arguments, that is, the arguments of scientists, we are waiting to see what new reasonings will turn up
to support the continuation of testing. We have already begun
to hear talk to the effect that the Soviet leadership's idea to
eliminate nuclear weapons is utopian, for in a world like ours
one can hardly do without these weapons.

Nor have we yet received satisfactory replies to our proposals on medium-range missiles and on strategic arms. We
have received only the declaration that SALT-II is dead. Thus,
not only are no efforts being made to find and work out new
international mechanisms to halt the arms race and subsequently begin disarmament; the only remaining brakes on
that race are being dismantled. SDI, so they say, is necessary, among other things, because many countries today are
capable of developing a nuclear bomb of their own and, allegedly, a countermeasure is needed in case some madman
launches a nuclear attack or makes an attempt at nuclear
blackmail.

Totally paradoxical arguments are used to defend SDI.
This, alas, draws a certain response from scientists and politicians. It is said that SDI is the way to the development of
science, to new heights in scientific and technological progress. But I will tell you that this type of thinking is warped—
everything is turned upside down. Can we not make advances
in science and technology, every part of scientific knowledge,
including the development of new materials, radio electronics, computer technology, mathematics, etc., through civilian projects? The Vega program is a recent and convincing
example of this. I heard the reports of Academician Sagdeyev
and other Soviet scientists who carried out this most interesting project with the participation of their foreign colleagues.
They needed new solutions and new materials. These were
found. They needed new solutions to the problem of controlling the maneuvers of a sophisticated craft over great dis-
tances. These were developed. They needed a stable radio and
TV communication link. This was established. They needed
new mathematical discoveries and computations to accomplish such a complex task. These were made. They needed
accurate information about the situation on Venus and near
Halley's Comet. This was obtained.

Many countries, Western included, participated in the project. Especially fruitful cooperation in that field was achieved
with scientists from France.

Now we have come to grips with the problem of developing
a dependable source of energy. The problems of energy, like
those of food and ecology, are the central, global problems of
the future. If there were no projects in the military field,

efforts in this peaceful sphere would be making progress at a much faster rate. Recently the Chairman of the Council of Ministers of the USSR, Nikolai Ryzhkov, submitted to the United Nations the Soviet Government's proposals on the development of international scientific cooperation in peaceful uses of outer space.

Thus, advances can be made in science on the basis of civilian projects. The argument that science and technology can be developed only through an arms race is simply absurd. The question to ask then is this: what is the problem? Who, God perhaps, has taken away the ability to grasp the realities of today's world, of the nuclear-missile space age? These two men [pointing to portraits of Marx and Lenin] taught us that in order to get to the heart of the matter, we must clear the surface of all sorts of rubbish and lay bare the motives and interests behind one position or another.

Whose interests are met by the proposals of political forces, scientists and the public, who are insisting on scaling down the arms race, on starting disarmament and on the eventual elimination of nuclear weapons? I believe these proposals meet the interests of all nations and there are no higher interests.

We realize that a group of countries which would like to use their superior arms arsenals for political pressure might have interests of their own. And there are other interests, I would say, of a lower order. There are the interests of the military-industrial complex, which are also very real. But, first of all, these are not the interests of any nation, let alone human civilization. And, second, neither civilian research, nor research into energy problems, nor anything else would suffer if military research and war production were stopped. The forces which are involved in the development of weapons today could work fruitfully in civilian areas. Neither science nor the industries currently involved in war production would be left idle. Everyone would only stand to gain.

So, we need a new way of thinking. It is impossible to solve the burning problems of today, let alone of the coming century, if one is to be guided by views characteristic of past centuries, past decades, or, in any case, of times prior to the emergence of nuclear weapons and the recent upsurge in the scientific and technological revolution.

I do not wish to impose my views on anyone. I do not expect you to accept them without careful thought. Our views were spelled out at the Congress. Their essence, in brief, is that we all live in the nuclear-space era, in a complex, interrelated and controversial world. And we must learn to live together, no matter how different we may be. Other countries have their own type of democracy; let them enjoy it. But do not let them encroach on our right to our democratic values. But then, these are matters of secondary importance.

The most important thing now is this: either we survive, cooperating and preserving the earth, the ocean, the skies, the whole environment, or we lead civilization to disastrous consequences. We must get rid of the outdated notion that the world is someone's domain. The world of today means coexistence of nations and states. It is a multitude of countries, each with a history of its own and each at its own stage of development. But everyone must recognize that each country has the sovereign right to choose its own type of state structure, to conduct its domestic affairs independently.

We recognize this right and will act accordingly. But we demand that others respect this right as well. International relations will become chaotic unless the sovereign right of every nationality and every country is recognized. Philosophical recognition is not enough; we must act according to this recognition. You can rest assured that the Soviet Union will uphold this conviction firmly. At the same time, we have absolutely no intention of placing the fate of the world, our country, and other nations at the mercy of those who expect to dictate their will to the entire world.

We are in constant debate with America, and at times this debate is heated. Nevertheless, we do not paint America all black, or even in just two colors, black and white. We see the real America, America as it is. And we realize that there are many people in American society who share a realistic approach to the problems of today.

We must work and create relations of a new type in international and interstate affairs. Neither the Soviet Union nor the United States will be able to be in command of the world. The world has changed. And unless this is recognized, gross blunders may be made in politics. We proceed from precisely this view, as you will witness for yourselves. I think the Soviet

Union has already advanced serious arguments confirming this viewpoint.

Returning to the subject of the forum, I would like to conclude by saying that I fully agree with your opinion that an end to nuclear testing would be a major step in the right direction, a step toward ending the arms race and the process of technically improving nuclear weapons, and toward their eventual elimination altogether.

The opinion was expressed that this forum should not become an isolated event, that the action group should continue its work. The initiative of the Soviet and American physicians has set a useful example. Their work began with what seemed a one-time meeting. This first meeting, however, laid the foundation at what has become a very influential movement of people competent in their field. I think that if the efforts started in Moscow were continued by scientists in yet another field, that of technology, their work would only be welcomed. But this, of course, must be your own decision.

I am most pleased with this meeting and, most importantly, with its spirit and content. Today it is more important than ever before that politics and science cooperate. Today it is essential that every field of science analyze the political consequences of its discoveries and achievements. And likewise, politics must be based on scientific achievements, on the strict analysis, objective evaluations and predictions offered by science.

I favor the unification of politics and science. Every country stands to gain from such a unification in regard both to domestic affairs and to the solution of the problems which we are discussing today.

Thank you. I hope that the work you have started will continue and will be supported by all those who are concerned about the present-day situation in the world.

XV

SPEECH

On Domestic and International Subjects

Vladivostok, July 28, 1986

Comrades,

I have long wanted to visit the Far East. This is not only because one is naturally drawn to places where he has never been and is motivated by a desire to see what he has never seen. It is also because one cannot have a complete picture of our Homeland, its past, present and future without getting to know your vast and beautiful part of the country.

The Far East is always associated in our thinking with the enormous expanses of the Soviet Union, stretching from the Baltic and Black seas to the Pacific, as well as with the courage, industry and fortitude of the people who have settled and defended this land, and with the novelty and scope of today's work. It was with special warmth that Vladimir Ilyich Lenin spoke of the city of Vladivostok, calling it "one of our own towns."

The feat of valor accomplished by our compatriots, the pioneers who have blazed the trail to the Pacific, will forever remain in the people's memory. The storming of Spassk and Volochayevka, the energetic development of the territory at the time of the first five-year plans, and the soldierly exploits of the border guards on those sacred frontiers will never be forgotten. The gallantry of the Far Eastern divisions and Pacific seamen who fought at Moscow and Stalingrad and in the final battles of the Second World War in the East will also live forever in the nation's memory.

History is made by people. The history of the Far East brings to mind the names of the intrepid pioneers Dezhnev, Khabarov and Nevelskoy. It is also associated with the glorious names of Lazo, Postyshev, Sukhanov, the Sibirtsev brothers, Bonivur, Chasovitin, Blyukher and Uborevich. I would like to mention among those who inspire others by their example today Party and Civil War veteran Ivan Andreyevich Chuprynin; Hero of Socialist Labor Yuri Petrovich Volkov, captain of fishing vessels; Hero of Socialist Labor

329

Anatoly Andreyevich Belov, leader of a hull-building team; Galina Vladimirovna Merkulova, head of a team of finishers and alternate member of the CPSU Central Committee; and Nikolai Nikolayevich Dubinin, holder of the honorary title of People's Teacher of the USSR.

The Far East, celebrated by Arsenyev and Fadeyev, has always been and will forever remain dear to the heart of every Soviet person. I am glad of this opportunity to visit Maritime Territory, to see how you live and work, and to learn what is being done here today and what will be done here tomorrow, particularly since the Far East and Siberia have been assigned a special place in the plans put forward by the 27th CPSU Congress.

I have had quite a few businesslike and interesting meetings, both preplanned and impromptu, at factories, on ships, at institutes and, finally, simply on the street these last few days. These have been useful, frank and friendly. The talking has been straightforward, as it should always be when discussing the business at hand, especially the current job of restructuring.

Our meeting today is in honor of a very special occasion: Vladivostok is being presented with the Order of Lenin. The city has been awarded this highest distinction for the achievements of its working people in economic and cultural advancement and for its great contribution to Far Eastern economic development.

I am very pleased to carry out the instruction of the Central Committee of our Party and the Presidium of the Supreme Soviet of the USSR. *(The audience applauds as Mikhail Gorbachev attaches the order to the city's banner.)*

From the bottom of my heart I congratulate you and all the people of Vladivostok, recipient of two orders. The Order of Lenin on your banner is a well-deserved award, earned by the dedicated and strenuous labor of this beautiful city's remarkable people—sailors, ship-builders, fishermen, workers in the mechanical engineering and the power industries, construction and transport personnel, scientists, physicians and teachers, veterans and young people alike. This honor is rightfully shared by the border guards, the troops of the Far Eastern military district and the seamen of the Red-Banner Pacific Fleet. It crowns the fine accomplishments of the many generations who have done much to settle, protect and develop the country's Pacific coast.

Vladivostok today is a modern industrial, cultural and scientific center, a major port, the heart and soul of Soviet Maritime Territory and one of the most notable cities in the country as a whole. May the Homeland's award be a fresh inspiration for you.

Please accept the congratulations of the Party's Central Committee, the Presidium of the Supreme Soviet of the USSR and the Soviet Government, their wishes for success in your work and for further great accomplishments in the life of the city, its work collectives and every family.

Comrades,

It has now been over a year since the April Plenary Meeting of the Central Committee and close to five months since the 27th Party Congress. This time has been marked by an active search for new approaches to solving the problems that have arisen in Soviet society and by principled assessments of our achievements and failures alike.

We now have a wide-ranging long-term program of action to accelerate the country's social and economic development, which takes into account both our own aspirations and the more important trends in world development. We also have more detailed guidelines for the shorter term—the State Plan for the 12th five-year development period, which has been drawn up following an in-depth analysis of the state of affairs and a probe for reserves and ways and methods of ensuring dynamic development for Soviet society.

The time has come for us to look to ourselves for the fulfillment of the plans. We must be strict in this, making no allowances for anybody. The results of the nation's economic performance in the first half of the year have already been summed up. They show that the positive trends initiated in the economy are gaining momentum, even if they are not of equal strength throughout. We have been able to impart greater dynamism to economic processes and to raise production growth rates and labor productivity. Measures to improve the situation in mechanical engineering, the fuel and energy sector, the agroindustrial complex, the iron-and-steel industry, the chemical and petrochemical industries, and other sectors have begun to take effect.

Social tasks have also been tackled better. More housing has been built, and a greater number of social and cultural facilities have been made available. Where the local authorities work resourcefully and energetically, the population has become better provided with foodstuffs, manufactured goods and consumer services. Changes like these can only be welcomed.

But let us be frank, comrades: these pleasing and encouraging shifts have been achieved primarily as a result of measures to tighten up labor, state and planning discipline. We have imposed higher standards on how the plans are worked out and met, demanded greater order in production, begun to work better and effectively cracked down on drunkenness—and the positive results have been quick to show.

Though the indices for the six months are basically good, growth rates in some sectors dropped in May and June, and a number of ministries failed to cope with their plans. An irregular rate of production is still a major problem, as is rather inefficient use of what we have. There has been no apparent improvement in the quality of goods, which, you know, is our common problem.

This all leads to one definite conclusion: the qualitative change needed to truly consolidate the trend for accelerated growth has yet to take place. But then I think you understand and will agree that it could not have come about, considering the fact that the vital economic, social, organizational, ideological, and other measures are just beginning to come into force and cannot, of course, have an immediate effect. Consequently, the increased rates of national economic growth are not yet stable and perhaps, as I have said, we cannot yet expect them to be so.

Therefore it is inadmissible now to go to either of the two extremes. It is naive, and harmful, to assume that since economic indicators have improved, the effort to restyle our work has already begun in real earnest and is proceeding at full tilt everywhere. This is still far from the case. In a number of regions and economic sectors, they are just talking about the work of restructuring but making no progress.

It is equally inadmissible, however, to give in to the difficulties of restructuring and to the resistance or indifference of those accustomed to drifting with the tide and working in the old manner. As was rightly stressed at the 27th Party Congress, we are embarking on a difficult job and setting ourselves realistic but challenging goals which can only be attained if we learn from life, constantly ponder its experience, lessons and new developments.

We are in effect only beginning this work, successfully in some areas and not so successfully in others. The further we go, the more clearly we see the complexity of our task and the enormity of the workload at hand. But we cannot—we shall not—back out, as we simply have no alternative to the acceleration strategy. I have said this on many occasions and I would like to repeat it once again here in Vladivostok.

Of course, we must not, by either prodding or poking people, awake in them a desire to act against the laws of social development or to try somehow to get around and "outwit" those laws and objective conditions. In pursuing a policy of restructuring, the Party and its Central Committee proceed from a different premise—the need to get to know those laws more quickly and thoroughly and competently take them into account in our activities, and the pressing need to remove all impediments and obstructions artificially created on this road.

The tangible, objective results achieved in the first six months of the five-year-plan period testify to the Soviet people's support of the acceleration policy, and they have expressed this support in the most valuable way—through practical action.

Here in Vladivostok, as elsewhere, I have also been carrying out what may be called my new duties; I have been asking people one and the same question: are they clear on the policy worked out by the Party and presented to the nation, or do they have doubts? I have been pleased to hear people here on Far Eastern soil speak out emphatically in support of the Party's people-oriented policy, a policy followed in the interests of every Soviet family and every Soviet person, in the interests of the country's future. It is essential that this support, this popular resolve to grapple with difficulties and eliminate them, should be used to full effect and with the greatest possible return to fulfill the tasks set forth by the 27th Congress of the CPSU. It is in this light, comrades, that I would like to touch upon some of the issues of development in the Far East and consult you, as a continuation of the discussions I have been holding for the third day with you Far Eastern people, on how we can more quickly transform this region and put its riches at the service of the Soviet people and more fully satisfy the needs of those living here.

The Far East has been traditionally referred to as the country's outpost on the Pacific. This is certainly true. But this view of the region is no longer broad enough. Maritime Territory and the Far East should be made into a highly developed economic complex.

I see that you are very ready to tackle this task. I think that, perhaps, you who have lived here for years or even decades, know even better that the full-scale development of the Far East is not an easy job. But since you have responded so favorably to what I have said, you must be confident that we are equal to this task now. The real basis for this is everything that has been done in the past years. A major scientific and production potential has been formed here. Large factories representing all industries have been built. Mines, electric power stations, new railroads, ferry crossings and ports have been commissioned. Hundreds of thousands of hectares of land have been improved. The USSR Academy of Sciences has set up an affiliate in the Far East with its own network of research centers. Skilled workers and specialists have been trained.

As a result, the industrial output here has nearly trebled in the past two decades, agricultural production having risen by more than 50 percent. Today the Far East accounts for 40 percent of the country's fish catches. In the past four five-year-plan periods, 62 million square meters of housing have been built—enough to accommodate the population of Vladivostok about seven times over. While the growth in the labor force remains insufficient, the population has grown by 40 percent in the past 20 years. In short, the country's economy now has an extensive base on the Pacific.

Guided by the principles of the 27th Congress and the acceleration policy, we should, however, ask ourselves squarely: do the pace of economic and social development, the performance of scientific institutions and the scope of research work in the Far East today really correspond to its growing role and the new targets set by the Party? Is the potential amassed here really being used efficiently enough?

The strategy of accelerating social and economic development also demands a new regional policy. In this strategy the
Party stresses the need to give priority to the development of
eastern regions. Therefore we should, among other things,
take a careful look at the economic prospects of the Far East.
This should be done promptly, in the light of the region's
special significance.

This should be done without delay also because the Far
Eastern economy has begun to show growth rates below
those of the national economy as a whole, though it would
seem this should be the other way round. As a result, the
region's share in the country's production, far from increasing, is diminishing. The lag in solving social problems, especially in housing, has become more pronounced. I have
heard quite a few remarks and suggestions on this score
directed at the Party's Central Committee and the Soviet
Government. These remarks have been justified.

It cannot be said that the development of the Far East has
been neglected. Over the past few years the Central Committee and the Council of Ministers of the USSR have taken
decisions specifying measures to advance the power industry,
ferrous and nonferrous metallurgy and coal mining, to further develop fisheries, forestry, the woodworking industry,
transport and other economic sectors, to increase the production of rice and soya, to restructure the countryside, and to
improve the state of affairs in the cultural field. So far, unfortunately, much of what was planned has been badly executed.

This reflects a failure to understand the role and significance of the Far Eastern economy and, in the final analysis,
the political shortsightedness of some highly placed officials
at the State Planning Committee and the State Committee for
the Supply of Materials and Equipment; the Ministries of
Non-Ferrous Metallurgy, Coal Mining, Power Development
and Electrification; and a number of other departments. The
government agencies of the Russian Federation and those on
the local level also bear a large part of the blame.

We have to amend the situation in a fundamental way, make
certain that growth accelerates rather than slows down, and
change over from extensive development factors to all-out
intensification through scientific and technological progress.

It is essential to slash the time it takes to solve problems and sharply increase the contribution of the Far East to the country's economic potential. Above all, this requires that priority be given to raising the standard of living in the Far East, substantially improving working conditions and the provision of housing, foodstuffs and manufactured goods, and upgrading the entire social sphere. The latter is clearly lagging, though it is of key importance to having people settle down in the Far East and ultimately has a bearing on the pace of its development.

The task now is to work out a concept for long-term Far Eastern development under a uniform state regional policy. This concept should obviously be embodied in a comprehensive program. Its aim will be to create a highly efficient economic complex in the Far East, which will have a solid resource, science, and production base of its own, optimum economic makeup and well-developed social infrastructure, and will become an organic part of the nationwide and international division of labor. Much has been done in this respect in the process of drafting the five-year plan. It is strenuous and will require quite an effort to fulfill.

However, this is just the beginning of the work to speed up the development of the entire region. Not to get ahead of what should be analyzed in detail by the experts with the participation of the broad public, I shall look at just a few of the most important trends in this work.

First, the geographic position of the Far East itself predetermines the course for setting up there a highly developed complex of branches of industries connected with tapping the resources of the ocean. For many reasons the country's fisheries will be increasingly shifted to the Far East. Substantial funds have been invested to set up a large-capacity fishing fleet in the area. Meanwhile, the equipment of on-shore services lags considerably behind. Mechanization of arduous work is at a low level. As a result, a considerable number of expensive vessels are idle or not effectively used. The capacities of the repair base, storage facilities, fishing ports, and processing enterprises are chronically insufficient. In a word, serious measures are needed across the board to develop the fishing industry in the Far East. Special attention must go to producing biologically active substances from sea products.

This trend is developing in other countries and has proved highly effective.

Second, the issue of the comprehensive use of the rich natural resources of the region. The attention of the Ministry of Non-Ferrous Metallurgy must be directed to the potentialities of the Far East. Geologists have established that the region abounds in large deposits of nonferrous metals, gold and silver, and many other valuable elements and minerals. Their mining and processing can be widened substantially if approached in a thrifty and confident way. We must begin working in earnest on the development of large-scale nonferrous metallurgy in the Far East. Complete production cycles for manufacturing various finished products must be created here. The Far East should no longer be regarded solely as a raw material base. I think that you should not put up with this. This should be well realized in the central administrative bodies: I mean those on the all-Union and Russian Federation levels. We must use the territory's huge raw material reserves to build complete-cycle enterprises here and produce at least semifinished products, or, even better, finished goods. What I have said about nonferrous metallurgy applies even more so to the Ministry of the Timber and Pulp and Paper, and Woodworking Industry, which must decisively begin the intensive processing of timber. In this connection, there are large-scale economic development tasks posed in the zone of the Baikal-Amur Mainline. A special decision of the Central Committee and the government on this matter is now being drafted. You face major undertakings in this area, too.

Third, a chronic lag in the fuel and energy complex of the Far East is holding back other branches of industry and must be overcome quickly. You must not live without looking to the future, expecting that no matter what, fuel and energy assistance will come from the center. You have huge resources of fuel and hydrocarbon raw materials. There has been talk for more than a decade, for instance, of tapping the gas in North Sakhalin, yet that work has just started. Solution of the problems of operation of the oil and gas deposits of the Sakhalin shelf has also been delayed. Meanwhile, hundreds of trainloads of oil go to the Far East from Western Siberia. We have to bring millions of tons of oil from other parts of the country into the Far East.

The implementation of the measures to develop the fuel and energy sector in the Transbaikal and Far Eastern areas, which were drawn up previously, are way behind schedule.

The Far East can and must fully meet its energy needs through its own resources. People in the Far East must make an effort to create a reliable base for developing power engineering, speed up the building of a complex of thermal and hydropower stations, and form a large unified power grid. We must proceed from the view that the Far East, in the long term, will not only supply nearby areas with fuel and energy but become a major exporter of them.

Fourth, concerning a higher pace for the course of development of the production infrastructure. Certainly this is not only a problem for the Far East, but it is perhaps particularly acute here. It is essential to accelerate the development of a modern construction industry in your region. I would say that this is the basis for the plans that we are outlining here in the Far East. The large teams of the railway builders who so quickly laid the Baikal-Amur Mainline have arrived in the Far East. They can and must be employed, for instance, in the reconstruction of old railway lines that presently have a low capacity, or in the construction of highways and ports, or other necessary facilities.

Marine transport must also be used more effectively. Its infrastructure must be strengthened. Advanced forms of carriage should be developed. You have experience in this respect. Just today I saw the port of Vostochny in Nakhodka at work. It is an excellent modern port. It can serve as an example for many. The ferry to Sakhalin, for instance, operates well. Measures should also be taken more quickly for enhancing the economic effect of the through navigation along the Arctic route.

Fifth, the resolution of matters involving the regional policy with regard to science and technology and the installation of the latest equipment at enterprises, with the conditions of their maintenance in the area taken into account, has a specific character. It appears that there are numerous machine-building enterprises here, many having highly skilled personnel and a good name.

But because of a lack of coordination between departments, a considerable part of the machinery manufactured in the Far

East goes to the European part of the country, and a stream of equipment comes from there to meet the needs of the Far East. These questions should be promptly analyzed. The specialization of machine-building plants here should be decided with the emphasis on large-capacity, well-equipped facilities to turn out machinery for the needs of the region and for export.

Sixth, possibilities for developing the Far Eastern economy with an export trend should be utilized in full measure. The region's share in the country's exports is today very low, far below its potentialities. Cardinal changes are needed in this sphere, along with new approaches to invigorate coastal and border trade and the use of progressive forms of economic ties with foreign countries, including cooperation in production and joint enterprises. A specialized export base needs to be set up.

Seventh, the principle of allocating leftover funds to the social sphere came in for sharp criticism at the Party Congress. This is an old ailment. It has also become widespread in a number of eastern areas of the country, including the Maritime Territory. Some 7.7 million people inhabit the vast territory of the region. Nearly half of all food is brought here. In the past 20 years the per capita output of milk, potatoes, and vegetables has dropped in the Far East. Many officials in territories, regions, areas, districts, and farms have resigned themselves to low harvests, small yields of milk, and slow weight gain in cattle, as well as to receiving supplies of fodder from other areas. Even the proposals for the plans for the next 15–20 years envisage increasing the food supply to the Far East through deliveries from other regions of the country.

I think this is a shortsighted line. There is one way out: to create a highly developed agricultural base and food industry in the area. For these purposes we must vigorously develop all branches of the agroindustrial complex, specifically the fertilizer industry, on the basis of intensification technologies, and cooperate with neighbor countries in the solution of agricultural tasks.

A tense situation has formed in the region as regards housing construction and the construction of social and cultural amenities. This is a hindrance to the settlement of those who arrive here for permanent residence. I think that the responsibility for such a state of affairs must be shared with the local bodies by the appropriate ministries and departments, both all-Union and republican.

I have reproved the authorities of the territory mainly for the insufficiency of what they are presently doing for the development of the social sphere. At any rate it falls short of the actually existing need. But I think that a substantial part of this reproof should be addressed to Moscow-based departments.

Many of them are most lavish when it comes to the development of production facilities in quite different spheres, but are very sparing in the funds allocated to develop the social sphere. As a result, manufacturing capacities are set up, but there is no one to use the production potential in a really efficient way. This is one of those "tricks" that cost the state dearly. Such is the political appraisal of that phenomenon.

You have a wonderful land, beautiful sea, unique nature, rich mineral springs. As I was flying to Nakhodka today the fog faded, the clouds vanished and the sun appeared and I saw the picturesque country from midair. The hills, the Golden Valley, and the ocean are close by. This produces a great impression. It is truly a wonderful land.

The Far East must become one of the leading health resorts of the USSR, a major center of domestic and international tourism, including oceanic and high-latitude tourism. This, by the way, would also replenish resources for accelerating construction in cities and villages.

Yesterday, on my way to a Young Pioneer camp, I met a group of holiday-makers. It turned out that the group included people from different parts of the country. And what is interesting is that for many of them it was not the first visit to this place. They have come to love this land and its nature. Their unanimous advice was to promote holiday facilities here.

The reason for the present situation is clear. Unsatisfactory construction of housing and social and cultural amenities is explained by a lack of the necessary basis, a lag in construction facilities, the weakness of collectives of builders. This can no longer be tolerated. If dealing with social matters is vitally needed for the whole country, this is two or three times as applicable for the Far East.

What should be done to overcome the difficulties which have accumulated over the years? Both central and local bodies are to blame for this. So, action has to be taken simultaneously from above and below in order to remedy the situation. I can assure you that the CPSU Central Committee and the government will be urging the all-Union and republican ministries to tackle the problems of the eastern areas of the country, including your territory.

The Soviet Far East has an unforgettable past, and, I am sure, a glorious future. This is a territory of vast natural wealth, huge social and economic possibilities, and great international prospects. It depends on you and, of course, on the attention of the central bodies, how we will run the affairs of that very important region of the country and what results we will achieve.

I understand that the remarks made, and the sharpness with which the problems were formulated, are not totally appropriate to today's occasion. But such is the constructive Leninist tradition: to look ahead while assessing what has been done. The most important thing now is not to lose our sense of perspective, to lay the foundation for scaling new heights. The main thing is to concentrate on your future tasks arising from the decisions of the 27th Congress. And I believe that even such a festive occasion as the presentation of a high award is suitable for this kind of approach, including critical analysis.

These are our common plans and concerns, comrades. They show the Soviet Union's true intentions better than any verbal subterfuges. However much the ruling forces of imperialism may try to distort them, we have said openly and honestly and will continue telling all peoples and governments: yes, we need peace; we again and again issue the call to end the arms race, stop nuclear madness and eliminate nuclear weapons, and to search persistently for a political settlement to regional conflicts.

We are witnessing phenomena of paramount importance. The realization that there should be *peace for all* is forcefully grasping the minds of the peoples even where the governments continue to think that weapons and war are tools of politics. It is precisely for all, since a nuclear war would not be a clash of only two blocs, two confronting forces. It will lead to a global disaster, in which human civilization will be threatened with destruction.

Our initiatives on nuclear disarmament, on a considerable reduction of conventional weapons and armed forces, verification, and creation of a healthier international atmosphere were met in different ways.

The friendly countries have expressed support for them. The countries of the socialist community regard them with good reason as a component part of the general policy of socialism in the world arena. And not only because these initiatives have been coordinated with them, not only for principled internationalist considerations, but also because we are both engaged in a purely peaceful undertaking—the perfection of our societies. The salutary process of our drawing closer together is intensified on that basis, economic integration is filled with new contents, concrete steps are made to create joint plants and amalgamations, human contacts are broadened. In a word, a progressive, mutually beneficial process of deepening cooperation and fraternity among the peoples of the community is under way.

The developing world shows much interest in our plans and intentions—both internal and international ones. We note that many developing countries wish to expand and deepen economic, scientific and cultural cooperation with the Soviet Union. We are prepared for that.

It would be fair to say that the Western public at large and representatives of the business community who have a realistic view of things, who do not suffer from anticommunist paranoia and do not associate themselves with profits from the arms race, regard our plans seriously and with interest. They also stand for peace and cooperation, for the development of healthy economic, scientific and cultural ties with the Soviet Union. We welcome such an approach.

Yet, in many capitalist countries the tone is set, as before, by forces that have been in the past and will in the future be blinded by animosity toward socialism, by imperial ambitions or close links with the war business. And this business, as is known, is extremely voracious and ruthless. Yesterday it needed millions, today it needs billions, and tomorrow it will need trillions. It will never start manufacturing, of its own free will, toys for children instead of missiles. Such is its nature.

The ruling circles of the U.S.A. and some countries allied to it are trying either to picture our peace initiatives as sheer propaganda or to make it appear that only the Soviet Union stands to gain from them. Yes, we stand to gain from disarmament, if we are to use that expression, just as all peoples whose governments now spend billions on the arms race stand to gain from disarmament. Yet, this is only a part of the truth. I will even say, a small part of the truth. The most important truth is that our initiatives stem from a profound concern for the future of humanity.

In the face of nuclear threat it is absurd and criminal to act according to an old, already dead scheme: what is good for the socialist countries must be rejected. Here one can clearly see class narrow-mindedness, a primitive ideological mechanical approach, and the growing political influence of militarism. Yet, I am not inclined to believe that the military-industrial complex is omnipotent. We see that the world public realizes ever more clearly the danger of militarism. We see that in the United States, too, despite the constant whipping up of chauvinistic sentiments, a sense of realism is growing, and the realization is deepening that the source of military threat to the U.S.A. is not the Soviet people, not the socialist countries, not the peasants of Nicaragua, not the faraway Vietnamese or Libyans, but its own arms manufacturers, the irresponsible politicians serving them, and the adventuristic military.

Of course we are aware that the arms race, which is gaining momentum, serves not only the aims of making superprofit and of war preparations, but also—and this is not of the least importance—other immoral aims, which are essentially to exhaust the Soviet Union economically, frustrate the Party's course for achieving a further rise in the living standards of the people, and hamper the implementation of our social program. We also know who are those that continue to cherish the hope of bringing about a planned, systematic destruction of the USSR and of other socialist countries, using to that end economic, moral-psychological, propaganda, political and military methods.

But it can be said that this is a futile attempt; it always has been and still is today. The time has come to reckon with the realities rather than to make policy on the basis of illusions and misconceptions. If no accords are reached, this will not bring relief to the world, no tranquility will set in. Fear will not disappear until some rulers in the West give up the attempts, which are perhaps consoling for them, but fruitless, and above all dangerous, to bring the Soviet Union to its knees, split the socialist society and hamper our advance.

The time urgently demands a new understanding of the present stage in the development of civilization, of international relations, of the world. The world is full of contradictions, it is complex, but it is objectively united by bonds of interdependence. International relations are such that, with all the differences and clashes of interest, one can no longer live according to the millennia-old traditions of "fist law." And civilization has demonstrated an unprecedented strength of the human mind and human labor and at the same time its own fragility, its vulnerability to the forces released by the human genius but placed at the service of destruction.

All that dictates the need for and makes urgent a radical break with many customary attitudes to foreign policy, a break with traditional political thinking, traditional views on problems of war and peace, on defense, on the security of individual states and international security. In this connection it is clear that our radical, global, in the full sense of the word, proposals such as the program for the elimination in this century of nuclear and other mass destruction weapons, a total ban on nuclear weapons tests, a ban on chemical weapons, proposals on cooperation in the peaceful uses of outer space, and a whole set of other proposals, concern the whole world, all countries.

The main problem confronting mankind today—that of survival—is equally acute and urgent for Europe, Africa, America and Asia. Yet in each part of the world it looks different. Therefore, while being here, in Vladivostok, it is natural to look at international policy issues from the Asian-Pacific standpoint.

Such an approach is justified for many reasons. In the first place, a greater part of our country's territory lies east of the Urals, in Asia—in Siberia and the Far East. It is here that many national tasks put forward by the Party Congress will be carried out. Therefore, the situation in the Far East as a whole, in Asia and the ocean expanses adjoining it, where we are permanent inhabitants and seafarers of long standing, is to us of a national, state interest.

Many major states of the world, including the USSR, the United States, India, China, Japan, Vietnam, Mexico and Indonesia are situated on the enormous expanses of this territory extending over almost half of the earth. Here are situated states which are considered to be medium-sized ones, but are rather big by European standards—Canada, the Philippines, Australia and New Zealand, and tens of comparatively small and tiny countries. Some of them have a history covering millennia or many centuries, others have formed in modern times, and still others have formed quite recently.

Asia, which woke up to a new life in the 20th century, has enhanced world progress with its diversified and unique experience in the fight for freedom and independence. This is not only history. This is a living legacy forming an important part of the foundations of the current political realities in this part of the world.

Every country has its own social and political system with all conceivable shades, its own traditions, achievements and difficulties, its own mode of life and beliefs, convictions and prejudices, its own understanding of spiritual and material values. Each country has something to be proud of and something to uphold in the treasure-house of human civilization.

This impressive diversity, this colossal human and sociopolitical massif calls for close attention, study and respect. We know well from our own, Soviet, experience what an immense creative force a renewed sense of national dignity becomes, what a constructive role is played by the national identity of a people in its organic interrelationship with other equal and free peoples. This process is now on the rise in Asia and the Pacific region: everything is in motion here, far from everything has settled. The new mixes with the old. A way of life which seemed unshakable only yesterday is giving way to the whirlwind of changes—social, scientific and technical, and ideological. This is, I would say, yet another period of renaissance in world history, a period harboring a huge potential of progress. And progress not only for Asia and Oceania.

Which direction will socioeconomic and political development take in the region? What processes will prevail in interstate relations? These issues will largely determine the destinies of the whole world.

Socialism is an inalienable factor in the large-scale and complex changes taking place in this region. It gained firm positions in Asia as a result of the Great October Socialist Revolution and the victory over fascism and Japanese militarism, as a result of the great Chinese revolution, as a result of the consolidation of the new social system in Mongolia, in the land of Korea, whose people displayed outstanding steadfastness in the struggle for the socialist future of their country, and then in Vietnam and Laos. But it is also in Asia where it met with the most brutal and cynical counteraction. Vietnam is the most graphic example of this. Its heroic experience, the lessons of its victory over imperialism accentuated once again the irresistible force of the ideas of freedom and socialism.

Here, in Asia, the concept of nonalignment, a movement which now includes more than a hundred nations, emerged. It is trying to come up with its own response to the challenge of the time, is actively working for overcoming the world's division into military blocs and is seeking its own ways of reducing the nuclear threat. In rejecting and condemning exploitation, the policy of aggression and neocolonialism, the nonaligned movement is urging mankind to work for unity, for cooperation in combating hunger and the acute poverty of hundreds of millions of people.

The great India, with its moral prestige and traditional wisdom, with its specific political experience and huge economic potentialities, is the recognized leader of this movement. We highly value its contribution to establishing standards of equal coexistence and justice in the international community. Friendly relations between the USSR and India have become a stabilizing factor on a world scale.

Japan has turned into a power of foremost importance. The country which became the first victim of American nuclear weapons has traversed a great path within a brief period, and has achieved outstanding successes in industry, trade, education, science and technology. These successes are due not only to the organizing ability, self-discipline and energy of the Japanese people, but also to the "three nonnuclear principles" which officially underlie its foreign policy, although lately— and this must be emphasized—they, as well as the peaceful provisions of Japan's Constitution, are being circumvented ever more openly.

But we also see many other things in Asia and Oceania. The fact that the peoples' dignity was insulted by colonialism, the legacy of poverty, illiteracy and backwardness, along with profound prejudices, preserve conditions for mistrust and hostility between peoples, including peoples living within one state. Imperialism takes advantage of the difficulties and prejudices, which leads to local conflicts, ethnic and religious strife and political instability.

Wherever independence becomes a tangible international value and a threat to the exploitative interests of imperialism emerges, it resorts to its favorite methods: economic blackmail, intrigues and plots against the leadership of the country in question, and interference in internal affairs; it backs separatists and finances and even directly arms counterrevolution and terrorists. Punjab, the Tamil problem, with attempts being made to turn this problem against India too, the undeclared wars on Kampuchea and Afghanistan, the annexation of Micronesia, interference in the Philippines, and pressure on New Zealand provide enough examples showing how the contemporary mechanism of imperialist intervention and diktat works.

The experience of history, the laws of growing interdependence and the need for economic integration urge one to look for ways leading to agreement and to the establishment of open ties between states in the region and beyond it. These states have tens, hundreds of glaring problems, problems inherited from the colonial past and emerging out of contradictions of present-day development. And these states are being dragged into blocs; the freedom of utilizing their own resources is being curtailed. They are being forced to increase their military budgets, and are being drawn into the arms race and the militarization of the economy and the entire social life.

All this deforms the processes of internal development,

creates tension and, naturally, hampers a normalization of relations between nations and states.

The Soviet Union is also an Asian and Pacific country. It is very much aware of the complex problems facing this vast region. They concern it directly. This is what determines its balanced and comprehensive view with regard to this huge part of the world where a large number of different nations and peoples are concentrated. Our approach to it is based on a recognition and understanding of the existing realities in the region.

At the same time our interest is not a claim to privileges and a special position, or an egoistic attempt to strengthen our security at someone else's expense, or a search for advantages to the detriment of others. Our interest is in the pooling of efforts and in cooperation, with full respect for the right of each nation to live as it chooses and resolve its problems on its own in conditions of peace.

We are in favor of building together new, fair relations in Asia and the Pacific.

Recently I have had many meetings with leaders of European states, with various political figures of European countries. I cannot help comparing the situation in Asia with that in Europe.

On the whole the Pacific region has not as yet been militarized to the extent Europe has. But the potentialities of its militarization are truly immense, and the consequences are extremely dangerous. One only needs to look at a map to be convinced of this. Major nuclear powers are situated here. Large land armies, navies and air forces have been established. The scientific, technological and industrial potential of many countries—from the western to the eastern fringes of the ocean—makes it possible to step up any arms race. The situation is being exacerbated by the preservation of conflict situations. Let us not forget: it is in Asia that American imperialism waged the two biggest wars since 1945—the war in Korea and the war in Indochina. In the last four decades there is hardly a period of even just a few years when the flames of war did not blaze in one or another part of the Asian and Pacific region.

In Europe, whether it is working well or not, the Helsinki

process of dialogue, negotiations and agreements is under way. This creates a certain stability and reduces the probability of armed conflicts. In the region under consideration this is absent, or nearly absent. If something has changed lately, it has not been for the better. Since the second half of the seventies the U.S.A. has undertaken large-scale measures to build up armed forces in the Pacific Ocean. The militarized triangle of Washington, Tokyo and Seoul is being set up under its pressure. And although two out of three nuclear powers in the region—the People's Republic of China and the USSR—pledged not to be the first to use nuclear weapons, the United States has deployed nuclear weapon-delivery vehicles and nuclear warheads in one of the zones of crisis—in the Korean Peninsula, and nuclear weapon-delivery vehicles on Japanese territory.

One has to state that militarization and the escalation of the war threat in this part of the world are taking place at a dangerously fast pace. The Pacific Ocean is turning into an arena of military and political confrontation. This is what gives rise to growing concern among the peoples living here. This is alarming also for us from all points of view, including for considerations of security in the Asian part of our country.

The Soviet Union's policy toward Asia and the Pacific region is an integral part of the general platform of the CPSU's international activity worked out by the April Plenary Meeting and the 27th Congress. But a platform is not a chart that can be applied to any situation. Rather it is a set of principles and a method based on experience.

How, then, should one envisage the process of establishing international security and peaceful cooperation in this vast region?

First of all, in keeping with its principled policy as approved by the 27th Congress, the Soviet Union will try to invigorate its bilateral relations with all countries in the region without exception. We shall strengthen friendship in every way and promote many-sided relations with the Mongolian People's Republic, the Democratic People's Republic of Korea, the Socialist Republic of Vietnam, the Lao People's Democratic Republic, and the People's Republic of Kampuchea. We regard relations with our friends, built on the principles of equality and solidarity, as an integral part of overall Asian and Pacific security.

At present, for instance, a question of withdrawing a substantial part of Soviet troops from Mongolia is being considered jointly by the Soviet and Mongolian leadership.

We are prepared to expand ties with Indonesia, Australia, New Zealand, the Philippines, Thailand, Malaysia, Singapore, Burma, Sri Lanka, Nepal, Brunei, the Republic of Maldives, and the youngest independent participants in the region's political life. With some of these—Papua New Guinea, Western Samoa, the Kingdom of Tonga, Fiji, the Republic of Kiribati, the Republic of Nauru, Tuvalu, and the Republic of Vanuatu—we already maintain diplomatic relations.

Speaking in a city which is but a step from the People's Republic of China, I would like to dwell on the most important issues in our relations. These relations are extremely important for several reasons, starting with the fact that we are neighbors, that we share the world's longest land border, and that for this reason alone we, our children, and grandchildren are destined to live near each other "for ever and ever."

Of course, there is more to the question than that. History has entrusted the Soviet and the Chinese peoples with an extremely responsible mission. Much in international development depends upon these two major socialist nations.

Relations between our two countries have improved noticeably in recent years. I would like to reaffirm that the Soviet Union is prepared—at any time and at any level—to enter into discussion with China on additional measures for establishing an atmosphere of good-neighborliness. We hope that the border dividing us (I would prefer to say linking) will become in the near future a line of peace and friendship.

The Soviet people respond with understanding and respect to the objective advanced by the Communist Party of China— to modernize the country and build in the future a socialist society worthy of a great people.

As far as it is possible to judge, the Soviet Union and China have similar priorities—to accelerate social and economic development. Why not support each other, why not cooperate in implementing our plans wherever this is clearly to the benefit of both sides? The better our relations, the more we shall be able to share our experience.

We note with satisfaction that a positive shift has become visible in economic ties. We are convinced that the historically established complementarity between the Soviet and the Chinese economies offers great opportunities for expanding these ties, including in the border regions. Some of the major problems of cooperation are literally knocking at the door. For instance, we do not want the Amur, which runs along the Chinese-Soviet border, to be viewed as a "water barrier." Let the basin of this mighty river unite the efforts of the Chinese and the Soviet peoples in using the river's rich resources for mutual benefit and in building water-management projects. A relevant intergovernmental agreement is already being jointly worked out. And the official border could pass along the main ship channel.

The Soviet Government is preparing a positive reply concerning the question of assistance in building a railway connecting the Xinkiang-Uigur Autonomous Region with Kazakhstan.

We have suggested cooperating with China in space exploration, which could include the training of Chinese cosmonauts. The opportunities for mutually beneficial exchanges in the sphere of culture and education are great. We are prepared for and sincerely desire all this.

On relations with Japan. Signs are emerging indicating a turn for the better here as well. It would indeed be a positive development if the turn did take place. The objective position of our two countries in the world demands profound cooperation on a sound and realistic basis, and in a calm atmosphere free from problems of the past. A beginning was made this year. Foreign ministers exchanged visits and an exchange of top-level visits is on the agenda.

Economic cooperation is of mutual interest. The main issue here is our coastal regions which already have business contacts with Japanese firms. It is possible to discuss the question of establishing joint enterprises in adjacent and nearby regions of the USSR and Japan. Why not establish long-term cooperation in the investigation and comprehensive use of the ocean resources, why not correlate programs of the peaceful study and use of outer space? The Japanese, it seems, have a method of making relations more dynamic which is called "economic diplomacy." This time let it serve Soviet-Japanese cooperation.

The Soviet Union also shares the border with the United States in the Pacific region. It is our next-door neighbor in the literal meaning of the word, with only seven kilometers dividing us—the exact distance between the Soviet island of Big Diomede and the American island of Little Diomede.

We recognize clearly that the United States is a great Pacific power. Primarily because a considerable part of the country's population lives on the shores of this ocean, the western part of America, gravitating toward this area, is playing a growing part in the country's development and is a dynamic force. Furthermore, the United States, undoubtedly, has important and legitimate economic and political interests in the region.

No doubt, without the United States and its participation, it is not possible to resolve the problem of security and cooperation in the Pacific Ocean to the satisfaction of all nations in the region. Regrettably, Washington has thus far shown no interest in this issue. It is not even contemplating a serious talk on the Pacific issue. If the issue is taken up, it inevitably leads to the trodden path of the "Soviet threat" and to saber-rattling corroborating this myth.

Our approach to relations with the United States is well known. We are for peaceful, good-neighborly, equitable relations, and mutually beneficial cooperation which offers, incidentally, considerable opportunities in the Far East as well as in the Pacific.

A few words concerning the most important aspect of our relations with the United States at present—on the termination of the arms race. Since the Geneva meeting the Soviet Union has put forward many large-scale proposals on the entire range of problems involved in reducing and eliminating arms and verifying this process. We have not noticed any movement to meet us even halfway. In fact, our proposals met the same response as before the Geneva summit.

In an attempt to overcome the standstill, we went a step further: new large-scale proposals of compromise were put forward in my June letter to the President of the United States. When visiting here, in the Far East, I received a reply from President Reagan. The reply sets one thinking and we have begun to study it. We shall treat it with responsibility and attention. The most important thing from our point of view is the extent to which the proposals contained in the letter meet the principle of equal security and whether they make it possible to reach effective joint solutions in ending the arms race and preventing its spread into outer space. We shall determine our further steps accordingly.

As far as a new Soviet-U.S. summit meeting is concerned, I can repeat: we favor such a meeting. But we are resolutely against interpreting the accords reached at the previous meeting in Geneva as a promise to have more meetings. No. The main thing on which we agreed last time with President Reagan and what we signed is the consent to strive for the normalization of relations between the USSR and the U.S.A. and for the improvement of the international situation, and to speed up the course of talks on the reduction of armaments. This should also be the purpose of a new summit meeting.

We frequently hear from abroad all kinds of stories to the effect that the Soviet Union is building up its military power in the east of the country. Let me state with full responsibility: we are not doing anything and shall not do anything over and above the level that corresponds to the minimal requirements of our own defense, and the defense of our friends and allies, especially in the light of the American military activity not far from our and their frontiers.

This applies in full measure to the medium-range missiles. Those who do not want to see the lessening of world tensions continue to allege that we will be able to move our SS-20 missiles from the west to the east and from the east to the west. This is why I emphasize one more time—we suggest that both American and Soviet medium-range missiles in Europe *be eliminated*. Eliminated—not moved somewhere else. This quite clearly promotes the interests of the Asian countries as well.

I would also like to state that the Soviet Union is a dedicated advocate of disbanding the military groupings, renouncing the possession of military bases in Asia and the Pacific Ocean and withdrawing troops from the territories of other countries. The USSR is a member of the Warsaw Treaty; but this is a European defensive alliance and it operates strictly within the stipulated geographical limits. In our turn we are strongly opposed to the U.S. attempts to extend NATO's "competence" to the entire world, including Asia and the Pacific Ocean.

Our views about security in the Asian-Pacific region did not come out of thin air. They take into account the experience of the past and of today. The principles of "Pancha Shila" and of Bandung have not sunk into oblivion. The positive examples of the truce in Korea, the 1954 Geneva meeting on Indochina, the Indo-Pakistani agreement in Tashkent live on in diplomatic experience. Nowadays, too, we have witnessed the efforts of a number of states to solve in practice common economic problems and the attempts somehow to regulate conflicts. In the activities of the ASEAN and in bilateral ties many positive steps have been taken. After the plan for a "Pacific community" had been rejected, the discussions began on the idea of a "Pacific economic cooperation." We approached this idea without bias and we are ready to join in the deliberations on the possible foundations of such cooperation: this is, of course, if it is not conceived in a forced, bloc-oriented, and antisocialist pattern, but is rather the result of free discussion without any discrimination. The sufficiently vast arsenal of scientific and political ideas on the issue of establishing a new world economic order and the experience of integration in the West and the East could become a solid foundation for such discussions.

For an objective, however remote, we would like to propose a conference, in the mold of the Helsinki Conference, to be attended by all countries gravitating toward the Ocean. When an agreement is reached on its convocation (if an agreement is reached at all, of course) it will be possible to establish the place for this conference. Hiroshima is a possible option. Why should that city, the first victim of nuclear evil, not become a "Helsinki" for Asia and the Pacific Ocean?

In summary, I would like to emphasize that we stand for integrating the Asian-Pacific region into the general process of establishing a comprehensive system of international security proposed at the 27th Congress of the CPSU.

What are our concrete views on this issue?

First of all, the issues of *regional settlement* inevitably arise. I'll speak of Afghanistan separately. Now let me speak of Southeast Asia and Kampuchea. The Khmer people sustained

terrible losses. That country, its cities and villages were victims of American bombing raids more than once. Through its
suffering that country has earned itself the right to choose its
friends and allies. It is impermissible to try and draw it back
into its tragic past, to decide the future of that state in the
distant capitals or even in the United Nations.

Here, as with other problems of Southeast Asia, much depends on the normalization of Sino-Vietnamese relations. It is
a sovereign matter of the governments and the leadership of
both countries. We can only express our interest in seeing the
border between these socialist states become again a border
of peace and good-neighborly relations, in seeing friendly
dialogue resumed and the unnecessary suspicion and mistrust removed. It seems that the moment is right, and all of
Asia needs this change.

In our opinion, there are no insurmountable obstacles in
the way of establishing mutually acceptable relations between the countries of Indochina and ASEAN. Given good
will and the absence of foreign interference they could solve
their problems, which would simultaneously benefit the
cause of security in Asia.

There is a possibility for not only relieving the dangerous
tensions in the Korean peninsula, but also for beginning the
solving of the national problem of the entire Korean people.
As far as the truly Korean interests are concerned, there are
no sensible reasons for evading a serious dialogue which has
been proposed by the Democratic People's Republic of Korea.

Second. We are for blocking the proliferation and buildup of
nuclear weapons in Asia and the Pacific Ocean.

As is known, the USSR has pledged not to increase the
number of medium-range nuclear missiles in the Asian part
of the country.

The USSR supports proclaiming the southern part of the
Pacific a nuclear-free zone and urges all nuclear powers to
guarantee its status in a unilateral or multilateral way.

The implementation of the proposal of the DPRK for the
creation of a nuclear-free zone in the Korean peninsula would
be a significant contribution. The idea of creating such a zone
in Southeast Asia has aroused well-deserved attention.

Third. We propose to start talks on the reduction of the
activity of *naval forces* in the Pacific, in particular, nuclear-

armed ships. Restriction of the rivalry in the sphere of anti-submarine weapons, specifically, the arrangement to refrain from antisubmarine activity in certain zones of the Pacific, would help strengthen stability. This could become a substantial confidence-building measure.

In general, I would like to say that if the United States gave up its military presence, say, in the Philippines, we would not leave this step unanswered.

We remain strongly in favor of resuming the talks on establishing *the Indian Ocean as a peace zone.*

Fourth. The Soviet Union attaches great importance to the radical *reduction of armed forces and conventional armaments in Asia* to limits of reasonable sufficiency. We realize that this problem should be tackled gradually, stage-by-stage, by starting with one certain region, say, the Far East. In this context the USSR is prepared to discuss with China concrete steps aimed at the commensurate lowering of the level of land forces.

Fifth. The Soviet Union believes that it is high time to switch to practical discussions on confidence-building measures and on the nonuse of force in this region. Simpler measures could serve as the beginning—for instance, measures for the security of sea lanes in the Pacific, and for the prevention of international terrorism.

A conference to discuss and work out such measures could be held in one of the Soviet maritime cities. By the way, with time the question of opening Vladivostok to visits by foreigners could be solved. If the situation in the Pacific actually changes for the better, Vladivostok could become a major international center, a commercial and cultural center, a city for festivals, sports events, congresses, and scientific symposiums. We would like it to be our window opened widely on the East. And then the words of our great Pushkin, "the ships of every flag and nation will hail our shores," will apply to Vladivostok as well.

And in conclusion, about Afghanistan. It was declared from the rostrum of the 27th CPSU Congress that we are ready to recall Soviet troops stationed in Afghanistan at the request of its government. As is known, the Party now firmly adheres to the principle that words should be confirmed by deeds.

Having thoroughly assessed the current situation and hav-

ing held consultations with the government of the Democratic
Republic of Afghanistan, the Soviet leadership has adopted
the decision which I officially announce today: six regiments
will be returned home from Afghanistan before the end of
1986—one armored regiment, two motorized infantry regiments, and three antiaircraft artillery regiments—with their
regular equipment and armaments. These units will be returned to the areas of their permanent deployment in the
Soviet Union, and in a manner that these moves will be
obvious to all those who take an interest in this.

Taking this serious step, of which we informed the states
concerned in advance, including Pakistan, the Soviet Union is
striving to speed up and give further impetus to a political
settlement. The Soviet Union expects that those who organize
and implement the armed intervention against the Democratic Republic of Afghanistan, will correctly understand and
duly appreciate this unilateral step we have taken. It must be
answered by the curtailment of outside interference in the
affairs of the Democratic Republic of Afghanistan.

Certain progress has been achieved recently at the Afghan-
Pakistani talks held through the mediation of a representative
of the UN Secretary-General. As soon as a political settlement
is finally worked out, the recall of all Soviet troops from
Afghanistan can be accelerated. Schedules for their stage-by-
stage recall have been agreed upon with the Afghan leadership.

But all who encourage and finance the undeclared war
against Afghanistan and from whose territory it is waged,
should know that if the intervention against the DRA continues, the Soviet Union will come to the defense of its neighbor. This position stems from our internationalist solidarity
with the Afghan people and from the interests of the Soviet
Union's security.

We support the policy of the present Afghan leadership
aimed at national reconciliation and at widening the social
base of the April National-Democratic Revolution. This includes the creation of a government in which would participate those political forces that have found themselves beyond
the country's borders but who are prepared to participate
sincerely in the nationwide process of building new
Afghanistan.

Comrades,

The present generations have inherited many difficult and painful problems. In order to reach a solution to these problems it is necessary to get rid of the burden of the past, to seek new approaches, guiding oneself by one's responsibility for the present and the future.

The Soviet state calls upon all Asian and Pacific nations to cooperate for the sake of peace and security. Everyone who strives toward these goals and who hopes for a better future for one's people, will find that we are willing to talk and are honest partners.

Humanity is living through a difficult and dramatic time. But it has a reserve of strength that allows it not simply to survive, but also to learn to live in a new, civilized world; in other words, to live without the threat of war, and to live in freedom, when the highest criterion will be mankind's benefit and the maximum development of the individual's abilities. But this requires a persistent struggle against the common enemy—the threat of universal annihilation.

Mobilization of the existing potential of common sense and the partnership of reason are now more important than ever before to stop the slide toward catastrophe. Everyone can rest assured, all peoples in all countries, that our resolve to do our utmost for this cause remains unchanged.

This, in brief, is the state of our domestic affairs at present and the state of the general international situation, in the development of which the Asian and Pacific part of the world is to play an ever-increasing role. We should draw practical conclusions from all this in order to act ever more vigorously to rebuild and improve our life.

Although there are no direct analogies in history, similar situations do arise. Therefore, we find past experience useful and edifying. In the article "Fourth Anniversary of the October Revolution" Lenin wrote:

"We have already started the necessary changes in our economic policy and already have some successes to our credit; true, they are small and partial, but nonetheless they are successes. In this new field of 'tuition' we are already finishing our preparatory class. By persistent and assiduous study, by making practical experience the test of every step we take, by not fearing to alter over and over again what we have already begun, by correcting our mistakes and most carefully analyzing their significance, we shall pass to the higher classes. We shall go through the whole 'course'. . ."

This is Lenin's advice, comrades, and a sample of his analysis with its typical depth, clear thinking, and self-criticism. We are advised how we should act in the present situation, how we should go about rebuilding, so that we might complete the whole course successfully and bring our country to a qualitatively new level. It is our duty to make full use of Lenin's wise counsel.

I wish you every success and achievement in putting our plans into effect. I wish you happiness, good health, and all the best in life.

I would like to take this opportunity to thank the people of the Soviet Far East for their kind words of trust and support, for their recommendations and suggestions, and for their warmth and cordiality. Thank you, comrades.

XVI

TELEVISED SPEECH
On Foreign Policy

Moscow, August 18, 1986

Good evening, dear comrades!

At our meeting tonight I would like to make a statement on one of the key issues of international politics.

The Soviet unilateral moratorium on nuclear tests, which the Soviet Union, as is known, had strictly observed for one year, expired several days ago, on August 6.

What was this not so simple, extremely responsible and, I would say, difficult decision based on? What prompted it?

In brief, it was based on the realities of the nuclear-space age.

What are these realities? How do we regard them?

First, mountains of nuclear and various other types of weapons have been stockpiled, but nonetheless the arms race continues unabated, is even escalating; the danger has emerged of its extension to outer space; the militarization of the United States and the entire NATO bloc is being carried out at full speed. It is important to stress that the pace of the development of military technology is so high that it leaves less and less time for people, states and politicians to become aware of the real danger, and limits humanity's possibilities for stopping the slide toward the nuclear abyss. No delay can be allowed, or else such sophisticated weapon systems will emerge that agreement on their control will become altogether impossible.

The situation is becoming increasingly intolerable. It is not enough today to preserve the existing treaties; major practical steps are needed which are capable of curbing militarism and reversing the course of developments for the better. The "balance of fear" is ceasing to be a factor of restraint, and not only because fear in general is no advisor to reason and may prompt actions that are unpredictable in their consequences. This fear is actually a direct participant in the arms race: by increasing mistrust and suspicion, it forms a vicious circle of heightening tension. There are many examples.

It has become crystal clear to all that the old notions of war as a means of attaining political objectives are outdated. In the nuclear age, these obsolete tenets are feeding a policy that may result in an all-out conflagration.

Second, our decision on the moratorium was based on the adherence of socialism as a social system to the cause of peace, and on the profound understanding of its responsibility for the destinies of civilization. The Soviet Union, as a socialist state and as a nuclear power, considers it its supreme duty to do everything possible to ensure a peaceful future for the planet.

Our striving to steer international development toward detente is dictated by our philosophy, our socialist morality. In the nuclear age, saving the earth from atomic annihilation is a universal human task, the cause of all peoples.

Third, the present-day world is complicated, diverse and controversial. At the same time, it is objectively becoming more interdependent and integral. This distinct feature of the human community today, at the end of the 20th century, cannot be disregarded in foreign policy if it is based on reality. Otherwise, there will be no normal international relations: they will be frenzied and will ultimately lead to catastrophic confrontation.

Prenuclear thinking essentially lost its significance on August 6, 1945. Today it is no longer possible to ensure one's own security without taking into account the security of other states and peoples. There can be no genuine security unless it is equal all around and all-encompassing. To think otherwise means to live in a world of illusions, in a world of self-deception.

The new way of thinking needed by the modern world is incompatible with the notion of the world as someone's domain, or with the attempts to "do others good" through patronage and instructions on how to conduct oneself and what path to choose—socialist, capitalist, or some other.

The Soviet Union believes that each nation, each country, has the right to be master of its own destiny and resources, to determine its social development autonomously, uphold its own security, and participate in the establishment of a comprehensive system of international security.

The aggravation of global problems is also characteristic of today's world. They cannot be resolved without pooling the efforts of all states and peoples. The exploration of outer space and the ocean depths, ecology and epidemics, poverty and backwardness are the realities of the age, and they demand international attention, international responsibility, and international cooperation. Many new world processes have thus become very tightly interwoven. Disarmament could play an immense role here by releasing considerable funds and the intellectual and technical potential for constructive purposes.

Our foreign policy draws inspiration from the fact that throughout the world, the conviction is becoming increasingly rooted in the consciousness of the peoples and of political and public forces of various orientations and world outlooks that the very existence of the human race is at stake, that the time for resolute and responsible steps has come. It calls for a complete mobilization of reason and common sense.

Two tragedies involving nuclear-space age technology occurred recently: the death of the Challenger crew and the accident at the Chernobyl nuclear power plant. These events heightened the feeling of alarm, and served as brutal reminders of the fact that people are just beginning to master the fantastically potent forces they themselves created, are only learning to make them serve progress. They showed what would happen if nuclear weapons were used.

Everyone, above all statesmen, should draw specific and obvious lessons from that. The most important lesson, perhaps, is that weapons devised by man should never be used and that today it is downright suicidal to build interstate relations on the illusion that superiority in horrible means of annihilation can be attained.

The only way toward genuine peace is to eliminate these weapons altogether. To embark on this path means to pass a historic maturity test. This applies to all political leaders who have been entrusted with this lofty humane mission.

One must learn to face the facts with courage: experts have

estimated that the explosion of the smallest nuclear warhead would be equal in level of radioactivity to three Chernobyls. This is most likely true. If this is the case, the explosion of even a small part of the existing nuclear arsenal will become a catastrophe, an irreversible catastrophe. And if someone still dares to deal a first nuclear strike, he will doom himself to an agonizing death—not even from a retaliatory strike, but from the consequences of the explosion of his own warheads.

This is not propaganda, political improvisation, or the heightening of "fear." This is a reality which it is simply irresponsible to reject and criminal to ignore.

An objective and honest analysis of all these realities prompts different approaches to world politics. They underlie the principled conclusions we have drawn recently, particularly at the 27th CPSU Congress.

Soviet foreign policy, including issues of disarmament, is based on the comprehension of the profound changes in the world.

We believe that the Soviet proposals of January 15 of this year for eliminating nuclear weapons worldwide by the year 2000 fully meet the demands of the time.

We have demonstrated our readiness to search for compromise solutions to the problems that are the cause of debate and suspicion.

The Soviet Union has placed a package of constructive proposals on the table of Soviet-American talks on nuclear and space armaments.

Together with our Warsaw Treaty allies, we have submitted a set of measures for reducing the armed forces and conventional armaments in Europe from the Atlantic to the Urals. In this sphere, too, we would like to see advancement— mutual and consistent—toward lower and less dangerous levels of military confrontation.

New proposals relating to chemical weapons have been advanced, making it possible, in our view, to sign a convention on banning chemical weapons and eliminating their stockpiles, as well as the industrial base for their production, before the end of this year or in the next year.

At the Stockholm Conference, the socialist countries, constructively cooperating with other participants, did a great deal to find solutions to such key issues as nonuse of force, notification about military exercises and troop movements, exchange of annual plans of military activity, invitation of observers, and inspection.

We have advanced a broad platform of ensuring security and cooperation in the Asian-Pacific region, and we invite all to participate in this process.

We have showed initiative for cooperation with all interested states in establishing international conditions for the safe development of nuclear power engineering.

We have recently submitted to the United Nations a program for building Star Peace, for establishing a world space organization, as an alternative to the Star Wars program.

The 27th CPSU Congress formulated the foundations of a comprehensive system of international security. This system is a generalization of our new approaches in foreign policy. The other day, the group of socialist countries submitted the issue of establishing such a system to the regular session of the UN General Assembly for consideration.

At the same time, I would like to stress that we understand that no matter how important and significant our proposals might be and how committed we are to them, we will not be able to do everything by ourselves. The problem of international security is a common problem and, therefore, a common concern and common responsibility.

When working out our proposals, we study and take into account points of view and initiatives of other governments and of public and political movements. We make every effort to provide equal security to all at each stage of the proposals' implementation. And nevertheless we do not at all consider these proposals final or not open to further discussion. Confrontational deadlocks can be overcome through dialogues and contacts, discussions and talks. This is the only way the ice of mutual mistrust will thaw and real results can be achieved.

This is what we base our position on in the issue of control in the solution of all the disarmament problems. For example, when we put forward our proposal to discontinue all nuclear explosions, we offered no objections to international verification. We agreed to the installation of American monitoring devices in the area of Semipalatinsk and this serves as convincing proof of our openness to international verification. It would seem that the issue of verification has ceased to be an obstacle in reaching agreements. However, this issue continues to be used in a persistent fashion in order to conceal the true position—an unwillingness to disarm.

People of good will welcomed our decision concerning the moratorium on nuclear explosions. People from all over the world approved and supported this decision. Politicians and parliamentarians, public figures and public organizations regarded this step as an example of the correct approach to the problems facing the world today. They saw in this step the hope that the world might rid itself of the fear of nuclear catastrophe. The Soviet moratorium was approved by the UN General Assembly, which is the most representative assembly of states in the world.

We were supported by outstanding scientists—physicists and doctors—who understand better than anyone else the dangers inherent in the atom. I saw for myself at a recent meeting with scientists in Moscow that our moratorium had inspired scientific workers from various countries to take concrete action on the nuclear issue.

However, all these definite and encouraging manifestations of a new way of thinking are in confrontation with the militarization of political thought, and in the United States in particular. The politics of the Western ruling circles is dangerously lagging behind the profound transformations taking place in international relations, while scientific and technological progress is rapidly overtaking social and moral progress.

The right-wing militaristic group in the U.S.A. representing the powerful military-industrial complex seems to have gone mad with the arms race. Their interests seem to have three purposes: to continue to profit from the manufacture of arms, to secure U.S. military superiority, to exhaust the Soviet Union's economic potential and to weaken its political position. Finally, the long-term goal is to ensure U.S. world domination, to realize the long-sought imperial ambitions, and to continue to pursue the policy of plunder in regard to developing countries.

This all leads to the formation of a foreign policy which with all its intricacies and verbal camouflage continues to be based on the following dangerous delusions: the underestimation of the Soviet Union, other socialist countries and newly free states, and the overestimation of its own potential, which nourishes technological self-confidence and political permissiveness.

Some American politicians contend that our participation in the talks is the result of the growing military might of the U.S.A. and its program of Strategic Defense Initiative. Basing its policy on such erroneous premises, the U.S. Administration cannot begin to enter into honest agreements or to improve international relations. And nevertheless the realities have to be considered, for they cannot be avoided.

As to our proposals, I repeat that they stem from the realities of the modern world; their source is not one of weakness but rather an awareness of our lofty responsibility for humanity's destiny.

This is the situation at the present moment.

On the one hand, our moratorium is in operation. Our compromise and extensive proposals have been announced and presented at the negotiating table of various forums. The forces for peace have gained considerable strength. Political leaders, including those in official positions, are giving greater attention to the issues of international security out of concern for the seriousness of the situation.

On the other hand, we are faced with the refusal to stop nuclear testing, with a stubborn resistance to peace initiatives and ostentatious disregard of public demands and the opinions of many authoritative parties and organizations. The concerns of the people and allies from other countries are even being ignored.

This is the state of affairs that we, the Soviet Union's leaders, are faced with as our moratorium has expired.

What is to be done? What choice is to be made? What decision will be the most correct and most appropriate in consideration of the situation? What decision will be most apt to promote positive processes and lessen the threat of military confrontation?

Our people resolutely support the foreign policy of the CPSU, of the Soviet state, and insistently demand that the foreign policy course taken at the 27th Party Congress be continued. At the same time, the Soviet people are justifiably expressing in both written and spoken form a deep concern: is it expedient to continue the moratorium when nuclear explosions reverberate one after another through the Nevada desert? Is not the risk too great? Is not the security of our country lessening with time?

Indeed, the United States has been the champion in regard to the number of explosions over the period of 40 years. Throughout the year during which the Soviet Union adhered to the moratorium, another 18 nuclear devices were exploded in the United States. I repeat: 18, three of which were unannounced. Furthermore, these explosions as a rule were used as a demonstration, timed to correspond either with a Soviet announcement of the extension of the moratorium, or with some other new Soviet initiative. And we were even invited to Nevada to watch the proceedings. It should be added that the present U.S. Administration is implementing the broadest of military programs.

In a word, the Soviet Union has sufficient reasons for resuming its nuclear testing. And yet we are still convinced that the ending of nuclear testing by both the Soviet Union and the United States would be a real breakthrough in stopping the nuclear arms race and would accelerate the process of entirely eliminating nuclear arms. The logic in this is simple: without nuclear testing the nuclear weapons, which both sides have stockpiled in abundance, cannot be upgraded.

The appeals made by a significant and authoritative sector of the world community to the United States and to the Soviet Union support the simplicity of this logic. Those who have made such appeals include the Delhi Six, a permament forum of leaders representing countries of the four continents—Argentina, Greece, India, Mexico, Tanzania, Sweden. A few days ago in Ixtapa the Mexican Declaration was adopted calling once again for an end to all nuclear explosions. This is also the demand of the majority of the countries participating in the nonaligned movement.

We have received messages from politicians and public figures, from individuals and organizations of many countries, including the United States and other NATO countries. They are also asking us not to resume nuclear testing and to give those who adhere firmly to nuclear testing one more chance to come to reason.

We are certainly aware, and I have spoken about that already, that the forces refusing to disarm are taking strenuous actions in the U.S.A. Moreover, they are making every effort possible to draw the Soviet Union into ever new spirals of the arms race and to provoke us into abandoning negotiations.

But we would like to hope that realism and the awareness that mutual efforts are required to find ways to improve the international situation, to end the senseless arms race and to eliminate nuclear weapons will prevail as the United States makes assessments and takes action.

At the same time, we know with whom we are dealing. The security of our country is therefore sacred to us. A matter of principle, this must be clear to all.

We proceed from this position as we respond to any challenge presented by the United States, including the notorious SDI. In this, too, it would be wrong to hope to intimidate us or to induce us into making needless expenditures. If need be, we shall promptly come up with a response, but it will not be the one the United States expects. It will, however, be a response which will devalue the Star Wars program. I say this with one aim: let those in the U.S. Administration weigh again and again the real value of the new military programs and of the arms race as a whole from the point of view of the United States' interests and its security. After all, SDI is most damaging in that it undermines the prospects of the talks and leads to increased mistrust. This is the entire problem. It is no less a political problem than it is a military one. That is why we once again are calling for measures to change the world armed to the limits into a world free of weapons.

Thus, comrades, the Politburo of the CPSU Central Committee and the Government of the Soviet Union have comprehensively and scrupulously weighed all the pros and cons and, guided by their responsibility for the world's destiny, have decided to *extend the unilateral moratorium on nuclear explosions until January 1, 1987.*

In taking this step, we believe that the people of all countries in the world, the political circles and the international public will correctly evaluate the long-reigning silence of the Soviet nuclear test ranges.

On behalf of the Soviet people, I am appealing to the

wisdom and dignity of the American people not to miss another historical chance which could lead to an end to the arms race.

I am asking the U.S. President, Ronald Reagan, to evaluate the present situation once again without bias, to discard everything extraneous and to overcome delusions about the Soviet Union and its foreign policy.

The Soviet Union is confident that an agreement on ending nuclear tests can be reached soon and signed even *this year at the Soviet-American summit meeting*. That event would, undoubtedly, be the *main real outcome of this meeting*, a considerable step toward ending the arms race. The signing of such an agreement would serve as a prologue to future progress at the talks on nuclear weapons and on their elimination and to a radical improvement of the entire world situation.

With its moratorium on nuclear explosions the Soviet Union hasn't simply made a proposal, but has taken definite action. It has proved the seriousness and sincerity of our nuclear disarmament program and of our calls for a new policy—one of realism, peace and cooperation.

More than a half of 1986, which the United Nations organization declared as the Year of Peace, has passed. By extending its unilateral moratorium, the Soviet Union is making another weighty contribution to the common striving to ensure that this year go down in history worthy of its name.

This is the essence of the Soviet Union's new political initiative.

This is the message which our country is sending to the governments and peoples of all countries, and in particular to the government of the United States of America and to the American people.

Thank you. Good night.

XVII

SPEECH
To the Indian Parliament

New Delhi, November 27, 1986

Esteemed Mr. Vice President,
Esteemed Mr. Prime Minister,
Esteemed Mr. Speaker,
Esteemed Members of Parliament,

You have accorded me the honor of speaking from India's main rostrum. This rostrum remembers Jawaharlal Nehru, Indira Gandhi, and other great leaders elected by the Indian people.

The teachings of peace and nonviolence that have been expounded here for several decades now are identified in the minds of people with the country itself and the philosophy of life espoused by this ancient nation.

On behalf of my country I would like to share with you our vision of the world, closely linking it with the thoughts and aspirations of millions of people in your country.

I shall speak of things that are equally cherished by our two peoples and of things that are equally disturbing to them. And since our two great nations make up a substantial portion of mankind, I would like to think that what I am going to say from this rostrum will be heard not only in India.

Joint action and cooperation of the Soviet Union and India are a significant factor in world politics and perform a constructive role in the system of international relations.

The positions held by the Soviet Union and the great India on the fundamental problems of our time are very close; this is indisputable, as is their commitment to peace and equitable cooperation, to disarmament and the prevention of nuclear war.

Nor is there any doubt that at this alarming juncture in the life of mankind we are equally determined to work persistently for saving the nations of the world from a nuclear catastrophe, for building a world order that would rule out diktat or violence and enable every people to choose freely its own road of development.

To me personally, it is quite obvious that much of what we call new political thinking manifested itself internationally for the first time in relations between the Soviet Union and India.

The fact that differences of sociopolitical system and ideology, and our national, cultural and other distinctions have not hampered our dialogue is extremely important as a guiding example for others.

Today every people, every country, without giving up the least bit of its national pride, its values and interests, should be able to channel them toward the main goal, that of saving human civilization.

In this respect, I trust, we are of one mind. And I am pleased to recall here the wise Indian saying that truth brings friends closer together. The truth of our times lies in our responsibility to achieve equal security for all. This is what brings us closer together as never before.

The truth of the nuclear and space age calls on all of us, whatever our political allegiance, ideological convictions or religion, whatever our other differences, to think about a problem common to all mankind, the problem of survival, and act accordingly.

It is from this obvious truth that we draw our optimism. And although this truth is not yet quite indisputable to the leaders of some countries, we are not discouraged. Sooner or later they will have to reckon with this truth and this reality. What is important is that they should not come to realize this too late.

Our ancestors made a "voyage beyond three seas" to reach India and reveal to their countrymen the treasures of India's soul and mind.

Now we have come to India to strengthen the principles of our diversified bilateral cooperation and open up new vistas for it.

A new agreement on economic and technological cooperation, the largest in scope in the history of Soviet-Indian relations, has been signed.

We have come here in order to promote, together with the leaders of India, the affirmation of the concept of peace as the supreme and universal human value.

The Declaration of Principles for a Nuclear-Weapon Free

and Non-Violent World signed this morning by the Prime Minister, Mr. Rajiv Gandhi, and myself serves this noble goal. Yes, it serves this goal since our two great powers do not merely proclaim the principles of a world free from nuclear weapons and violence but are putting those principles in practice in international relations.

The Soviet program for a phased elimination of all nuclear arms and other weapons of mass destruction before the end of this century, announced on January 15, the concept of building a comprehensive system of international peace and security, our moratorium on nuclear tests, our various other peace initiatives—all this, as we see it, is consistent with the positions of the Delhi Six and with India's belief in the power of common sense and the possibility of ensuring peace and progress for the present and future generations.

What the world saw six weeks ago in Reykjavik was not a mirage of a nuclear-free world looming on the horizon, but a reality within reach, which the two sides could attain even tomorrow, if they have the will and act responsibly.

A great deal was accomplished in Reykjavik in the building of a bridge of a historic accord.

Regrettably, that did not prove possible—the Strategic Defense Initiative stood in the way.

I do not think, however, that mankind will accept this.

Whatever the situation may appear now, the fact remains that in one year we have made a huge step forward in our way of thinking and in our perception of what is necessary, what is realistic and what is possible.

During this year we have had two meetings with the Prime Minister of India, Mr. Rajiv Gandhi. Our discussions with him, our exchange of ideas and information make us confident that a breakthrough can be achieved and the nuclear danger removed.

We highly appreciate the position taken by the Government of India on the issue of the complete cessation of all nuclear weapons tests. Both on its own and as a member of the Delhi Six, India supported the Soviet moratorium on all nuclear tests.

We are gratified to note that the Soviet Union and India share the same approach to the idea of establishing a comprehensive system of international security. The Delhi declaration is a new step in promoting this concept of a durable and assured peace, a peace with a new quality.

To us peace is indivisible and integral, which also means that conflicts and explosive situations in any given region must be settled in the interests of the entire international community. The fact is that a fuse smouldering in one part of the globe might cause an explosion that would tear our planet apart.

For every nation world peace begins at the threshold of its home. That is why stability and security in Asia are a common concern for both India and the Soviet Union. Let me emphasize—for the Soviet Union too. For over one-third of Asia's territory is in the Soviet Union, and important sea lanes linking the east and the west of our country stretch across the Indian Ocean.

Peace in Europe and peace in Asia are of equal significance in our policy. In this context the title of Rabindranath Tagore's remarkable novel *The Home and the World* suggests an apt image for describing our actions.

For our national homes to be strong they need peace, and for peace in the world to remain unimpaired we must reinforce all the supports on which a house is built.

India is an acknowledged leader of the nonaligned movement; what is more, it enjoys great prestige as a member of the world community.

Therefore, today we intend to make some suggestions here, addressing them both to India as a major world power and to most other countries which want to bring international affairs to a more constructive level.

First. In a nuclear age, when the threat to people's lives is of a universal character, when an understanding of interdependence and mutual responsibility is becoming vitally important for everyone, such international institutions and organizations as the nonaligned movement, the Organization of African Unity, the South Asian Association for Regional Cooperation and others come to acquire an increasing significance. And, obviously, in these circumstances the work of the United Nations becomes even more important.

Lately the community of states has grown, in the United Nations the voice of sovereign states, which have gained strength and experience, has become more firm and independent, and the attempts to tell them how to vote and what to support are in most instances no longer successful, while an arbitrary behavior in international affairs is being unequivocally condemned.

Some people find this not to their liking, and there is now talk about the United Nations being "in crisis." What is more, they are taking actions aimed at actually hampering the normal functioning of the world organization. But it is our belief that, on the contrary, the role of the United Nations has been increasing owing to the significant growth of its membership and the independent attitudes of its members.

We are convinced that in the nuclear and space age the United Nations, which comprises 159 member states, can and must make a bigger contribution to strengthening peace than that envisaged at the time it was founded, and above all, for this purpose, to molding new political thinking and behavior.

The Soviet Union would like to see the potential of this universal international organization used more effectively than in the past; this can be achieved by (among other things) making its proceedings and its main bodies more democratic.

Specifically, we support the proposal of the UN Secretary-General to set up within the organization a multilateral center for reducing the risk of war.

We also consider it essential to ensure the full use of all the methods of peaceful settlement of disputes between states that are envisaged in the UN Charter—through negotiation, inquiry, mediation, conciliation, arbitration, legal settlement and resort to regional bodies or on the basis of accords.

In general, we are in favor of enhancing in every way the authority of the United Nations, of strengthening its political, legal and moral standing. The Soviet Union will do all it can to help the organization overcome its financial problems.

Second. Outer space surrounds the whole of mankind and no one should be indifferent to how it is used.

It is our profound conviction that space, this common property of mankind, should be entirely peaceful, and that what we need is "Star Peace" and not "Star Wars."

We are prepared to cooperate with any country in exploring outer space. We can, for that matter, cooperate with the United States, with which we have recently worked out a draft bilateral agreement to that effect, which provides for the implementation of 16 specific projects that can bring invaluable benefits to mankind.

The Soviet Union has already submitted to the United Nations a proposal to launch, jointly by all its member states, a program of "Star Peace," a program for the peaceful exploration and use of outer space. This should not be a prerogative of developed countries alone.

We believe that the developing countries, with their prestige and their desire to cooperate in coping with these tasks and their interest in putting space exploration on the track of peace and broad-based international cooperation, will play an important role in this endeavor.

Therefore, today we propose the establishment, with the help of the leading space powers, of an international center to carry out joint research and to develop space technologies at the request of developing countries, for example satellites for exploring natural resources. At such a center a school could be set up for training specialists from developing countries, including cosmonauts, and it would also have facilities for launching spacecraft.

If India were to express a readiness to host such a center on its territory, we would welcome it.

Third. As you know, the Soviet Union and India support the United Nations decision to convene not later than 1988 an international conference for the purpose of implementing the United Nations Declaration proclaiming the Indian Ocean a zone of peace. Demilitarization of the Indian Ocean must finally get under way.

In calling for increased military and political stability in the Indian Ocean region, the Soviet Union is prepared:

—to begin negotiations at any time with the United States and other nonlittoral states which have naval vessels on a permanent basis in the Indian Ocean on substantially reducing the size and activities of naval forces there;

—to hold negotiations with the United States and interested Asian countries on confidence-building measures in the military field applicable to Asia and the adjacent waters of the Indian and Pacific oceans. In particular, we have in mind notification of transfers and exercises of ground (amphibious), naval and air forces of those countries;

—to take part in multilateral negotiations involving all

states that are maritime users of the Indian Ocean in order to work out guarantees of the safety of sea lanes, including the Persian Gulf and the straits of Hormuz and Malacca, as well as guarantees of the sovereignty of littoral countries over their natural resources;

—to take part in working out a long overdue multilateral agreement on the safety of air traffic over the Indian Ocean;

—to participate in drafting, and to become a party to, an international convention to combat terrorism on the seas and in the air.

Of course, this list does not cover all problems related to ensuring peace in the Indian Ocean region, and we are prepared to discuss proposals of other countries to this effect. But the implementation of the aforementioned proposals would undoubtedly help improve the situation in the region.

Distinguished Members of Parliament, there is much that brings the peoples of our two countries closer together. But among the reasons for this mutual sympathy I would single out the continuous and profound search for the meaning of existence, which is common to our spiritual cultures. The question of what a human being should be like is not an idle one. Reflections on man's destiny and on the right path to take in life, on the individual's quest for self-perfection have dominated the thinking of the great men of genius in our two countries. In the popular traditions of our two countries the search for the meaning of life revolved around the eternal triad: human being—humanism—humanity. It may be for this reason that creeping pragmatism is not typical of our peoples' national characters.

A high degree of humanism is also evident in the policies of our two countries; both the Soviet and the Indian people tend not only to think in terms of their own security or interests, but also to relate them to universal security and the aspirations of all mankind.

And today, when we are making every effort to abolish nuclear weapons and to build a nonviolent world, we regard the well-being of man as the primary and main purpose of the development of our civilization.

Today, the danger of war means more than severe stress, which is injurious to mental health. The arms race absorbs enormous material, intellectual and various other resources and consequently denies people the necessary means to improve their life, and thus limits their possibilities of enriching society through creative work.

If the life of billions of people is to be changed for the better in a most radical way, the means required for this should be derived from what is not spent for military purposes. In other words, it is necessary to reduce material expenditures on the arms race and channel resources thus saved to peaceful development.

We cannot but recall in this connection that Indira Gandhi, the great daughter of the Indian people, was among the first political leaders who realized that this is the way to meet the global challenges facing mankind. The Soviet Union, too, has been consistently emphasizing that disarmament would not only lead to a more secure world, but also improve the quality of life.

Our positions on this matter coincide with the positions of India and of the Delhi Six. We are for the early convening of a UN conference on the interrelationship between disarmament and development. Regrettably, it has not yet been possible to hold such a conference because of the opposition virtually of one country, which spends on the arms race more than any country in the world.

Only the elimination of nuclear arms, a ban on space weapons, and the destruction of chemical weapons, and only the principle of sufficiency in defense needs would provide the necessary resources for improving the life of nations.

Should this be achieved, it would be possible within the lifetime of the present generations to come to grips in a practical way with the task of abolishing hunger, poverty, illiteracy and other social and economic ills.

When millions of people suffer, when they are deprived of the necessities of life, one cannot go on living as if this is not one's concern.

Ending the arms race would also promote the effective implementation of the idea of a new world economic order. It would also make it easier to solve the problem of foreign debt, which for many countries is fraught not only with grave economic but also political consequences.

Therefore, the problem of disarmament has many facets, each of them accentuating the need for its solution. But what is particularly unacceptable is replacing the race in some types of weapons with a race in other types of weapons. If we were to disarm in one area only to build up weapons of mass destruction in another area, that would not be disarmament but a fraud.

I am referring to SDI which, according to the world's leading experts, threatens yet again to cut deep into the "pockets" of the peoples of many countries. The world public is being told that besides being a defensive program SDI also stimulates the development of civilian economies and would lead to higher employment and even greater prosperity. This is not the place to engage in polemics. I would just say that the cynical proponents of this program make no secret of the fact that with the help of SDI they intend not only to dictate to other countries how they should live but also to increase their national product by impoverishing others.

Allow me, in conclusion, once again to turn to Soviet-Indian relations. They rest on the reliable foundation of our Treaty of Peace, Friendship and Cooperation.

The treaty has not only opened broad prospects for a steady development of mutually beneficial ties and contacts.

Its greatest significance lies in the reciprocal commitment to take action should a difficult situation arise for one of the sides or for both sides.

There have been such situations. And both the Soviet Union and India have remained faithful to their commitments and acted in accordance with the spirit and the letter of our treaty.

Friendship and cooperation between the Soviet Union and the Republic of India have stood the test of time. Instrumental in this have been the ties and contacts between our parliaments, which should be further developed. I am saying this on behalf of the USSR Supreme Soviet.

"The only real victory is one in which nobody is defeated and all are equally victorious."* You no doubt know these words, you know who spoke them. This great maxim, proclaimed on Indian soil more than 2,500 years ago, turns out to be even more relevant today. In the age of nuclear arms

---

*In a September 1961 speech at a meeting in Moscow, Jawaharlal Nehru quoted these words by the Buddha.

the only possible victory is the victory of reason. Let us jointly work for it!

Distinguished Members of Parliament, I wish you success in your work planned and carried out for the benefit of the Indian people and for the sake of universal peace.

May friendship between the peoples of the Soviet Union and India grow further! Thank you.

XVIII

INTERVIEW
Answers to
Joseph Kingsbury-Smith

December, 1986

Following is the full text of Mikhail Gorbachev's interview with U.S. journalist Joseph Kingsbury-Smith.

Q: What would you like to tell the American people on the occasion of the new year 1987?

A: I would like, first of all, to say that Soviet people want to live in peace with the Americans and do not feel any hostility toward them. On behalf of the leadership of the USSR, I could add that when working out our policy in matters of war and peace we are as honest with the American people as with our own people.

Our age—that of nuclear weapons and high speeds, and of growing economic and political interdependence—rules out the security of one to the detriment or at the expense of the security of another. I shall repeat once again: Only together can we perish or survive. Security nowadays is conceivable only as a mutual thing or, to be more exact, as a universal thing.

So, whether we like one another or not, it is essential to learn to coexist, to live in peace on this tiny and very fragile planet.

Q: Are you in favor of continuing the Geneva talks between Soviet and U.S. representatives in 1987 with a view to achieving progress in matters pertaining to limiting and reducing arms?

A: Yes, we are. We are for talks which would get out of the state of being fruitless and inert and would acquire real dynamism or, in a word, become real talks on reducing nuclear arms and on preventing an arms race in outer space.

We pressed for this in Reykjavik, and we shall press for it

still more vigorously in 1987. I am convinced that a radical turn in the talks would meet the vital interests of the American people as well.

At the same time the U.S. Administration's stand on this issue disappoints us deeply. Following the Reykjavik summit, the American delegation in Geneva even moved backwards.

Although the USSR has not conducted nuclear explosions for a year and a half, the United States has continued tests and declined to negotiate a comprehensive ban on them, and this despite the fact that the United States undertook to conduct such negotiations under two treaties, those dated 1963 and 1974. The defiant act of abandoning the important Strategic Arms Limitation Treaty (SALT-II) by the White House was added to that in November. Deliberately and pointedly wrecking old treaties does not help the conduct of successful talks on new agreements. This is a serious problem which deserves the closest attention.

I reaffirm once again: We are for agreements on the most radical reductions in arms, both nuclear and conventional. Now the ball is in Washington's court.

Q: Should the two sides show mutual flexibility, do you envision the possibility of reaching a compromise agreement during the next two years on antimissile defense matters if there is an accord on nondeployment of a space-based strategic defense system within a mutually agreed-upon period of time?

A: Under all conditions, nothing should be done which would erode or undermine the ABM Treaty. That would deprive us of any hopes for a reduction in nuclear arsenals and would upset strategic stability.

We are for the ABM Treaty of unlimited duration signed in 1972 to be maintained and maintained indefinitely. Article XV of the treaty envisages only one cause for denouncing it: extraordinary events jeopardizing the supreme interests of a party to the treaty. It depends only on the two of us, the Soviet Union and the United States, for such extraordinary events never to occur.

We regret that the U.S. Administration adheres to a different line which allows for the possibility of the U.S. abandoning the ABM Treaty if it deems that advantageous to itself during the implementation of the SDI program.

The Soviet Union is not just for the preservation of the ABM Treaty but is for consolidating it. This is precisely what would be promoted by an accord with the U.S.A. on defining the limits on allowed laboratory research in the ABM field, as is being suggested by the Soviet side.

This treaty is important in itself, but it is doubly important because without this treaty it is impossible to come to terms on cuts in strategic nuclear arms.

So, in this issue, too, things depend not on us but on Washington. People in Washington should finally decide very clearly what they want: a runaway arms race or reduction and elimination of weapons? No one will do that for the American Government or instead of it. A good deal depends on this choice, including the peace and well-being of the American people. We wish them peace and happiness, just as, of course, we do to all the other peoples.

TIPTREE
506236A
5-11-87